W9-ADP-937

GHOSTS, DEMONS, AND HENRY JAMES

GHOSTS, DEMONS, AND HENRY JAMES,

The Turn of the Screw at the Turn of the Century

Peter G. Beidler

University of Missouri Press
Columbia, 1989

Library of Congress Cataloging-in-Publication Data

Beidler, Peter G.
Ghosts, demons, and Henry James : The turn of the screw at
the turn of the century / Peter G. Beidler.
p.   cm.
Bibliography: p.
ISBN 0-8262-0684-0 (alk. paper)
1. James, Henry, 1834–1916. Turn of the screw.
2. Demonology in literature. 3. Ghosts in literature. I. Title.
PS2116.T83B39   1989   88-39776
813'.4—dc19   CIP

FOR KURT DAVID

CONTENTS

FOREWORD
David Kirby

Almost from the moment of its serial appearance in *Collier's Weekly* in 1898, *The Turn of the Screw* has occasioned a controversy seemingly without resolution, for either the ghosts are real and the governess a would-be heroine or they are imaginary and she insane. The battle has been so even over the years that it looked as though neither side would prevail unless new evidence were gathered.

Now Peter Beidler has that evidence. Beidler has settled the issue conclusively; he is the new master of Bly and its occupants. Specifically, Beidler read and analyzed a mind-numbing array of ghost stories (some two thousand in all) that were published in James's day, accounts of actual sightings that seemed to prove that there were such things as ghosts. After Beidler, readers will be convinced that *The Turn of the Screw* is an extended and highly literate ghost story that grows out of the reports of ghostly visitation that appeared by the thousands in the last half of the nineteenth century. Indeed, it is just those qualities—the nightmare fantasy of popular Victorian thinking made artistic by James's skill as a psychological realist—that make *The Turn of the Screw* the best ghost story in the world. Beidler goes well beyond the usual pro-ghost reading, however, by demonstrating that Peter Quint and Miss Jessel not only appear as ghosts in the story but also at times possess the bodies of Miles and Flora.

The reading public has long owed a debt to James, and now scholars owe a debt to Beidler as well. The main readership of this book will be James specialists, but it has much to say to students of the supernatural and of Victorian literature and psychology as well. For Beidler does more than merely interpret; he has gathered all the source material, done the homework for a generation of scholars to follow—and, along the way, compiled a splendid anthology of hair-raising tales.

Of course, no scholars, and certainly not Beidler, believe that

James's sole aim was to frighten his reader. That would seem to lower the Master to the level of a stagey Magwitch; perhaps worse, the sophisticated Jacobite would be demoted to a mere Pip, a child with his teeth a-chatter. To such readers, James figures as his own worst enemy, insisting that *The Turn* is a "bogey-tale" without any greater significance (letter to Dr. Louis Waldstein, 21 October 1898), "a pot-boiler and a *jeu d'esprit*" (letter to H. G. Wells, 9 December 1898), "a very mechanical matter . . . an inferior, a merely *pictorial* subject" (letter to F. W. H. Myers, 19 December 1898). James's most revealing confession to a correspondent is that *The Turn* is but a "fantaisie absolue dans le genre *recherche du frisson*" (letter to Auguste Monod, 17 July 1907).[1] James did tend to shield himself from self-revelation, and, characteristically, he hides this confession in French, a liberal translation of which would be "pure fantasy of the *thrill-seeking* school." In other words, one of our most daring pioneers in technical experimentation is confessing here (though years later and in another language) not only to mere pot-boiling but also to writing according to formula.

Such frank admissions by James convince the pro-ghost camp that they are in the right. On the other hand, the pro-insanity advocates will see these confessions as hasty and not very effective cover-ups designed to throw the literary sleuth off a trail that might lead to something James himself was unable to face, some psychosexual dimension of his own life having to do with the suffering of children or the fear of dementia, perhaps, or simply the embarrassment of having to grub for money now that he wanted to buy Lamb House and had failed in his condescending attempts to write plays for the masses.

The best way to arrive at James's true attitude toward his creation is to trace his references to it throughout the voluminous notebooks he kept, which are now available in their entirety. The first mention occurs on 12 January 1895, just a week after his public humiliation at the premiere of *Guy Domville*, and is a simple

1. Gerald Willen, ed., *A Casebook on Henry James's "The Turn of the Screw,"* 2d ed. (New York: Crowell, 1969), 379, 381, 382, 303.

outline of the *donnée* given him by the Archbishop of Canterbury, an anecdote notable to James primarily for the "strangely gruesome effect in it." On 23 January 1895, a still-shaken James noted that "I have only to *face* my problems," even if "all that is of the ineffable—too deep and pure for any utterance."[2] In the next five years, James was to produce some of his most technically innovative work, fiction that would form a bridge between the years he worked in the theater and what Louis Auchincloss calls James's period of "high, golden light," the era of *The Ambassadors*, *The Wings of the Dove*, and *The Golden Bowl*.[3] This experimental period also includes a number of thematically disturbing works, stories of terror and hauntings and, above all, the abuse and death of children. By 1900, James seems both to have worked out his personal crisis and to have prepared himself for a final outpouring of fiction in what F. R. Leavis describes as "The Great Tradition" of Jane Austen and George Eliot.[4]

On 9 August of that year, James sketched in his notebook a plan for *The Sense of the Past*, noting that he wanted to write a ghost story again, something "as simple as *The Turn of the Screw*, only different and less grossly and merely apparitional." In this entry, *The Turn* figures as a formula piece that is best put behind one; James dismisses it as a "squeezed sponge."[5] He eventually shelved *The Sense of the Past* and did not return to it until 1914; the unfinished novel appeared in 1917, a year after James's death. But lengthy notes dictated by James in 1915 show how much he had changed his mind about *The Turn of the Screw* in the interim.

Now he wanted the hard-to-manage *Sense of the Past* to be more like *The Turn*, not less. He thought *The Sense of the Past* should have "the tone of the 'Screw' point of view, should be intensely in the note of that tone, should be a concrete and definite thing." Earlier, James seemed to regard *The Turn of the Screw* as little more than a ghost story. Now he seems to be looking back at it wistfully as a

2. *The Complete Notebooks of Henry James*, ed. Leon Edel and Lyall H. Powers (New York: Oxford University Press, 1987), 109.

3. Louis Auchincloss, "A Strategy for James Readers," *Nation* 190 (1960): 367.

4. F. R. Leavis, *The Great Tradition* (New York: New York University Press, 1963).

5. James, *Notebooks*, 189–90.

story whose ghosts are precisely its strength as well as an anti-
dote to an "excess of the kind of romanticism that I don't want" (in
The Sense of the Past).[6]

Ever a child of Hawthorne, even in his old age, James was
aware of the seductive snares set by the romance genre. In his
preface to *The House of the Seven Gables*, James's American master
advises other authors not to be carried away with melodramatic
effects but then observes that no writer could be said "to commit a
literary crime even if he disregard this caution."[7] To give *The Sense
of the Past* a palpability greater than moonshine, James promised
himself to instill it with "the unfailing presence, drawing in
everything to itself, of that force of 'tone' which makes the thing
of the parenté of the 'Screw.' "[8]

His final, his best work, then, was to be the best because it
would be "parenté" to *The Turn of the Screw*. In the intervening
years, James came to realize just how much of his mastery he had
put into his ghost story. For *The Sense of the Past* to share con-
sanguinity with *The Turn of the Screw* is to ensure the aesthetic
success of the former. In addition, by having the two works share
the same bloodline, James acknowledges at last the legitimacy of
the one born earlier.

A main argument against the pro-insanity reading of *The Turn
of the Screw* is that it makes the work James is best known by into a
sort of literary bastard. To see the governess as mad and her story
as a psychological sketch is tempting; it lets one bring to bear the
techniques of close analysis learned in school and then paraded to
the astonishment of one's own students. But this reading is the
real dismissal of the work, the reduction of it to the status of an
innovative experiment in viewpoint and little more. As paradox-
ical as it may seem initially, the pro-ghost reading is the one that
moves *The Turn* back to the center of the canon, to the heart both of
James's own writing and of American literature as a whole.

A consideration of the genre, themes, and imagery of *The Turn*
from the pro-ghost viewpoint make this clear. As E. A. Sheppard

6. Ibid., 517

7. Nathaniel Hawthorne, *The House of the Seven Gables*, ed. William Charvat et
al., Centenary Edition (Columbus: Ohio State University Press, 1965), 1.

8. James, *Notebooks*, 532.

observes in *Henry James and "The Turn of the Screw,"* our author worked in the tradition of the English novel of manners as described by Leavis but also in "the American tradition of storytelling and its literary equivalents." In isolated communities, especially those in northern latitudes, people gather to tell ghost stories in self-defense—to, "as it were, hypostatize their fears." Thus ghost stories flourished in the Scottish highlands, in Scandinavia, and in the early New England communities; James invokes this tradition in his frame story by having *The Turn of the Screw* read aloud to a group of people at a country home in winter. Too, American literature began to take form at a time when there was a vogue in Europe for tales of terror told by Horace Walpole, Mrs. Radcliffe, and "Monk" Lewis. The first professional novelist in America, Charles Brockden Brown, was a Gothic romancer, as were Edgar Allan Poe and the Hawthorne who served as literary model for the young Henry James.[9]

Thematically, few themes are more central to American literature than detachment and its opposite, self-assertion. Because America, perhaps more than any other country, is associated with individual action and progress, and because writers often run counter to their culture's dominant themes, American literature is peopled with a cast of unusually detached characters: Poe's Pym, Bartleby, the Thoreau of *Walden*, Hester Prynne, Ishmael, Uncle Tom, Huckleberry Finn, Emily Dickinson's persona ("I'm Nobody—Who Are You?"), the Henry Adams of *The Education*, the heroes of *The Red Badge of Courage* and *The Ambassadors* and *The Sun Also Rises* and *Catch-22*. All these are passive or retiring figures in a world too busy for its own good. And whenever characters decide to do something about their lot, to go the way of Adam, say, or Faust, they remind us that action and self-assertion almost always lead to downfall. In *The Portrait of a Lady*, for example, the man Isabel Archer decides to make into a husband turns out to be a monster in disguise. Similarly, the governess decides that she too must assert herself (she could have run away and even thinks about doing so until a reappearance of Miss

---

9. E. A. Sheppard, *Henry James and "The Turn of the Screw"* (Auckland: Auckland University Press, 1974), 3.

Jessel stops her), but the turn of the screw is that it is little Miles who is lost, not she. James is putting some spin on a theme as old as Genesis and as new, to him, as Hawthorne's "The Birthmark," another story in which someone kills the thing he loves by dispossessing it of its life-giving flaw.

Imagistically, James puts at the center of his story the organ of sight, which is a hallmark of American writing. In this way, he makes *The Turn* a tale as American as "The Purloined Letter," in which right and wrong ways of seeing are crucial, and the governess herself as much a see-er as the Emerson who wrote "I am become a transparent eyeball" and the Whitman who asked, in "Salut au Monde," "What do you see Walt Whitman?" and then answered himself, using the phrase "I see" eighty-three times. Indeed, the governess may be using the right sensory organ but in the wrong country, for as Tony Tanner has pointed out, if the eye is central to American writing, the ear is central to English, as it is for Keats listening to the nightingale he cannot see and Wordsworth recalling the song of "The Solitary Reaper" long after his vision of her has faded.[10]

So the governess is the heroine of a Gothic tale, one who is safely detached (and then dangerously self-assertive), who looks when she should be listening. By "limiting" himself to a popular formula, James managed to write one of his most characteristically American tales.

But does this mean that the governess is possibly seeing something that isn't there? Of course it does. James couldn't write badly if he tried, as he did on occasion; the *Guy Domville* fiasco proved that. As James wrote in a letter of 30 August 1876 to Whitelaw Reid resigning the post of travel correspondent for the *New York Tribune*, "if my letters have been 'too good' I am honestly afraid that they are the poorest I can do"; remarkably, James was to recall this episode nearly twenty years later in a notebook entry made just three weeks after his humiliation in the theater and two weeks after recording the anecdote that became *The Turn of the*

10. Tony Tanner, "Notes for a Comparison Between American and European Romanticism," *Journal of American Studies* 2 (1968): 88.

Screw.[11] His personal writings at the time reveal a badly injured James, one who, like the governess, wondered whether he should rely on the evidence of his senses or doubt his own sanity and who, like the children, felt helpless, threatened. Some of James's strongest writing derives from an overlap of three stimuli: a story he has been told, a story he has read, and a fear in his own life. For example, *The Aspern Papers* derives from anecdotes told him by intimates of the Shelley-Byron circle, but it also has in it elements of works by Balzac and Pushkin as well as James's personal anxiety of being compromised by letters he had written to Constance Fenimore Woolson. *The Turn* seems to offer a parallel case: James had read and heard of many a ghostly visitation, and the *donnée* given him by the Archbishop acted as a catalyst, but the story also dramatizes James's fears about his own state of mind following the *Guy Domville* calamity.

From such depths any reading may rise to the surface—of course the pro-insanity critics have a case (Harold C. Goddard, Edna Kenton, Edmund Wilson, and their numberless epigones), as do those who have discovered that the true villain is the evil, manipulative Mrs. Grose (Eric Solomon, C. Knight Aldrich), and that Douglas, the narrator in the frame story, is actually the escaped Miles grown up (Louis D. Rubin, Jr.).[12] But to say that these are the only readings or even the most interesting ones is to sell short the abilities of the Henry James who needed money for his new home in Rye and who therefore set out, thoroughly within the spirit of his time, as Beidler establishes beyond doubt, yet fueled by his own serene genius as well as the fires of psychic turmoil, to acquire the pounds that had escaped him in his playwriting venture and, along the way, to write one of his most American fictions and the most riveting ghost story ever, yet a story he himself thought of as a "bogey-tale," "a pot-boiler and a *jeu d'esprit.*"

11. *Henry James: Selected Letters,* ed. Leon Edel (Cambridge: Belknap Press of Harvard University Press, 1987), 136; James, *Notebooks,* 110.

12. All these essays are included in Willen, *Casebook on "Turn of the Screw,"* except for Eric Solomon, "The Return of the Screw," *University Review* 30 (1964): 205–11.

PREFACE

Henry James made a great many revisions when he prepared the text of his 1898 story *The Turn of the Screw* for the 1909 New York Edition. Two very capable scholars have compared the two versions and published their conclusions. Leon Edel's comparison showed that James's conscious intention in the story was to focus the readers' attention on what the narrator felt, not on what she saw. The implication of Edel's finding is that James wanted his readers to know that when the narrator sees ghosts, she merely *feels* that she sees them. Not long after, E. A. Sheppard made a similar comparison of the two texts. She concluded that James's alterations were merely stylistic, tell us nothing about his conscious intentions, and offer no support to those who think the narrator merely imagines that she sees ghosts.

Readers who want to know more about this controversy are referred to the first appendix of Sheppard's book, *Henry James and "The Turn of the Screw."* All I want to say about the controversy is that it is typical of the criticism that has grown up around *The Turn of the Screw*. Two different scholars read exactly the same words but reach exactly opposite conclusions about what the words say. My point is not to criticize Edel or Sheppard. It is that modern readers of a century-old James story need something besides the text of the story itself if they are to understand the story as its author meant it to be read. We need to try to understand something of the context out of which it grew and something of the attitudes of the audience for which it was written. The purpose of this book is to reveal something of that context and those attitudes.

In accomplishing that purpose I shall in the coming pages be quoting prose selections from a great many books and journals contemporary with Henry James. I do so knowing that I myself often tend to skip or skim block quotations in scholarly works, preferring to read what the author himself or herself has to say. I

would urge readers of this book to do the opposite. The selections
I quote are, after all, interesting in their own right. Many are fun
to read and engagingly "creepy." Indeed, this book will be valuable to some readers as a kind of anthology of "factual" spiritual
cases. More important for my purposes, the selections are crucial
to an understanding of the interest in spiritualistic phenomena
that prevailed at the time that Henry James wrote *The Turn of the
Screw*. Readers who give serious attention to the selections will be
better prepared to read *The Turn of the Screw* next time around, for
they will have been carried back a century, into works now long
out of print and available only in old or specialized libraries.

I am grateful to Marion Egge for editorial assistance in preparing the text; to Carole Brown, James R. Frakes, Jan Fergus, Kath-
leen Mayberry, and Simon Smith for help with various aspects of
this book; to the staffs of the libraries at Lehigh University, the
University of Kent at Canterbury, the Society for Psychical Research, and the British Museum for their help in locating many
elusive materials; to Lehigh University for letting me go on sabbatical; to the University of Kent at Canterbury for letting me
come on sabbatical; to the Society for Psychical Research in
London for permission to quote from its *Proceedings*; to Professor
Alan Gauld, professor of psychology at the University of Not-
tingham, for directing me to Letter No. 1540 in the Lodge Collection in the archives of the Society for Psychical Research; and to
the Modern Language Association, in whose *PMLA* (100 [1985]:
96–97) I first published an excerpt from that letter, with brief
commentary.

A NOTE TO THE READER

In this study, I cite many narratives, most of them anonymous, of
ghosts and demons. Because most of these narratives are quite
short—rarely more than a few pages—I give only the titles, without page numbers, in the text of the book. Full bibliographical
information associated with each of these titles is given in my
Bibliography of Cases at the end of this book.

All citations to *The Turn of the Screw* itself are given paren-

thetically in the text by page number, referring to Robert Kimbrough's text in the 1966 Norton Critical Edition. Secondary
sources are cited in footnotes and in complete form in the Works
Cited, following the Bibliography of Cases.

P.G.B.
November 1988
Bethelehem, Pa.

INTRODUCTION
Two Readings of *The Turn of the Screw*

It is almost as if Henry James wrote two stories. They were both published in installments in *Collier's Weekly* in 1898. They are both exact transcripts of a first-person account written by a governess and read aloud by a man named Douglas, who knew the governess. They have exactly identical texts and titles and pagination. The only difference is in how the stories are read. I present below my own summaries of the two readings of *The Turn of the Screw*. The first reading makes the story a thrilling narrative about evil ghosts. The second reading, which did not begin to be fully articulated until the 1920s, makes the story a thrilling psychological study of a deluded governess.

READING 1: *Evil Ghosts*

One spring an attractive, sensitive, but naive young woman, the daughter of a country parson, answers an advertisement for a job as governess. She is interviewed by a handsome man of property and wealth in London's fashionable Harley Street. She discovers from him that the position involves the supervision of Flora, an eight-year-old girl. During vacations from his school, Miles, Flora's ten-year-old brother, will also be in the governess's charge. This young woman is enthralled with the handsome bachelor in Harley Street, uncle of the two children, with whom, by the death of their parents and grandparents, he finds himself burdened. Though troubled by the apparent mystery of the previous governess's death, the young woman nevertheless accepts the position. She even acquiesces in the uncle's primary condition: that she handle everything herself and never bother him in any way with any problems or decisions relating to the children. She cannot know that she will never see the uncle again. Nor can she know that, blessed or cursed with an unusual perception, she will soon see ghostly personages who will both terrify her and challenge her almost to the limit.

The newly appointed governess goes to Bly, the uncle's country estate. She is greeted warmly by Flora, the little girl who is to be under her care and tutelage, and by Mrs. Grose, the stout, illiterate housekeeper, who tries not to show how inordinately glad she is to see the new governess arrive. During her first night in the old house the governess hears faint noises that puzzle her—the cry of a child, a footstep outside her door.

On her second day at Bly the governess receives a letter from the headmaster of Miles's boarding school announcing that Miles shall absolutely not be permitted to return to school. No reasons for the expulsion are given, and the governess, not yet having met the boy, assumes that he must have caused some sort of injury to the other pupils. When she meets Miles on his return the next day, she is so charmed by him that she decides it is grotesque to imagine that such a lad could do any harm to anyone. She resolves not to inquire about the expulsion, either from the headmaster or from Miles himself.

One day, outdoors in the last daylight hour of a June evening, the governess daydreams about the dashing man who has hired her. She wishes he might appear and notice what a good job she is doing as governess of his niece and nephew. Looking up, she sees a man on the old square tower of the house. At first she thinks it is the handsome uncle, but a more careful look shows it to be, instead, a stranger, someone she has never seen before. The man stares down at her, moves to the opposite corner of the tower, then disappears. The governess puzzles about the intruder but finds no explanation. He is neither one of the servants nor one of the men she has seen in the small village near Bly. Concluding that he must be a traveler, curious about old houses, who has taken the liberty of coming in for a private look around, she trusts that she will never see him again.

On a Sunday many days later, before joining the others for the short walk to church, the governess comes into the dining room to pick up gloves she had left there. While there, she is startled to see this same strange man looking through the window. He looks at her, then looks around the room in a way that suggests he has really come seeking someone or something else. She gathers up her courage and rushes out to confront him, but finds him unaccountably gone. Meanwhile, Mrs. Grose has come into the dining room to see what has detained the governess. They discuss what the governess has seen.

The governess, having had a much closer look at the stranger this time, is able to describe him in detail: hair, eyes, eyebrows, whiskers, mouth, clothes. Mrs. Grose, from this description, identifies the stranger as Peter Quint, the personal valet of the Harley Street uncle. The governess learns, further, that Peter Quint had been in charge of the children for a time, that he was a rascal involved in assorted vices, and that he had died in an accident on the way home from a pub on a cold winter night. The governess comes to understand that Peter Quint must have returned from the dead in an effort to appear to, and even get hold of, Miles. She decides that it is her duty to protect Miles and his sister from this intruder.

Not long afterward, sitting with Flora beside the pond, the governess becomes aware of a second intruder, this time a woman. Dressed in black, the woman appears across the pond, a good way off from the governess and her pupil. The pale and dreadful intruder stares at Flora with a fury of intention. Flora keeps her back to the apparition, but the governess senses that Flora knows she is there. She also senses that the intruder is her predecessor, Miss Jessel, who had left Bly after a year and died in a manner not specified. Mrs. Grose later confirms, from the governess's description of the lady in black, that she is indeed very like the beautiful but infamous Miss Jessel. In subsequent weeks the governess sees both apparitions again: Peter Quint on the stairway; Miss Jessel also on the stairway and later in the schoolroom, sitting at the governess's own desk.

The two children, meanwhile, are perfect little pupils. Curiously, however, they never make any allusion to their former friends Peter Quint and Miss Jessel. And Miles never mentions anything about his experiences at the boarding school.

The governess, meanwhile, learns from Mrs. Grose about the

relationship between Peter Quint and Miles, and between Miss Jessel and Flora. She concludes that there were suspicious and unsavory dealings between Peter Quint and Miss Jessel and that the two children were probably aware of, if not a party to, certain details of that most inappropriate relationship. The governess decides that the two children cleverly continue, both night and day, to sneak out for what she assumes are meetings with their ghostly cohorts. She also senses or assumes that Peter Quint and Miss Jessel seek to entice the children to their destruction so that they may share the torments of the damned. As the governess becomes more and more certain of this, she considers appealing to the children's uncle for help. She decides, however, that he would see that appeal merely as an attempt to draw his attention to her own slighted charms. She resolves to keep her promise and to handle the matter on her own, even though she scarcely knows how to cope with the two evil spectres and can scarcely hope to succeed in protecting from them the two children, who seem determined to get into their clutches. But she knows she must try.

Summer yields to autumn after what appears to be a temporary cessation of direct or visible interaction between the ghosts and the children. The governess is still reluctant to try to discuss Peter Quint and Miss Jessel with the children or to ask Miles the reason for his dismissal from school. Indeed, these subjects have never been mentioned between them. When the governess finally does touch on these subjects, however delicately and indirectly, the disturbances begin anew. One night she asks Miles to tell her what happened before he left Bly to go to school and what happened at school before he came back. The whole room shakes and a gust of frozen air blows out the candle. Miles tells the governess that he blew the candle out.

Not long afterward, Miles entertains the governess with conversation and music in an effort to divert her attention from Flora, who seizes the opportunity to steal off and row a large boat across the lake for a rendezvous with Miss Jessel. When the governess realizes what is going on, she and Mrs. Grose rush out, find the boat missing, and walk around the lake to look for Flora. They find the boat hidden in a small inlet. Nearby they find Flora pretending to gather withered fern fronds. The governess sees

Miss Jessel observing them from the opposite bank, but Mrs. Grose, who has never seen any ghosts, does not now see one. Flora, insisting that there is nothing to be seen and never has been, begs Mrs. Grose to take her away from the governess.

Mrs. Grose does so, and the governess sees no more of Flora. The child grows feverish that night, and the next day Mrs. Grose takes her to the uncle in Harley Street. Before she leaves, however, Mrs. Grose confesses to the governess that though she has not seen ghosts herself, she believes the governess, for she has heard Flora speak dreadful horrors, in appalling language similar to language she had months earlier heard Miss Jessel use. Mrs. Grose promises to report favorably in Harley Street about the noble efforts of the governess.

The governess, meanwhile, resolves to win a confession from Miles about what went on at school and about the details of his relationship with the corrupt Peter Quint. She feels that if she can get Miles to confess he will be saved. Miles, who had earlier asked for freedom from the domineering presence of the governess, has been granted that freedom. Now, however, he seems reluctant to leave her. Miles seems to want to tell her about his experiences at school, but when he begins to do so, Peter Quint appears at the window, his white face of damnation ominous and threatening. The governess grasps the boy so that he cannot see the window and draws from him the admission that he "said things" to some of the other students. He cannot remember what they were or to whom he said them, but says that they must have been too terrible for the headmaster to put into his letter.

The governess sees that Peter Quint is still—or once again—at the window and shrieks, "No more!" Miles, apparently unable to see anything at the window, asks her if it is Miss Jessel. She says it is not Miss Jessel, but rather the coward horror. Finally Miles chokes out the name "Peter Quint—you devil!" The governess is triumphant, for this is the all-important confession of Miles's knowledge of the ghostly horror and proof that she has rescued Miles from him. Miles, apparently still seeing nothing, screams like one hurled over an abyss and dies in her arms. His little heart, dispossessed, has stopped.

READING 2: *Deluded Governess*

One spring a naive and sheltered young woman, the daughter of a whimsical, repressive country parson, answers an advertisement for a job as governess. She is interviewed by a handsome man of property and wealth in London's fashionable Harley Street. The position involves the supervision of Flora, an eight-year-old girl, and of Miles, her ten-year-old brother, during his vacations from school. The young woman falls in love with the handsome bachelor in Harley Street, uncle of the two children, with whom, by the death of their parents and grandparents, he is burdened. Although she is troubled by the mystery of the previous governess's death, her passion for the uncle persuades her to accept the position. She does so despite his primary condition: that she must handle everything herself and never bother him in any way with any problems or decisions relating to the children. Her passion for the uncle controls most of the actions of the story, which centers upon the deteriorating mental state of this dangerously impressionable governess.

When she arrives at Bly, the rich bachelor's country estate, the new governess is greeted by the delightful, warm, and open Flora, and by the stout housekeeper, Mrs. Grose. The governess is a little nervous about whether she will be able to assert her authority over Mrs. Grose because, like many victims of genteel poverty, the governess knows that all she really has to recommend her is caste. She is, therefore, jealous of the authority the uncle in Harley Street has given Mrs. Grose and is more than a little patronizing and haughty to her. The governess is pleased to note that Mrs. Grose curtsies and speaks to her with due deference. That night she fancies she hears noises about the house—the first real evidence that the governess is mad.

On her second day at Bly, the governess receives a letter from the headmaster at Miles's boarding school announcing regrets that Miles will not be able to return after the holiday. The precise contents of the letter are not revealed, but they probably bear reference to nothing more serious than that, at ten, Miles is too young to be sent away to school. The governess, however, perhaps because she is the daughter of a man whose profession is to castigate sin, has a habit of thinking the worst of people. She assumes that Miles has been expelled for doing harm to others. When she meets Miles, her propensity for ascribing wickedness to others is temporarily allayed by the boy's warmth and charm, and she resolves not to make any inquiries about what happened at school. Still, the letter upsets her and gives her a sleepless night. Sleeplessness, prolonged reading, and general nervousness about her new duties and strange surroundings soon reduce the governess to a state of exhaustion.

In just such a state, late on a June day, the governess looks up to the top of the old tower on the house and sees the Harley Street uncle gazing down at her. Startled, she looks again and sees not the man she loves, but a stranger. He soon also disappears from her view. This is the first of eight seizures during her time at Bly, seizures in which the mad governess, gripped by her paranoia and exhausted beyond measure, thinks she sees ghosts. Not sure what to make of what she imagines she has seen on the tower, she decides not to mention her experience.

Many days later, on a Sunday, just before joining the others for the walk to church, she comes into the dining room to pick up gloves she had left there. Startled by that same stranger looking at her through the window, the governess behaves in a very curious manner. Instead of screaming and running for help, she proves just how insane she is by mutely rushing outside to try to apprehend the intruder herself. Not surprisingly, she finds no one there. Mrs. Grose, meanwhile, comes to see what has detained the governess. They discuss what she has seen.

The governess, after a hysterical and deranged account of her two experiences with this stranger, proceeds to a detailed description of his clothes, his face, his demeanor. Mrs. Grose, apparently seizing on only the most general features of the governess's description—his handsomeness, his wearing no hat, his borrowed clothes—identifies him as the dead valet, Peter Quint. The housekeeper had distrusted and hated Peter Quint when he was alive. Herself something of a snob, she had been annoyed beyond measure that a mere valet had been sent to Bly to take charge of the children and the house. Her resentment had not ended even with his death, and at the first suggestion of a horrid-looking intruder at Bly, she jumps to the conclusion that the governess has seen the ghost of the despised Peter Quint. Her identification of the governess's imagined visitor is unfortunate, for it simply feeds the governess's delusions and helps to set the stage for her further mental deterioration.

The governess suffers other seizures. In one she imagines that a ghostly woman in black watches Flora from across the pond. She even imagines that Flora is aware that the ghost is there and that it is the ghost of Miss Jessel, the previous governess. The governess discusses the experience with Mrs. Grose, who is surprised, but does not try to dissuade her from her beliefs. Mrs. Grose is by now beginning to suspect that the governess is insane, but cannot be sure. She would not know what to do even if she were sure. During the next weeks the governess has three more seizures. In one she sees Peter Quint on the stairway; in two more she sees Miss Jessel, first on the stairway, then in the schoolroom at the desk.

The children, meanwhile, are perfect pupils. They behave well and do their lessons impeccably, even for this maniacal governess who behaves so irresponsibly both as guardian and as school-mistress. They are puzzled by her gushy, overprotective behavior, put up with her crushing embraces and frenzied kisses, and wonder silently when she laughs hysterically at unfunny things. They refrain from speaking about subjects they suspect she will find upsetting, like Peter Quint and Miss Jessel, and make no mention whatever of Miles's experiences at his boarding school.

The governess grows more and more demented as her imagination, sorting hysterically through a few unfavorable comments made by Mrs. Grose, conjures up nasty suspicions about the relationship between the children and their former protectors. She does not name all of her suspicions, but she is sure that the details, were they all known, would be shocking. She is sure, also, that Flora and Miles try to deceive her so that they have time, individually, to sneak off to meet their ghostly friends, who are trying to woo the children to destruction and to the eternal torments of hell. The governess considers, or pretends to consider, sending to the uncle in Harley Street for help, but in the end she determines not to do so. She is afraid he will think her crazy and either fire her or try to have her committed to an asylum. Also, of course, when she took the job she had promised not to bother him about the children, and she still has hopes of winning his approval by adhering to the main condition of her employment. She determines to ride out the crisis on her own, not realizing that there is no crisis.

As summer yields to autumn there seems to be a lull in the governess's propensity to imagine ghostly disturbances. Eventually, however, she feels that she must take some action to force the children to admit their complicity in wicked actions. One night she does ask Miles what happened at Bly before he went to school and what happened at school before he came back. Her only desire, she says, is to save him. She then imagines that the room shakes and that the candle is blown out. Miles, not sure how to behave in the face of such violent lunacy on the governess's part, meekly tells her that he blew out the candle. The governess's martyr complex is by now obvious: she insanely seeks to win a kind of sainthood by saving the two children from evil, pain, and damnation.

Not long afterward, Miles tries to calm the governess by playing the piano. She is soothed for a time, but then her paranoia takes over again, and she believes that he has been playing merely to distract her so that Flora can run off for a secret meeting with Miss Jessel. The governess gets Mrs. Grose, and the two rush down to the lake, where the governess had earlier imagined she had seen Flora and Miss Jessel meeting. The governess thinks the boat is gone and that Flora and Miss Jessel have rowed it across the lake. The boat, however, is right there where it always is—for again the insane governess sees only what she wants to see. The governess and a reluctant Mrs. Grose rush around the lake, where they find Flora gathering ferns. During another seizure the governess imagines that she sees Miss Jessel watching them. She is distressed to discover, however, that Mrs. Grose does not see the ghost and that Flora pretends not to. The delicate Flora, alarmed by the ranting governess, begs Mrs. Grose to take her away.

Mrs. Grose does so, and the governess sees no more of Flora. The child, severely frightened by the insane governess, grows feverish in the night, and the next day Mrs. Grose moves her to safety at the uncle's house in Harley Street. To calm the governess, Mrs. Grose pretends to believe in the ghosts, even though she cannot see them, and promises to put in a good word about the governess to the children's uncle.

The demented governess, having failed to save Flora from Miss Jessel, now determines at least to save Miles from Peter Quint. Trying to protect the poor boy, she really becomes his jailer. She prowls the halls at night to make sure he does not escape. Her final seizure comes after dinner with Miles. She insists that he confess, and the boy, to appease and calm her, blurts out some vague story about how he must have said terrible things at school. He does not remember what those things were or to whom he said them, but he supposes them too terrible for the headmaster to mention in a letter.

The governess, now far gone, thinks she sees Peter Quint once again at the window. Presumably afraid that Miles is about to be carried off by Quint, she determines to save Miles from his demonic clutches. She seizes Miles, holds him desperately to her, and shrieks at the window, "No more!" Miles asks her if it is Miss Jessel she sees. She tells him it is the coward horror. Miles, now thoroughly terrified by his grimacing, shrieking jailer, chokes out the words, "Peter Quint—you devil!" The governess takes this as evidence that she has saved him by wringing from him the name of his former friend. She does not realize, in her insane frenzy, that she has wrung from him also his life. Miles lies dead in her arms, having been frightened literally to death by this terrifyingly insane governess.

My synopsis of the second reading is a somewhat generalized summation of the readings of a number of "nonapparitionists"— critics who do not believe James wrote a ghost story. Among these critics are Harold C. Goddard, Edna Kenton, Edmund Wilson, and Leon Edel, who have all argued that the governess is insane. My synopsis is based especially, however, on a 1965 study by Thomas M. Cranfill and his nephew, Robert L. Clark, Jr.: *An Anatomy of "The Turn of the Screw."* Cranfill and Clark sort out and consolidate the work of previous writers who prefer to focus on the mental state of the governess rather than on the mysterious dangers she encounters at Bly. Cranfill and Clark extend the psychological interpretation somewhat in their own directions, adding particularly their views of Mrs. Grose and the role she plays in the story of the governess's developing lunacy.

There are other ways to read the story. One is that *The Turn of the Screw* is the story neither of ghosts nor of the governess's insanity but rather of the deception of the governess by skilled manipulators. Another is that it is a satire of the Gothic novel. Another is that it is a love letter to the uncle in Harley Street. Another is that it is a fairy tale. Another is that it is merely the governess's nightmarish dream. Still another is that the story tells us less about ghosts or governesses than about Henry James's own psychological state. None of these interpretations have held much sway, and all are sufficiently wide of the Jamesian mark that they require little comment. There remain, however, the two dominant and opposite ways to read the story: that the ghosts are real and the governess sane; and that the ghosts are imaginary and the governess insane.

In the pages that follow, I shall have little to say about the second reading, the reading that finds the real kernel of the story to be less in the malignant influences of two dead servants than in the demented psyche of the observer of those influences. This second reading is now—at least on the American side of the Atlantic—the dominant reading, and it requires little more commentary than it has already received. It satisfies the modern demand for literary complexity and ambiguity, and it results in what is for most of us a quite pleasing way to see the story. It may be of interest that I began my pedagogical years with *The Turn of the Screw* as an enthusiastic advocate of the second reading. It was, after all, the more sophisticated reading, and I confess that I rather enjoyed springing on my students a reading that few of them had thought of. I found that I was skillful at overlooking or explaining away certain key facts of the story that did not fit gracefully into the notion that the governess is insane: Miles's expulsion from school; Miles's blowing out the candle; Flora's boat trip across the pond; Mrs. Grose's ability to identify Peter Quint from the governess's detailed description; Mrs. Grose's final assertion that she believes the governess; Douglas's insistence on the governess's good character; and the governess's own ability— quite strange if she were so unbalanced—to go on to become a successful and admired governess in other respectable families. As I began to discover and to analyze the evidence I present in this book, however, I reluctantly yielded to that evidence and began to see that, whatever else it may be, *The Turn of the Screw* is also a ghost story. But I also came to believe that this reading is insufficient unless it is expanded to include the concept of demon possession.

In developing these ideas I will not attempt still another extended "close reading of the text." Nor shall I attempt a full and complete review of the scholarship done by previous critics. Anyone who has read the critics knows that, armed with certain assumptions, they can prove almost anything by a close reading of the text: that there are ghosts in the story; that there are no ghosts in the story; that the children are good; that the children are evil; that the governess is insane; that the governess is a liar; that the governess is a saint; that the governess is an emotional cannibal; that the governess is a novelist; that the governess is possessed by the devil; that Douglas is Miles; that Douglas is gay; that the narrator of the opening frame story is a woman; that Douglas had proposed marriage to the governess but had been rejected; that Miss Jessel is alive and locked in the tower; that the tower is a phallic symbol; that Mrs. Grose is the mother of Flora; that Peter Quint is not dead after all; that the governess's father is mad; that the governess feels an incestuous attraction for Miles; that the governess accidentally chokes Miles to death; that the governess suffocates Miles; that the governess murders Miles to keep him from carrying tales to his uncle; that the governess has frontal-lobe epilepsy; that the governess spends the decade after

Miles's death in an insane asylum; that Bly is the setting for a Faustian allegory; that Bly is an allegorical Garden of Eden; that Bly is James's own haunted mind; that James had once witnessed his parents making love; that James was horrified by his own attraction to little boys; and so on. I shall from time to time refer both to the text of James's story and to the published opinions of certain other critics. I shall not, however, offer an exhaustive discussion of either.

The time has come in the history of the criticism of *The Turn of the Screw* to turn away for a moment both from the slender text of the story and from the fat volumes of scholarship on it. The time has come for us to try to reorient ourselves, away from the assumptions prevalent at the end of the twentieth century and toward the assumptions prevalent at the end of the nineteenth. The time has come to consider not what *we* know about ghosts and young women who see them but what men and women in Henry James's time knew about ghosts and about the young women who saw them. The time has come, in other words, to look at the context out of which *The Turn of the Screw* was written, and to reconstruct the intellectual climate that James and his first readers shared.

As a first step in that reconstruction, let us look at three assumptions that many modern readers have been taught to bring to a reading of the story:

Assumption 1: Narrators who lie are pathological liars. The governess lies to Mrs. Grose after seeing Miss Jessel at her desk in the schoolroom. Although Miss Jessel said nothing, the governess reports to Mrs. Grose that she had "a talk" with Miss Jessel in which Miss Jessel said that she suffered the torments of the damned and wanted Flora to share them with her. Why does the governess lie? She lies because she feels the need to keep the literal-minded and skeptical housekeeper informed about what the governess's more subtle powers of perception reveal to her. We must recall that we know the governess lies only because she herself reveals, even admits, that she did. When Mrs. Grose asks if Miss Jessel really spoke, the governess clarifies her hasty statements by saying, "It came to that" (p. 60). "It came to that" seems to mean "I knew what she would have said" or "she might as well have spoken, for her looks said everything." I shall have more to say about this lie in connection with the Miss Lister narrative in chapter 2. For now I suggest only that such lies to another character in the story are not proof that the governess is a pathological liar. For now I suggest only that the governess has many faults. She is a poor judge of the character and intentions of handsome bachelors. She allows herself to be used. She is naive. She is rather too full of her own importance. She sometimes thinks that small matters are large and that large matters are small. She is afraid to confront certain puzzling questions directly. She is a bit snobbish. She is slow to act. She fibs when she thinks she needs to. She is fallible. She is human. But we cannot therefore conclude that when she reports that the boat is missing, she is lying, or that she sneaks into town to learn enough on the sly about Peter Quint so that she can subsequently draw Mrs. Grose into the subtle web of her own delusions. If we do not accept the facts the governess reports, we are left with no story at all: there was no uncle in Harley Street, no job offer, no Bly, no tower, no Peter Quint, no lake, no boat.

Assumption 2: Good fiction forces readers to work hard. When Edna Kenton proclaimed the traditional ghost-story reading of *The Turn of the Screw* to be "lazy,"[1] she began the serious questioning of the prevalent view that James wrote a scary story about corrupt dead servants who try to woo two young children. Surely, Kenton implied, it is a ghost story only to those who lack the energy to probe further. Surely, if we *work* hard enough, we will discover James's true intentions, his subtle meanings and sophisticated modern characterizations. Yet perhaps we should recall that *The Turn of the Screw* was written for a popular audience in a popular magazine, and was serialized over several months. Can we be so sure that James wanted or expected his audience to work hard to interpret a story that he himself called "a pot-boiler"?[2]

1. Edna Kenton, "Henry James to the Ruminant Reader: *The Turn of the Screw*," 253.

2. Henry James, *Letters*, ed. Leon Edel, 4:86.

Perhaps we should also recall that Henry James wrote this story shortly after an unsuccessful foray into writing plays, shortly after the audience booed and hissed him on the opening of *Guy Domville*, and shortly after he signed a long-term lease on Lamb House in Rye. Henry James needed the reassurance of a popular success and he needed cash. In such a situation, would he have been likely to write a super-subtle work that would elude and confuse all but the most sophisticated, careful, and workaholic of readers?

Assumption 3: Because there are no ghosts, Henry James would not write a ghost story. Many of the modern readings of *The Turn of the Screw* begin with this assumption. Gerald Willen, in the preface to the second edition of his casebook on the story, summarizes his own views thus: "All this is not to say that we cannot read the story as a ghost story. . . . But if we do take the ghosts to be 'real,' we are simply deluding ourselves, since ghosts, realistically speaking, do not exist."[3] And Edwin Fussell feels that it would strain a "normal reader's normal expectations" to believe that the governess had actually experienced the events she depicts in her story.[4] Readers who begin with this assumption about ghosts have little choice but to conclude that the governess is lying, or is writing fiction, or is deceived, or is insane, when she says she sees ghosts. My purposes in the first four chapters of this book are to question the validity of this assumption by presenting documentary evidence that ghosts were taken seriously by many sophisticated men and women in the last half of the nineteenth century, and to show that in portraying Peter Quint and Miss Jessel as he does, Henry James was aligning his fiction with a substantial body of published evidence showing that ghosts in some sense do exist.

My purpose in the fifth and sixth chapters is to show that in portraying Peter Quint and Miss Jessel as demons who possess the living, James was aligning himself with a more questionable,

---

3. Gerald Willen, ed., *A Casebook on Henry James's "The Turn of the Screw,"* vii.
4. Edwin Fussell, "The Ontology of *The Turn of the Screw*," 119.

but still abundant, body of published opinion. My purpose in the last chapter is to show that James's own comments, written after completing his story, reveal a sophisticated writer who thought he had made ghosts and demons characters in a serious fiction.

I should like to make clear, right from the beginning, that I do not believe that Henry James read all of the cases I cite in the coming chapters. I am certain, however, that he read some of them, and I believe that the many cases I cite are evidence that an interest in spiritualism was prevalent among thinking men and women in the last half of the nineteenth century. Furthermore, I wish to make clear that it is no part of my argument that James himself personally believed in either ghosts or demons. He may or may not have believed in them. He may have believed in ghosts of some sort, but not in demons. He may have changed his mind on such matters over the years. I cannot say, and it does not matter.

What does matter is that we come to an understanding of the artistic uses to which Henry James puts his ghostly personages. To approach such an understanding, we need to determine whether Henry James portrayed Peter Quint and Miss Jessel in such a way that they would have been recognized as realistic by his contemporary readers. The following several chapters are an attempt to make that determination. They will show us that Henry James knew the people who were at the very center of certain controversies about ghosts and demons, that he had read widely in the published books and articles about such subjects, and that he was careful to write *The Turn of the Screw* in such a way that it would have sounded realistic to those at least generally familiar with spiritualism and psychical research.

1

THE RISE OF SPIRITUALISM
AND PSYCHICAL RESEARCH

Beliefs akin to spiritualism and activities akin to psychical research can be traced back thousands of years. It is not necessary to do so for an understanding of the attitudes and controversies that surrounded both phenomena during the last few years of the nineteenth century, the years in which Henry James planned and wrote *The Turn of the Screw*. It will be sufficient for our purposes to begin with two events that took place in the year 1848, when Henry James was a lad of five. Fifty years later he would publish, in a popular journal, a story that grew out of forces set in motion in that year.

The first event took place on the last day of March 1848 in the village of Hydesville, in New York State. A blacksmith named Fox had just moved into a house in Hydesville with his wife and two daughters, aged fourteen and twelve. After the family had been there for a few months, they began to hear unexplained rappings in the bedroom. That was strange enough. Even stranger was the fact that one evening the two Fox daughters and their mother, Margaret, found a way to get the maker of the rappings to communicate with them. But let us hear the story in the words of Margaret Fox, the mother, who made a statement about the experience less than two weeks after that strange evening:

My husband had not gone to bed when we first heard the noise on this evening. I had just laid down. It commenced as usual. I knew it from all other noises I had ever heard in the house. The girls, who slept in the other bed in the room, heard the noise, and tried to make a similar noise by snapping their fingers. The youngest girl is about 12 years old; she is the one who made her hand go. As fast as she made the noise with her hands or fingers, the sound was followed up in the room. It did not sound any different at that time, only it made the same number of noises that the girl did. When she stopped, the sound itself stopped for a short time.

The other girl, who is in her 15th year, then spoke in sport and said,

"Now do this just as I do. Count 1, 2, 3, 4," &c, striking one hand in the other at the same time. The blows which she made were repeated as before. It appeared to answer her by repeating every blow that she made. She only did so once. She then began to be startled; and then I spoke and said to the noise, "Count ten," and it made ten strokes or noises. Then I asked the ages of my different children successively and it gave a number of raps, corresponding to the ages of my children.

I then asked if it was a human being that was making the noise? and if it was, to manifest it by the same noise. There was no noise. I then asked if it was a spirit? and if it was, to manifest it by two sounds. I heard two sounds as soon as the words were spoken. I then asked if it was an injured spirit? to give me the sound, and I heard the rapping distinctly. I then asked if it was injured in this house? and it manifested it by the noise. If the person was living that injured it? and got the same answer. I then ascertained by the same method that its remains were buried under the dwelling.[1]

Neighbors were brought in to verify the strange rappings. Depositions were taken from previous occupants of the house, including Jane Lape, who had once visited the house as a guest of the Weekmans, former occupants of the house. She stated that one afternoon she had seen a ghostly man in the house:

I saw a man in the bed-room joining the kitchen. The bed-room door was open, and I saw the man distinctly. . . . I had been in the kitchen some time at work, and knew that no one had gone into that room. The man stood facing me when I saw him. He did not speak, nor did I hear any noise at any time, like a person walking or moving about in the room. He had on grey pants, black frock coat and black cap. He was about middling size, I should think. I knew of no person in that vicinity who wore a similar dress. Mrs. Weekman was in another part of the house. . . . I was very much frightened and left the room, and when I returned with Mrs. W. there was no person there.[2]

Additional stories were brought to light, about a peddler who was last seen entering the house, about human bones discovered buried in the basement, and so on. I cannot tell the full story here. Interested readers can conveniently read more about it in Alan Gauld's *The Founders of Psychical Research*.

1. Alan Gauld, *The Founders of Psychical Research*, 4.
2. Ibid., 6.

The serious study of modern spiritualism, a study later called psychical research, can be said to have originated with the Foxes. The sisters became famous. They were invited to other towns and cities, where they took part in remarkable seances. Crowds gathered. Newspapers did interviews. Skeptics searched for hidden devices or wires. Horace Greeley, then editor of the *Tribune*, invited the Foxes to stay at his home for several days and later wrote that most of the people who had seen them were convinced that the strange noises were not produced by any human means. The Foxes were so beset with requests for seances that they began accepting money for them and so became, in effect, the first professional mediums. Soon other mediums began to admit to having had similar experiences. Some of these were proved to be fraudulent con artists, but even so, it was evident that something big had begun.

By 1853 there were no less than ten spiritualist newspapers in the United States. Soon it was fashionable to have opinions about spirit rappings and table tappings and even to have had personal experiences that tended to prove or to disprove their reliability. In 1869, in a review of a book on spiritualism, Henry James's brother William wrote:

We see tens of thousands of respectable people on the one hand admitting as facts of everyday certainty what tens of thousands of others equally respectable claim to be an abject and contemptible delusion; while other tens of thousands are content to stand passively in the dark between these two hosts and in doubt, the matter meanwhile being—rightfully considered—one of really transcendent interest.[3]

By 1880 the transcendent interest in spiritualism had taken such hold on both sides of the Atlantic that Wirt Sikes, in his book *British Goblins*, could say with remarkable matter-of-factness:

This age is superstitious with regard to ghosts. . . . The "controls" of the modern spiritualistic seance have the world for their audience. The United States, a land generally deemed—at least by its inhabitants—to be

3. Ibid., 30.

the most advanced in these directions of any on God's footstool, gave birth to modern spiritualism. . . . With the masses, some degree of belief in the spirits is so nearly universal that I need hardly qualify the adjective.[4]

Even when allowances are made for exaggeration—Sikes was eager to show that the Welsh were not the *only* superstitious people in the world—these statements suggest that within a few decades after the Fox sisters had heard those rappings, spiritualism was a major force in American intellectual life. And it had all begun in Henry James's home state.

The second crucial event of 1848 was the publication of Catherine Stevens Crowe's *The Night Side of Nature: or, Ghosts and Ghost Seers*. This book went through several editions and many, many printings in the fifty years before Henry James published *The Turn of the Screw*. It was the classic collection of "real" ghost narratives and was the most influential single book about ghosts in the second half of the nineteenth century. Catherine Crowe brought to the early stirrings of psychical research a wide knowledge of the writings of German intellectuals. Not an original researcher herself, she did more than anyone else to popularize ghost research in England and to bring it "out of the closet."

I can best convey the state of the art of ghost research in the middle of the nineteenth century by quoting from Crowe's introduction to the first edition of *The Night Side of Nature*. She begins with a brief history of classical and Christian theories regarding the survival of the human soul after the death of the body. Then she quickly brings history down to her own times. The rationalism of the eighteenth century, she says, had all but put an end to "belief," and even "science" had become the handmaiden of despotic prejudices that refused to consider theories about any kind of life after death:

To minds which can admit nothing but what can be explained and demonstrated, an investigation of this sort must appear perfectly idle. . . . Experience, observation, and intuition, must be our principal,

4. Wirt Sikes, *British Goblins*, 138–39.

if not our only, guides. . . . If scientific men could but comprehend how they discredit the science they profess, by their despotic arrogance and exclusive scepticism, they would surely, for the sake of that very science they love, affect more liberality and candour.[5]

A woman of strong opinion and ready generalization, Crowe finds the scientists of Germany to be more open-minded and courageous than those of her own England, at least regarding the possibility of life after death:

I wish also to make the English public acquainted with the ideas entertained on these subjects by a large proportion of German minds of the highest order. It is a distinctive characteristic of the thinkers of that country, that in the first place, they do think independently and cou- rageously; and, in the second, that they never shrink from promulgating the opinions they have been led to form, however new, strange, hetero- dox, or even absurd, they may appear to others. They do not succumb, as people do in this country, to the fear of ridicule, nor are they in danger of the odium that here pursues those who deviate from established notions.[6]

Although Crowe condemns British academics for being un- scientific, negative, and unwilling to consider the truths that intuition, observation, and experience offer to them, she finds more to hope for among the British common people, for they are more open-minded to the truth about ghosts:

I think I might venture to assert that I have the majority on my side, as far as regards ghosts—for it is beyond a doubt that many more are disposed to believe than to confess—and those who do confess are not few.[7]

Although Crowe does not claim to offer the public a book that has scientific merit, she nevertheless hopes her book will repre- sent a forward step toward a time when men of science will take seriously the kind of phenomena she reports:

It was the tendency of the last age to reject and *deny* everything they did not understand; I hope it is the growing tendency of the present one to

5. Catherine Stevens Crowe, *The Night Side of Nature; or, Ghosts and Ghost Seers,* 2–3.
6. Ibid., 5.
7. Ibid., 7.

examine what we do not understand. . . . There is a day yet brooding in the bosom of time, when the sciences will be no longer isolated; when we shall no longer deny, but be able to account for phenomena apparently prodigious; or have the modesty, if we cannot explain them, to admit that the difficulty arises solely from our own incapacity.[8]

There is a good deal more to Crowe's introduction than I have quoted, and a great deal more to her book, which runs to more than five hundred pages in most editions. Suffice it to say that her book is a compendium of what was at mid-century known or believed about dreams, trances, wraiths, doubles, apparitions, survival, will, spirits, hauntings, poltergeists, and possession. We shall glance in chapter 3 at brief selections from some of the cases Crowe cites, and in chapter 5 at what she has to say about possession. For now, however, I shall say no more except that Crowe's *The Night Side of Nature* was to psychical research in England what Stowe's *Uncle Tom's Cabin* was to the abolition of slavery in the United States. It got a lot of people thinking about a subject that had not much concerned them before.

Catherine Crowe must have been very pleased if she learned about what came to be called the "Cambridge Ghost Club." In 1851, just three years after her book was published, several members of Cambridge University, particularly those associated with Trinity College, formed a society the express purpose of which was to do precisely what she had recommended: investigate various matters previously referred to as either delusory or supernatural. Consisting of both faculty and students, members of the society sent out circulars describing the aims of the group and inviting individuals to write down and submit accounts of any supernatural experiences they had had. That circular, excerpted below, is interesting especially for the tone of the opening statement and for the closing request for information about the "natural temperament" of the person who had had the experience being reported:

8. Ibid., 11–12.

CIRCULAR OF A SOCIETY, INSTITUTED BY MEMBERS
OF THE UNIVERSITY OF CAMBRIDGE, ENGLAND,
FOR THE PURPOSE OF INVESTIGATING PHENOMENA
POPULARLY CALLED SUPERNATURAL.

The interest and importance of a serious and earnest inquiry into the nature of the phenomena which are vaguely called "supernatural" will scarcely be questioned. Many persons believe that all such apparently mysterious occurrences are due either to purely natural causes, or to delusions of the mind or senses, or to willful deception. But there are many others who believe it possible that the beings of the unseen world may manifest themselves to us in extraordinary ways. . . . The main impediment to investigations of this kind is the difficulty of obtaining a sufficient number of clear and well-attested cases. Many of the stories current in tradition, or scattered up and down in books, may be exactly true; others must be purely fictitious; others, again,—probably the greater number,—consist of a mixture of truth and falsehood. But it is idle to examine the significance of an alleged fact of this nature until the trustworthiness, and also the extent, of the evidence for it are ascertained. Impressed with this conviction, some members of the University of Cambridge are anxious, if possible, to form an extensive collection of authenticated cases of supposed "supernatural" agency. . . . From all those, then, who may be inclined to aid them, they request written communications, with full details of persons, times, and places; but it will not be required that names should be inserted without special permission, unless they have already become public property: it is, however, indispensable that the person making any communication should be acquainted with the names, and should pledge himself for the truth of the narrative from his own knowledge or conviction. . . . Every narrative of "supernatural" agency which may be communicated will be rendered far more instructive if accompanied by any particulars as to the observer's natural temperament, (*e.g.* sanguine, nervous, &c.,) constitution, (*e.g.* subject to fever, somnambulism, &c.,) and state at the time, (*e.g.* excited in mind or body, &c.).

Communications may be addressed to
REV. B. F. WESTCOTT, *Harrow, Middlesex*

I quote from this circular as it appears in the appendix of an 1869 book by Robert Dale Owen, *Footfalls on the Boundary of Another World*. Owen refuses to reveal the names of any of the members. He claims to have learned the names from "the son of a British peer, himself one of the leading members," and will say of these men only that "some of them [are] now at the head of well-known institutions, most of them clergymen and fellows of Trinity College, and almost all of them men who had graduated with the highest honors." Treating the club almost as if it were a secret society, he tells us that it "first came to my attention through the Bishop of —, who took an interest in its proceedings and bestirred himself to obtain contributions to its records."[9] Owen's refusal to publish the names of any of the members suggests that he was concerned that he might harm the reputations of men in high places. It also suggests that at least some spiritualists, even as late as 1869, were reluctant to face the ridicule that had often been the lot of people who expressed a serious interest in the supernatural. That attitude toward psychical researchers was to change considerably in the course of the next few decades.

The Cambridge Ghost Club is notable less for what it accomplished than for its bringing together, under a cloak of some respectability, a group of educated and serious men willing to admit, at least among themselves, that there might be something worth looking at in phenomena usually called supernatural. The club is perhaps most notable in that one of its early members, a young Trinity man named Henry Sidgwick, eventually agreed to become the founding president of the Society for Psychical Research.

The establishment of such a society was not Sidgwick's idea. Rather, it appears to have been originally suggested either by a journalist and spiritualist named Edmund D. Rogers or by a professor of physics named W. F. Barrett, who convened the original meetings at which the society was discussed in January 1882 in London. At those first meetings were Henry Sidgwick, Frederic W. H. Myers, and Edmund Gurney. All were interested in psychical phenomena, but none was particularly optimistic about the prospects for successful or conclusive investigations of such phenomena. Myers and Gurney agreed to support the new society on the condition that Sidgwick agree to become its president. Sidgwick, though not interested in doing active psychical research himself, agreed to take the office. That he did turned out to be most fortunate for the society. Soon to be named professor

9. Robert Dale Owen, *Footfalls on the Boundary of Another World*, 33–34.

of moral philosophy at Trinity College, Sidgwick brought to the new society a level-headedness, a dignity of bearing, a disinterestedness, and a public presence that were to help the fledgling organization weather many a crisis.

The stated aim of the Society for Psychical Research when it was established in 1882 was, "without prejudice or prepossession of any kind, and in the same spirit of exact and unimpassioned enquiry which has enabled Science to solve so many problems, . . . to investigate that large body of debateable phenomena designated by such terms as mesmeric, psychical and spiritualistic."[10] This aim was apparently widely applauded. Men and women of considerable eminence in many walks of British life became members of that early Society for Psychical Research. By the end of the decade its membership had risen to over seven hundred, and included prime ministers, bishops, titled persons, scientists of various persuasions, and even such literary men as Tennyson and Ruskin.

The society set up six special working subcommittees. Only two of them merit mention in connection with the present study. One was a "Literary Committee," charged with collecting and collating materials relating to thought-transference, mesmerism, and various other perceptual and psychical phenomena. The other was the "Committee on Apparitions, Haunted Houses, etc." The interests of both committees came together through the tireless work of Edmund Gurney, who wrote *Phantasms of the Living*, a book of central importance to a study of *The Turn of the Screw*.

Phantasms of the Living, published in 1886, consists of reports and discussions of some seven hundred individual cases possibly involving spirits. Most of the work of collecting, investigating, classifying, and analyzing these cases was done by Gurney, though he had some help from an associate named Frank Podmore, and even more from Frederic Myers, who wrote the lengthy introduction and other sections. Many of the cases dealt with visual apparitions that appeared to living persons ("perci-

10. Gauld, *Founders*, 138.

pients") before, at, or shortly after the death of the person
("agent") whose apparition appeared. Gurney and Myers provided complicated theoretical constructs designed to give appropriately scientific explanations of the reported phenomena. These
two men had somewhat different theories about the nature and
origin of the phantasms. I shall not here go into the sometimes
convoluted logic of their explanations or of the questions that
those explanations raised: Did people see apparitions because of
telepathic communication or because of clairvoyance? Were the
"hallucinations" subjective (merely in the mind of the perceiver)
or veridical (matched by an objective reality outside the perceiver)? I shall say only that the theories tended to be more
complicated than the phenomena they were designed to explain,
and that the narrative cases themselves were far more interesting
and concrete than the theories. There is no evidence that Henry
James was interested in those theories. There is, on the other
hand, ample evidence—as we shall see in the next two chapters—
of his interest in the narratives, in the many reported cases of
"real" ghosts.

Were they real, those ghosts reported to the investigators of the
Society for Psychical Research? That, of course, was the question
everyone was asking. The answer depended on what people
meant by "real." There were, of course, grave skeptics, even in
the ranks of the Society for Psychical Research, a body of individuals committed to investigating phenomena rather than to
proving that one view or another was correct. Most individuals
who studied the various cases, however, and who interviewed the
people who claimed to have seen ghosts, reached the conclusion
that there must be *something* real about *some* of the reported ghost
cases. Whereas it might be unreasonable to suppose that ghosts
appear to the living, they wrote, it was even more unreasonable
to assume that there was no validity to the accumulated evidence
that some kind of real communication could take place between
the dead and the living. Gurney believed, for example, that
though no single ghostly report was in itself fully persuasive, the
more reports there were, and the more individuals there were
who reported seeing ghosts, the less likely it was that the cases

were all false. To believe that there were nonspiritual "causes" for them all, Gurney said, was finally to believe the incredible:

> Common-sense persists in recognising that when phenomena, which are united by a fundamental characteristic and have every appearance of forming a single natural group, are presented to be explained, an explanation which multiplies causes is improbable, and an explanation which multiplies improbable causes becomes, at a certain point, incredible.[11]

Note that Gurney does not insist that all these cases definitely prove anything, merely that it is unreasonable to ignore so much carefully collected and substantially attested evidence.

While Gurney was working on the monumental task of organizing and interpreting the accumulated files on phantasms of the living, Eleanor Sidgwick, wife of Henry Sidgwick and later president in her own right of the Society for Psychical Research, took on the task of analyzing the 370 cases in the society's files on phantasms of the dead. It should be noted here that phantasms—those various visual, auditory, and tactile spirit phenomena—were somewhat arbitrarily categorized into one of two groups. For reasons I need not go into here, phantasms of dead people that had manifested themselves within twelve hours after death were classed as "phantasms of the living." A great many of the cases reported in Gurney's book, then, were really cases of spirit manifestations of the newly dead. The cases that Eleanor Sidgwick reviewed included only those that manifested themselves more than twelve hours after death. After analyzing the 370 cases, and after discussing four possible theories for explaining the evidence reported in those files, Eleanor Sidgwick published the most cautious and benign of conclusions in the 1885 *Proceedings of the Society for Psychical Research*:

> The evidence before us is quite inadequate to enable us to decide among these theories, or even to say that one of them is strongly supported by it. The only thing to be done, therefore, is to obtain more evidence.[12]

11. Edmund Gurney, Frederic W. H. Myers, and Frank Podmore, *Phantasms of the Living*, 163–64.

12. *Proceedings of the Society for Psychical Research* 3 (1885): 148. Cited hereafter as *PSPR*.

She was, indeed, so cautious that she annoyed some other members, who felt that she ought to have come forward at least with a hypothesis. Her conclusion about haunted houses, after she had reviewed the evidence and interviewed many witnesses, was a little more bold, but still almost amusingly circumspect:

I can only say that having made every effort—as my paper will, I hope, have shown—to exercise a reasonable scepticism, I yet do not feel equal to the degree of unbelief in human testimony necessary to avoid accepting at least provisionally the conclusion that there are, in a certain sense, haunted houses, *i.e.*, that there are houses in which similar quasi-human apparitions have occurred at different times to different inhabitants, under circumstances which exclude the hypothesis of suggestion or expectation.[13]

The extreme reluctance of the most serious members of the Society for Psychical Research to draw conclusions was well known to anyone who read their reports. It was almost as if they wanted to avoid criticism of their conclusions by not stating any. Method was everything, and caution was a key feature of the method. In an article in the 1889 *Proceedings*, for example, Gurney suggested a method for summarily excluding most of the reported ghost cases as evidence of anything except the imaginings of the person reporting the ghost:

There remain three, and I think only three, conditions which might establish a presumption that an apparition or other immediate manifestation of a dead person is something more than a mere subjective hallucination of the percipient's senses. Either (1) more persons than one might be independently affected by the phenomenon; or (2) the phantasm might convey information, afterwards discovered to be true, of something which the percipient had never known; or (3) the appearance might be that of a person whom the percipient himself had never seen, and of whose aspect he was ignorant, and yet his description of it might be sufficiently definite for identification.[14]

13. *PSPR* 3 (1885): 142.
14. *PSPR* 5 (1889): 404.

When Eleanor Sidgwick and others conducted their "Census of Hallucinations" in 1889, they asked some seventeen thousand individuals, from all segments of society, this question:

Have you ever, when believing yourself to be completely awake, had a vivid impression of seeing or being touched by a living being or inanimate object, or of hearing a voice; which impression, so far as you could discover, was not due to any external physical cause?[15]

They received 2,272 affirmative responses from the 17,000 respondees. By the time they had rejected the reported cases that were obviously suspect, probably coincidental, possibly contaminated in some way, or unacceptable for some other reason, they had a mere 32 cases that they felt able to put forward as evidence. Even these, however, they put forward as suggesting little more than that it was worthwhile to keep searching for more evidence. It would seem that the serious members of the Society for Psychical Research were more skeptical than the skeptics, more critical than their critics.

Skeptics and critics, of course, there always had been, though only a few of those who had strong opinions bothered to put them into print. Still, a surprising number of opinions did get published. Many appeared in the columns of the various general and spiritualist newspapers, but book after book also appeared. In the next few pages I shall cite a few of those books in an attempt to identify some of the cross-currents of the river into which James launched *The Turn of the Screw*.

Let us note, first, that there was a substantial body of men—mostly medical doctors—who wrote books opposing the view that there was anything "real" about ghosts. As far back as 1813, John Ferriar wrote in his preface to *An Essay Towards a Theory of Apparitions*:

It is well known, that in certain diseases of the brain, such as delirium and insanity, spectral delusions take place, even during the space of many days. But it has not been generally observed, that a partial affection

15. Gould, *Founders*, 182.

of the brain may exist, which renders the patient liable to such impressions, either of sight or sound, without disordering his judgment or memory. From this peculiar condition of the sensorium, I conceive that the best supported stories of apparitions may be completely accounted for.[16]

Another medical doctor named Samuel Hibbert, in the preface to his 1824 *Sketches of the Philosophy of Apparitions*, wrote:

My object has been to point out that, in well-authenticated ghost-stories of a supposed supernatural character, the ideas which are rendered so unduly intense as to induce spectral illusions, may be traced to such fantastical objects of prior belief as are incorporated in the various systems of superstition, which for ages have possessed the minds of the vulgar.[17]

After the Society for Psychical Research had been established and its members had begun their careful plodding work, similarly skeptical books were published. Members who read a book by Henry Maudsley, which appeared at just about the time Edmund Gurney and Eleanor Sidgwick were publishing the tentative results of their studies, must have thought Maudsley was frustratingly arrogant. The title of Maudsley's 1886 book, *Natural Causes and Supernatural Seemings*, proclaimed that natural phenomena were "caused," whereas supernatural ones were mere "seemings." In the concluding chapter Maudsley tells us:

Malobservation and misinterpretation of nature have been the unsound foundations of theories of the supernatural. . . . Lacking, therefore, any vestige of solid support in sound observation and reasoning, they survive in modern thought only by virtue of their pretensions to a supernatural authority above all observation and reasoning.[18]

To give just one more example of a medical man's view of the phenomena that psychical researchers took seriously, here is what

16. John Ferriar, *An Essay Towards a Theory of Apparitions*, 15–16.
17. Samuel Hibbert, *Sketches of the Philosophy of Apparitions; or, An Attempt to Trace Such Illusions to Their Physical Causes*, iv.
18. Henry Maudsley, *Natural Causes and Supernatural Seemings*, 354.

Lionel Weatherly had to say in the introduction to his 1891 book rhetorically entitled *The Supernatural?*:

To any common-sensed, thinking mind it must . . . be self- evident that almost all the tales of demonology and witchcraft, of haunted houses, ghostly walkings and visitations, of apparitions, and of visions, both individual and epidemic, owe their origin, in part at least, to what we call Hallucinations and Illusions. . . . Superstition has always reigned where ignorance has thrown her cloak over reason and judgment; and when to this we have added foolish credulity and love of all that is marvellous and extraordinary, can we not at once see the origin of many, if not all, the tales of apparitions?[19]

In view of such self-assurance about what people of common sense must of course think about the ignorant notions of super-stitious people, is it any wonder that psychical researchers were careful about publishing any but the most cautious and carefully phrased conclusions?

We must keep in mind, of course, that plenty was said with equal self-assurance on the other side of the debate. If medical men were predisposed to a dogmatically clinical view of ghostly phenomena, religious men were equally predisposed to a dog-matically biblical one. Indeed, the history of psychical research in the last half of the nineteenth century is in a sense the history of the conflict between the scientific and the religious ways of think-ing about the possibility that in some sense human beings survive death. We have been considering the medical or scientific view. Let us take a look at the spiritual or religious view.

As early as 1823 a layman named T. M. Jarvis published one of the first collections of "real" ghost narratives. Entitled *Accredited Ghost Stories*, Jarvis's book is of interest to us now less because of the narratives it contains than because of the arguments Jarvis advances for taking the narratives seriously. In his introduction, Jarvis mentions and then counters the three arguments that had been advanced against belief in ghosts: that it is irreligious to believe in them, that it would be unbenevolent of God to let

19. Lionel A. Weatherly, *The Supernatural?*, 2.

ghosts bother the living, and that there is no reason why the dead should be permitted to appear to the living. Let us read Jarvis's own words on the last of these arguments:

It is also continually demanded, for what reason the dead should be permitted to appear? To this I answer, for the most important reason that can possibly be imagined; to . . . preserve unfading, in the minds of the great and of the little vulgar, the belief in the immortality of the soul.[20]

It is impossible to say how many people were moved by such reasons, but presumably few were swayed who were not already convinced. Jarvis was no psychical researcher. Still, he gives us an interesting base line against which to measure the efforts of those who trod in his footsteps.

One of those was Newton Crosland, whose *Apparitions* appeared in 1873. Crosland opens his book with an autobiographical statement:

When, in the summer of 1854, my attention was first directed to the phenomena of Spirit-manifestations, and before I knew anything about them beyond what I learnt from mere rumour, I considered that they must necessarily be "the most impious buffoonery ever palmed upon the credulity of a nation." Further investigation, of a laborious and minute character, not only satisfied me that this hasty and insulting opinion must be retracted syllable by syllable, but I became convinced that "the manifestations" are among the most valuable and important indications of the principles of God's dealing with mankind. . . . The conclusion at which I have arrived is, that to doubt the reality of these manifestations, would be as ridiculous and foolish as to doubt the verity of the multiplication table. The fact that the spirits of the departed do return and communicate with living persons, I deem to be so thoroughly established by a host of witnesses in all ages, that I scarcely think it necessary to treat doubts on the subject with any great degree of respect; it is, however, an interesting topic of inquiry to ascertain what purpose is served by these Spirit-visitations. The argument of this Essay is intended to maintain that they clearly demonstrate the individual immortality of the soul; the certainty of a future state corresponding to our deserts and conduct in this life; God's government of the world through the instrumentality of

20. T. M. Jarvis, *Accredited Ghost Stories*, 12.

good and evil spirits; His individualising and incarnating Himself in the person of a Saviour, through whom our prayers are to be addressed; and the infallible efficacy of prayer.[21]

The circularity of arguments from religion was obvious enough to anyone reading them: ghosts are real because the Bible says the soul is immortal; the soul is immortal because there are ghosts; the Bible is true because the existence of ghosts proves the immortality of the soul. It is not difficult to understand why later investigators—even those who shared with some of these early writers an interest in religion and a profound curiosity about the possibilities for survival of bodily death—were eager to distance themselves from such arguments, and from the fanciful enthusiasm of such arguers.

Indeed, many of the early students of psychical phenomena found themselves in something of a dilemma. On the one hand, whether they admitted it or not, they hoped to discover proof of survival, proof that the human soul was immortal. On the other hand, they were committed to pursuing their proof by applying rigorous scientific methods of research and analysis. It is not difficult to see why the early psychical researchers felt peculiarly isolated, even paranoid. They were shunned by medical men for attempting to prove something that science in that age (Charles Darwin had died the year the Society for Psychical Research was established) had already largely disproved; they were shunned by religious men for suggesting that what for years had been taken on faith now needed to be proved by science. Psychical researchers frequently found themselves in troubled waters, uncertain where to find a port. As the century wore on, the psychical researchers tended to focus almost entirely on the scientific method and to abandon more and more the Christian orientation of men like Jarvis and Crosland.

More or less typical of this later class of writers is W. H. Harrison, publisher of a London weekly newspaper called *The Spiritualist*. In the preface to his 1879 book *Spirits Before Our Eyes*,

21. Newton Crosland, *Apparitions: An Essay Explanatory of Old Facts and a New Theory*, 2-3.

Harrison sets out his method, which sounds like an amalgam more of the judicial with the scientific than of the religious with the scientific:

The field and method of research united in this book are new in their present combination. In fact, since the publication of Glanvil's *Saducissimus Triumphatus* about the middle of the seventeenth century, no writer has brought forth an English book entirely devoted to proving the reality of spontaneous apparitions of the spirits of the departed. . . . So far as the authenticity of the facts contained in this volume is concerned, the attention of experienced lawyers is invited to the culture and education of the witnesses, to the absence of collusion among them, to the completeness of their separation by time, space, social position, motives for utterance, and want of knowledge of each other's existence; and, notwithstanding all this, the complete agreement in the general characteristics of the incidents they have recorded.[22]

One of the most interesting members of the Society for Psychical Research was William T. Stead. Because he figures so importantly in this study (especially in chapters 4 and 5 below), I must say a few words about him. The son of a Congregational minister, Stead was born in Yorkshire in 1849. He was a contemporary of Henry James, though I have seen no evidence to suggest that the two men were acquainted. They must have known of each other, however, for they were both among the foremost men of letters in their time. Stead made a name for himself in journalism very early. At twenty-two he was appointed editor of the *Northern Echo*. Succeeding at that position, he was named assistant editor of London's *Pall Mall Gazette* at the age of thirty-one. He became editor of the *Gazette* in 1883, at age thirty-four. He did as much as any other individual to transform journalism from its old "tell-what-happened" stance to what might be called its new "make-it-happen" stance. He was at the center of a number of political, military, social, and legal movements, and he did not hesitate to use his power as editor of a major newspaper to force the government's hand. At one point he was jailed for his efforts. In 1890 he gave up daily journalism and founded the *Review of Reviews*.

22. William H. Harrison, *Spirits Before Our Eyes*, vi–viii.

Shortly afterward he embarked on certain other publishing ventures, of which I shall have more to say in a moment. Stead died in 1912, having booked a cabin for the maiden voyage of the *Titanic*. He was last seen helping women and children into lifeboats. After his death there were many warm tributes. One British lord even declared, with perhaps forgivable hyperbole, that since the year 1880 no important events had happened in England that had not been influenced by Stead's personality.

Stead devoted the Christmas 1891 issue of the *Review of Reviews* to the publication of what he called "Real Ghost Stories." These stories were ghost narratives he had solicited from his friends, acquaintances, and readers. Some came from his own experiences. The Christmas issue ran to over a hundred pages of close-set double columns. He then published a sequel, or "New Year's Extra Number," in late January 1892. This one, entitled, "More Ghost Stories," also ran to more than a hundred pages. Why the sequel? The answer was simple enough. Stead wrote at the start of the New Year's number:

First, I was overcrowded with matter for "Real Ghost Stories"; and, secondly, the public demand for the Christmas Number exceeded the supply. The whole edition of 100,000 for the home market went off like snow in a fresh. We were not able to fill our orders. Some large agents were thousands short. Book-stalls which could have sold hundreds were compelled to be content with dozens, and in view of the demand I did not think it would be inexpedient to bring out this Sequel.[23]

Stead had apparently surprised himself in several ways with these collections of ghost narratives. For one thing, he was surprised at how interested he himself became in supernatural phenomena as a result of putting together the two issues. For another, he was surprised at how interested people were in reading about those phenomena—and in paying to read about them. On the strength of both of these surprises, Stead began to publish a new quarterly in 1894, *Borderland*. Its aim was to do for the general public what the Society for Psychical Research was doing for a

23. William T. Stead, "More Ghost Stories," *Review of Reviews* (January 1892): 7.

select few: call attention to various kinds of supernatural phenomena. At the end of the first year *Borderland* was operating at a
profit, and Stead was proud to announce that it was already "one
of the most widely-circulated quarterlies in the world."[24]

Borderland was a catchall for news about psychical investigations. It reviewed books and reported on various investigations of
clairvoyance, mediumship, haunted houses, hypnotism, palmis-
try, seances, automatic writing (writing by spirits through the
hand of a living person), and so on. In reporting on such subjects,
Stead was not as conservative as the "central management" of the
Society for Psychical Research or the editors of its various reports.
He was willing to publish narratives that had not been subjected
to tests and interviews and cross-checks. He was more interested
in capturing the imagination of his readers and supporting his
own intensifying convictions about the spirit world than in conducting rigorous and dispassionate investigations. Still, he was a
member of the Society for Psychical Research and a respected
seeker of the truth about psychical phenomena.

For reasons we need not go into here, Stead stopped publishing *Borderland* in 1897. In that same year, he republished the
Christmas 1891 and New Year's 1892 issues of the *Review of Reviews*
in book form under the combined title *Real Ghost Stories*. The book
contained most of what had appeared earlier in the two issues.
Stead dropped some material, rearranged other material, and
wrote a new introduction, but the book was essentially a reissue
of the 1891 and 1892 copies.

The book version of *Real Ghost Stories* is of particular interest to
us for several reasons. First, it was the most popular collection of
ghost narratives after Crowe's *The Night Side of Nature*. Second, it
appeared the year James wrote *The Turn of the Screw*. Third, the
preface emphasized the scientific nature of psychical research:

Eclipses in old days used to drive whole nations half mad with fright. To
this day the black disc of the moon no sooner begins to eat into the
shining surface of the sun than millions of savage men feel "creepy," and

24. William T. Stead, *Borderland* 1 (1894): iii.

begin to tremble at the thought of the approaching end of the world. But in civilised lands even the most ignorant regard an eclipse with imperturbable composure. Eclipses are scientific phenomena observed and understood. It is our object to reduce ghosts to the same level, or rather to establish the claim of ghosts to be regarded as belonging as much to the order of Nature as the eclipse. . . . It seems to me that it would be difficult to do better service in this direction than to strengthen the hands of those who have for many years past been trying to rationalise the consideration of the Science of Ghosts.[25]

Of particular interest are the opening lines of the introduction to Stead's book. These lines had not appeared in the *Review of Reviews* issues some years earlier and presumably represent the considered—if boldly stated—opinion of a mature and well-known journalist and psychical researcher who had spent most of the previous half-dozen years immersed in the study of ghostly matters:

Of all the vulgar superstitions of the half educated, none dies harder than the absurd delusion that there is no such thing as ghosts. All the experts, whether spiritual, poetical, or scientific, and all the others, non-experts, who have bestowed any serious attention upon the subject, know that they do exist. . . . There is endless variety of opinion as to what a ghost may be. But as to the fact of its existence, whatever it may be, there is no longer any serious dispute among honest investigators. If any one questions this, let him investigate for himself. In six months, possibly in six weeks, or even in six days, he will find it impossible to deny the reality of the existence of the phenomena popularly entitled ghostly. He may have a hundred ingenious explanations of the origin and nature of the ghost, but as to the existence of the entity itself there will no longer be any doubt.[26]

I do not suggest that Henry James knew all these books, though it seems entirely possible that a bookish author writing a story about real or imagined ghosts might well have wanted to have a look at some of them, especially that newly published and popular "latest word" on the subject, Stead's *Real Ghost Stories*. There

25. William T. Stead, *Real Ghost Stories*, viii–x.
26. Ibid., v.

can be no doubt, however, that Henry James knew about the
Society for Psychical Research. Henry James was personally acquainted with Henry Sidgwick, Edmund Gurney, and Frederic
Myers. He also knew Arthur Balfour, the brother of Mrs. Sidgwick
and an active member of the society. And just before Christmas
1886, James bought a copy of Gurney's *Phantasms of the Living*.[27]

Even if we did not have documentary evidence of Henry
James's knowledge of these men and their ideas, we might still
safely infer that he could scarcely *not* have known about psychical
research. He had been raised by his father in an atmosphere
charged with the teachings of Emanuel Swedenborg. It is of no
small interest that Edmund Gurney and Frederic Myers mention
Henry James, Sr., in a very early report of the Society for Psychical Research as one of two reporters of psychical phenomena who
"have obtained the highest reputation as acute and accurate
observers."[28] The novelist's brother William, with whom he was in
continual contact, was the guiding light of the American Society
for Psychical Research as well as being actively involved in the
English parent society. William became a member of the English
society as early as 1884, was a vice-president for eighteen years,
and was elected its president for 1894–1896. As we shall see in
chapter 5 below, Henry James even attended a meeting of the
Society for Psychical Research in London in 1890, where he read a
paper written by his brother William about certain psychical
phenomena.

Henry James's knowledge of some of the key ideas and person-
alities associated with psychical research leads me to call attention here to a fact overlooked by virtually all previous scholars:
that Douglas, the fireside reader of the governess's manuscript in
the frame-story of *The Turn of the Screw*, had gone to Trinity
College, Cambridge. In the opening chapter, in which Douglas
lays the narrative foundations for the governess's written account
of her experiences, Douglas mentions that he became acquainted
with his sister's governess on one of his college vacations: "I was

27. James, *Letters*, ed. Edel, 2:101, 255–56, 3:102, 116, 4:87–88; 3:41; 3:152.
28. *PSPR* 2 (1884): 123.

at Trinity, and I found her at home on my coming down the second summer" (p. 2). Given that the three prime practitioners of serious psychical research in England at the time were all Trinity men and that Henry James knew all three of them (as well as Arthur Balfour, another psychical researcher and also a Trinity man) personally, can there be any doubt that James's making Douglas a Trinity man was purposeful? By associating Douglas, the only person in the frame-story who had actually met the governess, with the very center of serious and scientific ghost research in England, was not Henry James setting him up as a reliable judge both of her and of the narrative she writes? If a Trinity man thinks that the governess is a trustworthy witness and that her ghosts are genuine, why should we doubt?

We must also recall, in connection with Douglas's association with Trinity College, that another friend of Henry James's had his roots there. Edward White Benson, blood relative of the Sidgwicks and later archbishop of Canterbury, not only studied at Trinity but also helped to organize the Cambridge Ghost Club in 1851. According to a biography of his father written by A. C. Benson, Edward White Benson "was then, as always, more interested in psychical phenomena than he cared to admit."[29] Archbishop Benson apparently did admit his interest to Henry James. In 1895 he told James the outlines of a ghost story that was to form the narrative nucleus of *The Turn of the Screw*. I shall have more to say about Benson's story later. For now I merely want to suggest that from its very inception, *The Turn of the Screw* had ties with ghost researchers at Trinity.

I also suggest that Henry James may even have been indicating, if only to certain "in" members of the anticipated audience for his story, that Douglas might himself have been a member of the Cambridge Ghost Club and a psychical researcher of at least amateur standing. Let us consider the dates. Douglas had met the governess some "forty years" (p. 3) before he read the manuscript in front of the fire. James's frame-story narrator says that he copied the manuscript "much later" (p. 4) when Douglas, near

29. Arthur Christopher Benson, *The Life of Edward White Benson*, 1:98.

death, sent him the handwritten copy the governess had sent to Douglas before her own death. If that "much later" was something like a half-dozen years, and was shortly before the story was published in 1898, then simple arithmetic suggests that Douglas could have been at Trinity in 1851, when the Ghost Club was started. Perhaps it is going too far to suggest that it may have been at Douglas's urging that the governess made a written record of her experiences, but we might recall that one of the stated aims of the Ghost Club was to "request written communications, with full details of persons, times, and places," from those who had had experiences with the "supernatural." Such a suggestion would account for certain puzzling features in *The Turn of the Screw*: why the governess wrote out her story in the first place; why she entrusted it to Douglas; and why her narrative has certain generic similarities with the narratives of other women who, often at the request of psychical researchers, wrote down first-person reports of their experiences. Let us now take a look at some of those other narratives.

2
SOME PRE-JAMESIAN GHOST NARRATIVES

I am not the first to suggest that Henry James was familiar with the people who investigated and discussed psychical cases. Nor am I the first to suggest that he drew from certain of the published ghost cases when he wrote *The Turn of the Screw.* In 1949 Francis X. Roellinger attempted to establish a link between James and psychical researchers. Roellinger's article, however, has not been generally influential. The primary problem is that it lacks sufficiently convincing evidence. Roellinger seems not to have read widely in the *Proceedings of the Society for Psychical Research.* Of the five cases he cites, four are taken from volume 3, one from volume 5. He apparently never consulted other volumes in this series, other periodicals, or the many books about ghosts that would have been available to Henry James by 1897, when he wrote *The Turn of the Screw.* Roellinger's most significant single omission was Edmund Gurney's *Phantasms of the Living,* one of Henry James's richest sources of information about the behavior of "real" ghosts. Roellinger's argument, in short, failed to convince most critics simply because, not having read widely enough in the reported ghost narratives available to Henry James, he failed to provide enough evidence to make his case credible.

The influence on Henry James of the researchers at the Society for Psychical Research was reexamined in the early 1970s. In 1972 Ernest Tuveson briefly mentioned a couple of ghost cases in connection with *The Turn of the Screw,* but he was less interested in proving James's awareness of such cases than in pursuing his own theory that the governess is a medium who unintentionally provides the means for Peter Quint and Miss Jessel to "get" Miles and Flora.

Howard Kerr, also writing in 1972, provided the most comprehensive analysis to date of the effect of spiritualism on American literature of the last half of the nineteenth century. His three-page treatment of *The Turn of the Screw,* however, is very sketchy indeed, and in the end he, also, finds the psychological state of the governess to be more noteworthy than the doings of Peter Quint and Miss Jessel. He calls the governess "a study in altered consciousness," and he speaks of her "neurotic complexity," her "nervous anomaly," and her "hysterical consciousness."[1]

Martha Banta's remarks about *The Turn of the Screw* also appeared in 1972. Those remarks are valuable in many ways, especially when Banta reminds us that Henry James wrote fiction about undeniably "real" ghosts both before and after he wrote *The Turn of the Screw.* This leads to her puzzlement about why scholars should so often be reluctant to accept the reality of the ghosts in James's most famous story. Again, however, like Tuveson, Banta was less interested in James's knowledge of and reliance upon ghost cases than in developing her own theory that the governess is the "most terrifying" presence of all. Banta's view that the ghosts would have been powerless if the governess had stayed away from Bly is highly questionable. Her opinion that James found the scientific approach of psychical researchers to be threatening to or antithetical to the interests of true literary art simply will not hold up, especially in view of the evidence I shall be presenting in this and subsequent chapters. Banta's work, then, cannot be said to have advanced very far the good work that Roellinger had begun.

One book that did go far toward finishing the work begun by Roellinger was E. A. Sheppard's remarkable *Henry James and "The Turn of the Screw,"* published in 1974. Sheppard immersed herself in the history and the reports of the Society for Psychical Research, and she established beyond any reasonable doubt Henry James's reliance upon the work of the men and women associated with that organization. She had at her fingertips information and cases that previous critics had not had. Serious readers of James's story will long be in Sheppard's debt for the massive amounts of information she collected and assimilated.

1. Howard Kerr, *Mediums, and Spirit-Rappers, and Roaring Radicals: Spiritualism in American Literature, 1850–1900,* 209–10.

It would have been pleasant to let the matter stand with Sheppard's book. Unfortunately, we cannot do so, for her book has several crucial limitations. For one thing, it is quite simply too exhaustive for its own good. Sheppard does not content herself with tracing relevant influences upon *The Turn of the Screw* in the reports of the Society for Psychical Research. She also argues for a curious array of apparently contradictory influences from literature and life. Indeed, half the book has to do not with psychical research but with highly speculative opinions about parallels between the governess and Jane Eyre, between the governess and Henriette Deluzy, and between Peter Quint and George Bernard Shaw—to name the most prominent of these proposed parallels. Not only are most of these parallels questionable in themselves, but they also throw into some confusion the connections Sheppard tries to make between James's characters and the people associated with the reported psychical cases.

Whereas on the one hand the book is too exhaustive and diffuse, on the other hand it is, curiously, too narrow. Sheppard is so eager to prove that Henry James had read Gurney's *Phantasms of the Living* and volumes 6 and 8 of the *Proceedings of the Society for Psychical Research* that she has neglected certain other volumes of the *Proceedings,* as well as the many other periodicals and books that would help us to understand the contemporary attitudes toward ghosts in the last decades of the nineteenth century. This narrowness leads Sheppard both to ignore many relevant ghost narratives and to push too hard for the influence of the ones she focuses on. A particularly serious limitation in her study is that she consulted only the works published by the conservative "central management" of the Society for Psychical Research, ignoring the published works of spiritualists and less methodologically careful researchers such as William T. Stead.

Another problem is that Sheppard does not let the narratives speak for themselves. Publishing short snippets from only a dozen narratives, she relegates to the obscurity of footnotes much of the most useful information she has uncovered. Many of those footnotes give the barest of information about the individual cases and merely refer the diligent reader to pages of volumes that have been out of print for nearly a century and are available in only the most complete of libraries. Readers seeking readily available reprints, excerpts, or citations from relevant cases will seek in vain in Sheppard's book. The result is that her book has been of limited usefulness to modern readers of *The Turn of the Screw,* and her arguments have unfortunately been only a little more influential than were Roellinger's.

Perhaps the most serious problem with Sheppard's book, however, is that, having painstakingly presented the best argument so far for James's awareness of psychical narratives and having alluded to many parallels between these narratives and James's story, Sheppard then turns her back on the evidence she has accumulated. Instead of concluding that the various parallels she draws suggest that James wrote an effective story about two ghosts who seek to lure two young children, Sheppard "rescues" him from charges of "naive superstition" by suggesting that *The Turn of the Screw* is not a ghost story after all.[2] What appear to the governess to be ghosts are merely her visual perceptions of the memories that Miles and Flora have of their former vice-ridden associates. According to Sheppard, the governess is essentially a good woman who desires to help the two children. By insisting upon shielding them from nonexistent evil influences, however, and by trying to make them perfect, the governess destroys them. In short, Sheppard succumbs to the modern temptation to read *The Turn of the Screw* as a story about a governess, not as a story told by a governess. We cannot, I am afraid, let the matter rest there.

In this chapter I present nine first-person ghost narratives written by women. My purpose is not to prove that Henry James had read any particular one of these narratives, though all nine appeared in print between 1878 and 1892, well before James began serious work on *The Turn of the Screw.* My purpose, rather, is to quote the nine narratives fully enough that readers at the end of the twentieth century can get a taste for the kind of ghost narratives that people were reading and discussing at the end of the nineteenth century.

2. E. A. Sheppard, *Henry James and "The Turn of the Screw,"* 208.

My first narrative is taken from the diary of Mrs. Vatas-Simpson, a woman who had troubling experiences with ghosts in an old London house. The narrative has a number of parallels with *The Turn of the Screw*: a woman left largely to her own devices with young children in an old house with secret places; the unexplained sound of an infant crying; the female cohort who shares some of the experiences; the reading of a book before one of the ghostly appearances; the appearance of two ghosts, one of each sex; the narrator's obvious relief when it turns out that there really are ghosts, thus justifying her own perceptions and proving that she is not crazy. We even find certain verbal parallels, for example with James's governess's interchange with Mrs. Grose: "Then how did he get in?" "And how did he get out?" (p. 23). It is puzzling that neither Roellinger nor Sheppard takes any notice of Mrs. Vatas-Simpson's narrative, which could have provided James with more stimulating source material than most of the narratives they do cite. I quote in full those portions of the diary that appeared in the 1885 *Proceedings of the Society for Psychical Research*. Full bibliographical references for this and the other narratives are given in the Bibliography of Cases at the end of this book. Titles appear in parentheses at the end of this and all subsequent narratives. These titles I have devised myself. I omit nothing from Mrs. Vatas-Simpson's diary that was present in the originally published account. All ellipses in this narrative, then, indicate omissions made by Eleanor Sidgwick, the original editor:

This is very strange. What can it mean? The servants say that they see queer things moving about, and that they hear peculiar noises. One servant has left us in consequence. To-day I was told by a neighbour that the people who lived here before we came could not remain, because there were always noises and sounds about the house at night, and that even his little children were disturbed by them. At last they became so very unbearable he was obliged to go elsewhere. One hardly knows whether to believe such reports or to laugh at them. At present we have had no nocturnal visitors, and I shall not tell my dear ones, to cause apprehension of ghosts and hobgoblins. . . .

There must be some foundation for the rumours regarding the sounds, noises, and appearances in this old house. It has stood here since the Fire of London. The lower part of the house is very extensive; and then, underground, dark, big, cavernous cellarage (which, it is said, has not been thoroughly explored or examined for years) where secret passages are believed to exist, and from whence issue sounds of moaning and sighing, clearly and quite unmistakably, after dark, when the hum of the busy world is hushed. Any one then, by placing themselves over the window grating may hear distinctly the peculiar noises within. I try to turn a deaf ear to all this, and to combat the fears such revelations inspire in the household, but am unsuccessful with the servants, as they leave me in consequence. My husband says the sounds are produced by the contrary winds careering through the gratings, and perhaps they are.

A severe illness has kept my pen idle for several weeks. Not so, however, events. To-day, L. told me that when the children are playing upstairs an old woman will persist in standing in the doorway, looking in very disconsolately. She believes in the reality of the occurrence; says that it is an annoyance; would I give orders to the servants to keep our gate on the staircase locked?—the iron gate that shuts in the private portion of the house from that which is below, making it thus quite impossible to pass up the stairs from the offices below. . . .

So late, so tired and weary. Every night now L. and I have to sit up long, dreary hours to wait my husband coming home, for we are afraid to go to bed till he returns. There is no feeling of security with only women in this big, grim, and hollow-sounding house, and though we are both free from all superstitious fears, and far from timid, we cannot but be sensible of our unprotected helplessness, left alone, as we are, till the night wanes into morning.

To-night, and for several nights now, we have had our courage put to the test, and most decidedly it has not been found wanting. . . . The first evening, about 11 o'clock, sitting with the drawing-room door open, a man's face was clearly seen above the balustrade, while the old-fashioned size and the carvings of the supports hid his form from our view. Instantly we both jumped up, and as instantly started forward. Both thought that he had come up by mistake, or purposely, perhaps, to see someone in the house. Ere we could speak he was gone.

The servants, not having gone to bed, were summoned, told to go and fasten the iron gate, and reprimanded for their negligence in forgetting to do so. The gas was alight, illuminating the house from the ground-floor to the very roof of the house. We stood upon the landing. The servants went down, protesting that they had locked and fastened securely the gate: and so they had—it was securely fast.

Then I went for the key, and downstairs, and satisfied myself of the fact, and also went below to satisfy myself that all doors and every place below were firmly secured for the night.

Now, then, how did that man get in?—or rather, how did he get *out*? It is possible he might have been concealed during the evening, and so have been on the stairs—but where could he go, instantaneously as he had been followed, and by both of us, neither of us suspecting anything more than that he had obtained entrance through the forgetfulness of the servants, and nothing doubting but that he would wait to be spoken to? Where could he go?—for in an instant, in the twinkling of an eye, the spot where he had appeared was vacant.

Well, when my husband came home I told him. He treated it as a good joke, laughed at our bewilderment, and said we must all have been asleep and dreaming. He has such a supreme contempt for any supposition of the supernatural. Has no belief in spiritual visions, in "ghosts," or visions of the night. He is far too practical, and only derides my credulity. At present I have been able to keep all suspicion of these things from the household. . . .

Twice late, sitting up during the night hours, my L. and I have been disturbed by that same appearance on the stairs, and each time have done our best to discover the mystery. The face is pale to sickliness, and the eye steady and mournful. The figure is shrouded in a sort of dark, shadowy indistinctness, and his departure is sudden and noiseless. The first time he came we slowly advanced to him, side by side, quite silently, and with firm decision of manner, intending to show him our determination to enforce an interview, and ask explanation for his intrusion. Ah! he is gone.

The second time I was reading an interesting book. L. looked up from her employment and, seeing him, touched me gently (we were close together), when both of us made a sudden dart forward, only to find the spot vacant which had, one instant previously, been occupied by his face and figure. It is impossible that we can be mistaken or deceived. No, No, we are not. There is no misapprehension, because no fear quells our courage; no cowardice prevents the full action of our powers of perception; no alarm frustrates our intention of grappling with him if we can, or of pursuing him, or of holding him if we can come up with him. We are on our guard against surprise, and our nerves steady, prepared to make a decided unequivocal effort to find out who and what this nocturnal intruder may be.

But nothing avails; he is not here; he is not anywhere near. Looking keenly at him one moment, the next he has fled, quick as a flash of lightning. But he *was* standing there; we both saw him, positively and undoubtedly. . . .

It is useless to contend against facts. Nervous terrors and timorous imaginations have nothing whatever to do in suggesting the various appearances and the indescribable sounds which pervade the rooms, the corners, and the recesses of this great house. Superstition might indeed supply one person with food for miracles or for belief in deception and witchcraft; but when there are several witnesses of all ages there must be a foundation of truth, and, at all events, each and every one could not be deceived. If all that is going on here is a strange delusion, then all would not be affected at the same moment. If it is but a mere sensation or impression, then it would only be conceived by *one* mind, not by all. If it were capable of detection, then so many persons gathered together would surely find out that it was imposture and deception.

Besides, there is nothing done to annoy any one of us; no attempt is made to frighten or even to surprise us. There seems no system or organisation in all these mysteries. In addition to the little old woman who goes about the upper floor, and the man who comes occasionally upon the stairs, there are other sights and sounds, and other nocturnal disturbances. Very often a babe is heard wailing and crying in the kitchen, generally in the evening. We heard these piteous wailings when we first came here to live, and then imagined that a babe was really within hearing; but when, after the lapse of many months, the sounds were still those of a new-born babe, no stronger in tone or different in expression, then we began to wonder, and to strive to penetrate the mystery, and are constrained to believe that no living infant causes those sounds.

Then again, close to my bedroom door, in a recess, there are notes of the most mournful singing the ear can hear—real notes—soft and sad, but clear and thrilling. Then, in an instant, the notes are prolonged, and change into short, sharp screams of agony. Then total silence.

All this takes place in the very interior of the house—in parts where there is no outside wall, but where the wall, thick and massive, divides one room from another.

Incredulous as my husband has always been when I have complained of our incomprehensible and spectral visitants, yet last night he was penetrated with the belief that there must be *truth* in our representations, at all events. So deeply is he impressed by the solemn assurance of his own scrutiny that a vision did really appear to him, that doubting, unbelieving, and sceptic as he is, he confesses himself thrilled and pervaded with unwonted sensations of awe and excitement. I must write it down. It all happened in this way:—

After all outer doors were shut and business hours over, my husband had for several evenings past devoted his leisure to writing, and to sorting the piles of letters and papers which had accumulated during his illness. Correspondence was behindhand; so shutting himself up in his own private office, he directed all his thoughts, energy, and attention to reducing the number of letters unanswered, and arranging papers and documents in their several places. His orders were peremptory to the servants to allow no one to disturb him, and I took my part in securing to him that perfect freedom from interruption, so absolutely needed in such an occupation.

This evening the silence in the house was almost oppressive. My husband had not once come up to the drawing-room since he left it after dinner. It was now 11 o'clock, and the hour for the servants to retire for the night, except when we had company. I sat with the door open that evening. I have a habit of doing this when I am alone. The large landing and the outlet gives more freedom and air. The door of the kitchen is in close proximity—an outer door—and always kept shut. Opposite the drawing-room door, across the landing, is the staircase, the balustrade of the stairs forming one side of the landing. All at once there was a great tramping upon the office-floor below; the door of the private office was flung open with much violence. My husband, in angry tones, called to the servant, and demanded "how they dare permit a stranger to come to him at that time of night?" Which servant had disobeyed him?

No one had done so.

"Don't deny it. Who is the woman? When did she come, and what does she want? I see no one at this hour of the night. Let her be here tomorrow if she wants me; show her out and fasten the gate again."

All this was spoken as if the person who had disturbed him was standing there still; addressed to the domestics that she might know his rules had been transgressed, and that she might hear him say so. It was in vain that the servants protested they had let no one in; and had seen no one pass up or down the stairs, that every door and window was fastened and secure. Astonishment kept my husband mute; he stood still, lost to all outward impressions for some time, like one in a dream. Then, with a sort of shudder he moved away from the door of his office, from whence he had not stirred, and told the servants to go to bed; he would find out on the morrow who had taken the liberty of intruding, or perhaps, the person would call again in the morning.

This was to them, but as soon as we were alone he told me all that had occurred: Absorbed in deep thought, searching amongst his papers for one of great importance, he raised his head from them, and saw, just within his office doorway, a little old lady standing. Even though an unwelcome intruder, his politeness did not fail; so rising directly he addressed her. Finding that she neither spoke nor moved, but only looked at him, he advanced a little, speaking again. This forward movement made no alteration; still she was mute, still not a finger stirred, the eyes still fixed upon him with a soft, sweet expression, the face very pallid. After allowing sufficient time for a reply (even if the old lady should be short of breath from coming upstairs), and still receiving none, he approached nearer, when she moved gradually and softly a little farther into the room, yet scarcely nearer to him, for the room is very spacious. Again he altered his position while she remained motionless, thus bringing himself into closer contact with her; still she was motionless.

Making now a quick step towards her, determined to ascertain the cause of her silence—lo! she was gone! To his amazement he lost all trace of her in one moment. It was then we must have heard the commotion below. After telling me thus far, my husband paused in his narrative. Again he was wrapt in deep meditation. His face was agitated, his lips quivered; evidently he was mastering strong emotion. Rousing himself from the reverie which I had allowed to remain unbroken, he continued to relate the incidents of the visit, and his own conclusions upon it.

Well, he said he didn't know whether his office door was open while she was there; he knew that he had shut it, and did not recollect opening it when he missed her from the room. The gas was giving a full blaze of light, and no shadow of darkness rested anywhere to deceive him. The whole place was illumined.

No suspicion entered his mind of anything like visionary object or apparitions; his whole attention was rivetted upon his letters and papers, and his only idea was that this old lady was in some great trouble, had come to him for advice, and that her age and probable distress might be the excuse for her untimely visit. It was with such considerations that he first addressed her as he would any lady who came to him upon office business, but afterwards, when he became annoyed by her silence, he permitted his irritation to be visible both in voice and manner.

His description of her appearance is this:—"A little old lady, with a very pale face, and her hands clasped before her, a cap round her face, and a dark bonnet, with strings tied under her chin." When I asked him what dress, then he is at fault. He only saw a dark form. Well, he cannot say, he was only looking at her face. It must have been a dark dress, he believes—it looked dark. She moved with a gentle, gliding motion; looked at him most intently; did not move her hands. His face is quite troubled, and he is much excited. Says that he feels bewildered and embarrassed, and is most unwilling to admit the reality of the vision.

I believe that he would not have named it at all could he have anticipated the termination of the scene. As it is, no explanation can do away with the fact, and it is useless to deny what he has once admitted. Either way, he is in a dilemma, from which he cannot escape. He sums it all up by saying, "I have told you exactly what took place. I know what I saw, and am quite aware that it cannot be explained. As it is, so let it rest." He will never again laugh at us for our absurd notions and experiences of "ghosts," I am quite certain. He is touched in a way that he himself cannot comprehend. He does not like it—his own feelings puzzle him. It will be a long time before he loses the novel impression aroused in his mind by that visit of our little old lady, who seems to wander about our house whenever and wheresoever she pleases. ("Mrs. Vatas-Simpson and the Two Ghosts")

My second narrative was written in French by Julie Marchand. It appeared in the *Proceedings of the Society for Psychical Research* in 1889, some thirty years after the events it recounts had taken place. Although it lacks the immediacy of Mrs. Vatas-Simpson's narrative, it is of interest to us, if only because Miss Marchand is a young governess charged with caring for two children with whom she shares a bedroom. It is also noteworthy that this governess is reading when she sees her ghostly visitor, that she "feels" his presence before she sees him, that she feels little or no fear in his presence, and that she experiences some difficulty getting one of her charges to "confess" that she too had seen the ghost. The woman who reported the case to Frederic Myers tells us that she had known Miss Marchand personally for twenty-two years, a fact apparently meant to suggest the witness's general reliability. I omit a paragraph or so at the start of the narrative, where Miss Marchand describes the bedroom, and several paragraphs at the end, where she reports that she and the children moved to another bedroom after she told the baron about the strange visitor. Perhaps it is worth mentioning that the baron subsequently reported to Miss Marchand that when the workmen were building closets in the room, they had discovered a man's skeleton in the wall. Here, then, is the central portion of the narrative, in my own translation:

One evening while I was in bed and the two children were sleeping peacefully, I felt that someone was near me. I looked up and saw—I can scarcely say a shadow because a shadow appears one-dimensional—the distinct shape of a man. I was not able to distinguish the features of his face, which were hidden in the shadow of a large hat. The extraordinary thing was that I did not feel at all frightened.

I looked at the figure for a long time, thinking it must be a figment of my imagination. I returned to my reading. After a while I looked up again. The shape was still in the same place, and the face still invisible. Finally I turned off the light, turned my back to the shape, and fell asleep, thinking it was just my imagination. The same thing happened several days later. Afraid that people would make fun of me, I did not tell a soul.

The children were very young, nine and ten years old. They had their supper at seven. I went down at nine to have supper with the baron and the baroness. I usually went to bed at ten. During that hour the light remained on the table, as it was always lit when the children were sleeping. Also, the light in the study remained lit. The eldest child was very fearful.

One evening when I went upstairs after supper, I heard distressed cries coming from the bedroom. I ran in and saw one of my pupils trying to tear her sister, who was in a deep sleep, out of bed, begging her to wake up. She said, "Dear Charlotte, please wake up." When she saw me she ran back to bed. I said to her, "I hope you will no longer make such a din."

The next day she appeared so miserable that she worried me a little. I asked her if she was ill. She answered, "No, I am well." It occurred to me to question her about her fright the night before, for I was sure her condition stemmed from her terror then. I took her into the bedroom alone to question her.

For a long time I could make her admit nothing. Finally, I promised that she would not be scolded, and she could tell me whatever nonsense she wished. I told her I wanted to know the cause of her fear in order to talk it over with her. Eventually, after some hesitation, she said to me, "I know it wasn't real, but it frightened me. As soon as you went down, someone knocked on the door of the bedroom, and at the foot of my bed I saw a man." That struck me. I said to her, "I would like to know how your frightened imagination saw him."

"I know it wasn't real," she said, but finally she told me he wore a long coat, with a long collar, and a low-topped hat with a wide brim. I was afraid the child could see my surprise, for that was exactly the same figure I had seen several times standing in front of my chest of drawers, between two lights, perhaps four or five feet from me. ("Miss Marchand and the Ghostly Man")

My third narrative, this one also by a governess, is set in Ireland. Only the initials of the governess and others involved in the narrative were given because the people involved wished to have neither their own names nor the name of the house generally known. I quote Miss C.'s original narrative in its entirety, though I omit certain statements she made subsequently in response to specific questions by the Society for Psychical Research investigator. I also omit corroborative statements by several of her pupils who also saw the ghost. Perhaps I should note that there were

vague reports by neighbors about a certain Miss M., who had
died in a fire in the house in 1752. Miss M. had apparently been
subject to certain fits or tendencies toward sleepwalking and was
said to have been locked in her room at night to prevent her doing
harm to herself or others. There was a vague hint that she had set
or caused the fire in which she perished. When Miss C. was asked
how she could be sure of the dates she cites in her narrative, she
replied that she had made brief notes in her diary and that she had
referred to them before writing her account. Miss C.'s narrative
has several interesting parallels with James's story: the governess
who shares a room with one of her pupils; the pale lady in black;
the ghostly visitor first thought to be a living one; the ghost's
appearing to look for something. Here is Miss C.'s narrative, as it
appeared in the *Proceedings of the Society for Psychical Research* in
1885:

On the 18th of April (Thursday), 1867, about 7.40 p.m., I was going to my
room, which I at that time shared with one of my pupils, when just as I
had reached the top of the stairs I plainly saw the figure of a female
dressed in black, with a large white collar or kerchief, very dark hair, and
pale face. I only saw the side face. She moved slowly and went into my
room, the door of which was open. I thought it was Marie, the French
maid, going to see about A.'s clothes, but the next moment I saw that the
figure was too tall and walked better. I then fancied it was some visitor
who had arrived unexpectedly (Mrs. S. had done so a few days previously), and had gone into the wrong bedroom, and as I had only been at
F. H. a short time, I felt rather shy at speaking to strangers, so waited
where I was a minute or two expecting to see the lady come out, but I
never lost sight of the door. At last I went in, and there was no one in the
room. I looked everywhere, and even felt the back of the hanging side of
the wardrobe to see whether there was any concealed door leading into
the next room. This idea would not have occurred to me had I been able in
any way to account for the lady's disappearance. She could not have gone
by the window, as the room was on the second storey. Going downstairs,
I met the cook and another maid, and asked them if any stranger had
arrived, and was answered in the negative. I had never heard of any
strange appearances in the house, and could not account for what I had
seen that evening.

Some years after, in December, 1874, as I was going to bed, about 10
o'clock (the house had been slightly altered), I saw most distinctly a lady

in black leaning over the fire in the room occupied by the eldest daughter. She was shading her eyes with her hand, and seemed looking for something by the fender; her other hand was on the chimney-piece. I walked slowly towards the room, and said, "Take care, C., you will burn your face, it is *so* near the flame." As there was no answer I spoke again, I suppose louder, for at that moment C., whom I supposed the lady to be, came out of her *sister's room* and asked what I was talking about and why I was in such a fright about her burning her face. There was no one in her room and no one could have passed me unobserved, as I was standing close to the door.

Another time, late one evening in September, I was sitting in the schoolroom with the door open, when I saw the figure again, standing on the far side of the stove in the lower hall. I at once got up to see who it was, but it had vanished. I think it seemed to go up one step of the stairs, but am not sure, as this was the only time I felt rather nervous when seeing it, and that, perhaps, from thinking it was someone who had no business in the house, or that someone was playing me a trick. Each time I have seen "the black lady" she has been dressed in what appeared to be black serge or cashmere—something soft and in heavy folds—with the same large white collar or kerchief on her neck. Whatever it was, I feel as certain of having seen it as that I am now writing this account of it, and it may be as well to mention that I am by no means a nervous person—quite the contrary. ("Miss C. and the Black Lady")

My fourth narrative was written by a woman of thirty-one who recalled certain experiences involving the apparition of a favorite aunt. Although this was a "phantasm of the living" rather than of the dead—the aunt was not yet dead when her apparition appeared to Miss W.—it is worth looking at for certain other features. I call particular attention to the plight of a child abandoned by parents and left in the care of one of the parent's siblings; to the very clever child, skilled at play-acting; to the child's attachment, bordering on idolatry, to the surrogate mother who subsequently dies; and to the banishment of the child to boarding school. It seems quite possible, because of these features, that Henry James might have been interested in this narrative, which was published in volume 2 of Gurney's 1886 *Phantasms of the Living*, a book that James owned:

When I was eight months old, my mother's younger sister, Mercy Cox, came to reside with us, and to take charge of me. My father's position at the Belgian Court, as portrait painter, obliged him to be much abroad, and I was left almost wholly to the care of my very beautiful aunt. The affection that subsisted between us amounted almost to idolatry, and my poor mother wept many bitter tears when she came home, to see how little I cared for anyone else. My aunt took cold, and for three years lingered in decline. I was a quick child, and could read well and even play prettily, so that I was her constant companion day and night. Our doctor, Mr. Field, of the Charter House, greatly disapproved of this close contact, and urged my parents to send me quite away. This was a difficult feat to accomplish, the bare mention of the thing throwing my aunt into faintings. At last Mr. Cumberland (the theatrical publisher) suggested that I should join his two daughters, Caroline, aged 16, and Lavinia, younger, at Mrs. Hewetson's, the widow of a clergyman resident at Stourpaine, in Dorsetshire, who only took four young ladies. This was represented to my aunt as something so wonderfully nice and advantageous to me, that she consented to part with me. My portrait was painted, and placed by her bed, and I remember how constantly she talked to me about our separation. She knew she should be dead before the year of my absence would be ended. She talked to me of this, and of how soon I should forget her; but she vehemently protested that she would come to me there. Sometimes it was to be as an applewoman for me to buy fruit of, sometimes as a maid wanting a place, always *she* would know *me*, but I should not know her, till I cried and implored to know her.

I was but nine when they sent me away, and coach travelling was very slow in those days. Letters, too, were dear, and I very rarely had one. My parents had sickness and troubles, and they believed the reports that I was well and happy, but I was a very miserable, illtreated little girl. One morning, at break of day—it was New Year's Day—I was sleeping beside Lavinia. We two shared one little white tester bed, with curtains, while Caroline—upon whom I looked with awe, she being 16, slept in another similar bed at the other end of a long narrow room, the beds being placed so that the feet faced each other, and two white curtains hung down at the sides of the head. This New Year's morning, I was roughly waked by Lavinia shaking me and exclaiming, "Oh look there! there's your aunt in bed with Caroline." Seeing two persons asleep in the bed, I jumped out, and ran to the right side of it. There lay my aunt, a little on her right side, fast asleep, with her mouth a little open. I recognised her worked nightgown and cap. I stood bewildered, with a childish sort of wonder as to when she could have come; it must have been after I went to bed at night. Lavinia's cries awakened Caroline, who as soon as she could understand, caught the curtains on each side and pulled them together over her. I tore them open, but only Caroline lay there, almost fainting from fright. This lady, Miss Cumberland, afterwards became Mrs. Part, wife of a celebrated doctor at Camden Terrace.

I never talked of what had occurred, but one day, after I had long returned home, I said to my mother, "Do you know, mamma, I saw auntie when I was at school?" This led to an explanation, but my mother, instead of commenting upon it, went and fetched her mother, saying to her, "Listen to what this child says." Young as I was, I saw they were greatly shocked, but they would tell me nothing except that when I was older I should know all. The day came when I learned that my dear aunt suffered dreadfully from the noise of St. Bride's bells, ringing in the New Year. My father tried to get them stopped, but could not. Towards morning she became insensible; my mother and grandmother seated on either side of her, and holding her hands, she awoke and said to my mother, "Now I shall die happy, Anna, I have seen my dear child." They were her last words. ("Miss W. and the Ghost of Mercy Cox")

My fifth narrative is interesting for several reasons, not the least of which is its setting: a wooded country estate not far from a village, and an old house with a square battlemented tower containing a little-used bedroom chamber. Other parallels will strike the reader: the sighting of a ghost at the end of a long summer day; the ghost-seer's own face, pale and agitated as she returns after seeing a ghost; the comparison of the distinctness of the ghost to the written page—recall the governess's saying of Peter Quint that "I saw him as I see the letters form on this page" (p. 17). I quote the whole of the narrative except a few sentences at the start and finish in which the narrator says that, although she believes "the spectral form was a reality," she desires not to have her name or the exact identity of the house revealed. I quote the narrative from an 1878 book by Frederick G. Lee, *More Glimpses of the World Unseen*:

I and my sister, with our maid, were invited to stay for a fortnight at an old-fashioned and well-known country house in Derbyshire, which had been taken for five years by some connections of ours; and we accepted the invitation with pleasure, anticipating a most agreeable visit, as well from the society of friends who were invited to meet us, as because of the beauty of the country in which the house stood.

Situated about three miles from a country town, it lay in a park of some dimensions, backed by a wood immediately behind, and a large extent of coppice and underwood on the western side. Part of the house was built in the reign of Henry VIII, other portions had been added later, and the whole had been from time to time renovated, refaced, and considerably altered. There was one part however,—a square embattled tower, containing three rooms one above the other, all panelled in oak, with elaborately-carved ceilings—which, it is said, remained still much as they had been when first erected three centuries and a half ago. This most picturesque part formed the south-east corner of the mansion, and was partly covered with ivy and creepers. The lower room, sparsely furnished, and seldom used, opened out on to the lawn; the room at the top contained only empty packing-boxes, disused portmanteaus, and a few ill-painted and not very valuable family portraits in a state of decay. The middle apartment was a bedroom, only used when all the others were occupied; and this was appointed to me. It was very old-fashioned in its appearance: the bed, which was raised on a broad platform, was large, with highly-carved bulbous posts, and a most elaborately-panelled back; the hangings were of faded blue velvet, with flowers in gold thread intertwined throughout, and it was surmounted by several stiff clusters of blue feathers, then much faded. The mantel-piece, which stood out from the side wall, was carved to correspond, and occupied the whole space up to the roof. On one side, in a recess, was a large cupboard, not very deep, but entirely filling up the recess. This too was panelled, and into the door of it was let a long rectangular piece of engraved Venetian looking-glass. A large cypress tree on the lawn somewhat darkened the room.

A queer feeling—which I cannot better describe than by these three brief words—came over me when first I was shown to my room. But the old place was so artistically interesting and curious that I took some time to examine all its points of interest with unusual curiosity and attention, so that the feeling in question soon passed away. Our maid unpacked my things, and later on, came in to help me to dress for dinner. This being done about half-an-hour before the dinner hour, the maid left the room, and I lay down to rest on the sofa at the end of the bed. It was the height of summer, the end of July, I think; and the evenings were of course perfectly light. Just as the gong sounded for dinner, I rose and mechanically glanced into the looking-glass; when, smitten with surprise, I suddenly saw the distinct reflection of a tall female figure gliding across the room behind me. Its face was thin and pale and careworn, and the style of dress as antique as that of King James I's age. The eyes, which looked tearful, were fixed firmly on mine, and for a moment, notwithstanding the unusual dress, I thought and made sure that someone who wanted me had come into the room. Turning suddenly, I distinctly heard the rustling of a lady's dress, saw her form as distinctly as I see the paper on which I am now writing, and beheld the apparition turning sharply round, walk, as it were, straight into the wall opposite. The motion of the spectre was not as that of a person walking, but as of a form gliding without energy or effort. For a moment I imagined that a door, as yet unnoticed, must have been opened, but on going to examine that side of the room where the figure vanished away, no door, nor anything like a door, was to be found. Hurrying out of the room, and being seen by the assembled people downstairs to be pale and agitated—and no wonder!— I was pressed for the cause. This I gave substantially in the above words.

During my visit, I saw nothing more, but night after night, I heard the most extraordinary, and unaccountable knocks, sharp, definite, and distinct, in all parts of the room; while overhead, I seemed to hear the ceaseless patter of feet, as on a wooden floor, from one side of the room to the other, sounds made with the regularity of a stately and steady march.

More than two years afterwards, I heard from a relative that a very old woman who had once been the wife of a lodge-keeper on the estate, asserted that she had often seen the "ghost-lady" in the old part of the house; and gave an elaborate description of her features and form, which exactly tallied with my own.

This is my apparition, the only one I ever saw, and the only one I ever want to see. ("Miss B. and the Lady in the Tower")

My sixth case involves a Miss Lister, who sees two different and unconnected apparitions, in different houses at different times. These are reported in letters of March 8 and March 13, 1888, to Edmund Gurney, and were published in the society's *Proceedings* the following year. They are interesting to us because of a number of parallels with *The Turn of the Screw*. The appearance of the husband of Miss Lister's friend offers enlightening parallels to the governess's seeing a ghost that perhaps tries instead to appear to another person. The wife's "lie" when she says, "I have seen my husband," followed by her clarification, "I didn't actually see him," recalls the governess's "lie" to Mrs. Grose that she had had "a talk with Miss Jessel," followed by the clarification, "it came to that" (p. 60). It might be noted that Miss Lister's friend said she saw, but merely heard, whereas the governess said she heard, but merely saw. The parallel is inexact, of course, but both women do seem to "know" more than their senses can verify. The account of the appearance of the old lady offers enlightening parallels with James's story also. Most obvious is the parallel with Mrs. Grose, offered by Phoebe, the servant who had also served the previous occupant of the house and who is able to identify the ghost from

Miss Lister's point-by-point description. Also noteworthy is the appearance of the old lady on the stairs in the final paragraph. This may be echoed in James's account of Peter Quint's appearance on the stairway: "The apparition had reached the landing halfway up. . . . It stopped short and fixed me. . . . There was nothing in me unable to meet and measure him. . . . The thing was as human and hideous as a real interview. . . . Our long gaze . . . was so prolonged. . . . I definitely saw it turn . . . straight down the stairway and into the darkness in which the next bend was lost" (p. 41). Can the parallels with Miss Lister's account—the long gaze exchanged between a live person who is not on the stairway and a life-like apparition who is, the bold feelings of the percipient, the turning disappearance of the apparition—all be coincidental? Edmund Gurney reports that he had had a long interview with Miss Lister and had found her to be "an accurate witness. She is certainly the very opposite of a nervous or superstitious person." I quote both letters as they appeared in the 1889 *Proceedings of the Society for Psychical Research*, excluding only an irrelevant paragraph at the beginning and an irrelevant four sentences at the end of the second letter. The first letter ends after the third paragraph below:

Some time ago a friend of mine had the misfortune to lose her husband. They had only been married about five years, and she expressed great grief at his loss, and asked me to go and reside with her. I went to her, and stayed six months. One evening, towards the end of that summer, I remarked that I would go upstairs and have a bath. "Do," she replied, "but first I wish you would fetch me that little book I left on the drawing-room table last night." I started without a light (having been naturally fearless all my life, I am accustomed to go about in the dark), opened the drawing-room door, and stood for a minute, thinking where she had placed it, when I saw, to my amazement, her husband, sitting by the table; his elbow was resting on the table close to the book. My first thought was to pretend forgetfulness, my second to tell her what I had seen and return without the book. However, having boasted that I did not know the meaning of fear, I determined to get it, and advanced to the table. He seemed to be smiling, as if he knew my thoughts. I picked up the book and took it to her without saying anything about it; then, going into the bathroom, I soon forgot it. But after being there about 20 minutes

I heard my friend go up and open the drawing-room door. I laughed, and listened to hear if he was still there, and very soon heard her run out of the room, and downstairs about four at a time, and ring the dining-room bell furiously. One of the maids came running up. I dressed as quickly as possible and went down to her, and found her looking very white and trembling. "Whatever is the matter?" I said. "I have seen my husband," she replied. "What nonsense," I answered. "Oh, but I have," she continued,—"at least, I didn't actually see him, but he spoke twice to me; I ran out of the room, and he followed and put his cold hand on my shoulder."

Now this seems to me a very strange thing, because I had only seen the gentleman about two or three times, therefore cannot understand his appearing to me, and I certainly was not thinking of him at the time.

The other apparition was of an old lady whom I had never seen, and I only discovered for whom it was intended by describing her to someone who knew her. She appeared to me on several occasions, and I happened to relate this to the gentleman alluded to, who informed me that it was my imagination, and added that if it had been a spirit I should have been too frightened to look long enough to describe its appearance. I told him in reply that I wished someone who had heard the tale would appear to me after their death and see if they could frighten me; and I thought of it when he appeared, and wondered if it had anything to do with my seeing him. . . .

The old lady's appearance was here. My father purchased the house in June, 1883, from Mrs. ——, whose aunt had died here—being found dead in bed one day, having died the night before, all alone. The lodger forced the door, fearing something was the matter; but I was not aware of this till a long time after. This appearance occurred on a special *fête* day at the "Fisheries"—the proceeds of which were, I believe, intended to build a church. Some friends of mine were going, and had tried to persuade me to accompany them, but the house would have been left with no one in it if I had gone. In the afternoon I had been sewing, and drawing my chair close to the window overlooking the garden at the back, I intended working as long as I could see. I sat for a few minutes looking out, and trying to imagine how the exhibition looked, and, upon turning, saw the old lady standing looking at me. "Who can that be?" I thought (and looked out again); "some one must have come here by mistake—possibly a neighbour." I looked at her again, long enough to take in all the details of her costume. Again I turned to the window, wondering whether I had left any of the doors open, and how it was I had not heard her come in. Then thinking how stupid not to ask her, I got up to put the question—but she had gone, as noiselessly as she came. I looked all over the house—in cupboards, under bedsteads, &c., but not a trace of anyone or anything could be found.

The servant I had at that time had been a servant at the house before, I knew; so I resolved (of course without telling her why) to describe the old lady. I made several casual remarks about her, then I said, "I fancy I saw her one day, Phoebe, let me describe her. She was rather short, thin, had brown eyes, a long nose, and wore a black cap with a flower or red bow at the side, a black dress, black mittens, and a white neckerchief, edged with lace, folded cornerways and fastened with a brooch." Phoebe interrupted me several times by saying 'That was her, miss!' and ended by saying she always wore one of those kerchiefs.

About three weeks after, I happened to be again alone, and was hurrying out of the breakfast-room into the room where I had seen her, when, glancing up the staircase, I beheld my old lady coming down. This time she was attired in a lavender dress. I stood at the foot of the stairs, thinking as she passed I would take hold of her. We seemed to be looking at one another for 10 minutes, when she went backwards up the stairs like a human being. I now felt certain someone was playing me a trick (though I had heard no sound); I ran up quickly, but at the turn in the stairs, she vanished. I searched the house as before, with the same result. ("Miss Lister and the Apparitions")

My seventh narrative was probably the most widely known of them all. It was extensively researched by "Miss Morton," the primary percipient, and by Frederic Myers, an acquaintance of Henry James.[3] Because the account published in the 1892 *Proceedings of the Society for Psychical Research* is so long (it runs to some seventeen pages of small print) and repetitious, I can give here only selected extracts. "Miss Morton" was a nineteen-year-old woman who adopted this pseudonym because she and her father did not want to harm the owner of the house by allowing the identity of the house to be traced from the report. Haunted houses were difficult to rent, even when, as so often happened, the owner reduced the rent. The house was an ordinary "modern" house, more or less typical of the period. A few years before the Mortons took up residence there, a certain Mrs. S., the second wife of Mr. S. and a former resident in the house, died and was buried in the churchyard not far away. Mr. S. had died a few

3. See David S. Miall, "Designed Horror: James's Vision of Evil in *The Turn of the Screw*," 309ff., for a discussion of certain similarities between the Morton case and James's story.

months earlier. Their marriage, not a happy one, had been full of drinking, quarrels about the children of the first marriage, and suspicious accusations about who rightfully owned the first Mrs. S.'s jewelry.

Following Miss Morton's lengthy narrative are many pages of additional testimony from a half-dozen relatives, friends, and servants of the Mortons. Because these testimonies add little of importance to the basic narrative, however, I have not reprinted them. I would call attention only to Frederic Myers's description of Mrs. Twining, the charwoman, as a "sensible, trustworthy person, who has worked for the Mortons for 8 or 9 years. She is illiterate." Might Mrs. Twining have suggested to Henry James the characterization of the sensible, trustworthy, but illiterate Mrs. Grose? Miss Morton's account follows, with ellipses indicating my own omissions in her narrative:

My father took the house in March, 1882, none of us having then heard of anything unusual about the house. We moved in towards the end of April, and it was not until the following June that I first saw the apparition.

I had gone up to my room, but was not yet in bed, when I heard someone at the door, and went to it, thinking it might be my mother. On opening the door, I saw no one; but on going a few steps along the passage, I saw the figure of a tall lady, dressed in black, standing at the head of the stairs. After a few moments she descended the stairs, and I followed for a short distance, feeling curious what it could be. I had only a small piece of candle, and it suddenly burnt itself out; and being unable to see more, I went back to my room.

The figure was that of a tall lady, dressed in black of a soft woollen material, judging from the slight sound in moving. The face was hidden in a handkerchief held in the right hand. This is all I noticed then; but on further occasions, when I was able to observe her more closely, I saw the upper part of the left side of the forehead, and a little of the hair above. Her left hand was nearly hidden by her sleeve and a fold of her dress. As she held it down a portion of a widow's cuff was visible on both wrists, so that the whole impression was that of a lady in widow's weeds. There was no cap on the head but a general effect of blackness suggests a bonnet, with long veil or a hood.

During the next two years—from 1882 to 1884—I saw the figure about half a dozen times; at first at long intervals, and afterwards at shorter, but I only mentioned these appearances to one friend, who did not speak of them to anyone.

During this period, as far as we know, there were only 3 appearances to anyone else.

1. In the summer of 1882 to my sister, Mrs. K., when the figure was thought to be that of a Sister of Mercy who had called at the house, and no further curiosity was aroused. She was coming down the stairs rather late for dinner at 6.30, it being then quite light, when she saw the figure cross the hall in front of her, and pass into the drawing-room. She then asked the rest of us, already seated at dinner, "Who was that Sister of Mercy whom I have just seen going into the drawing-room?" She was told there was no such person, and a servant was sent to look; but the drawing-room was empty, and she was sure no one had come in. Mrs. K. persisted that she had seen a tall figure in black, with some white about it; but nothing further was thought of the matter.

2. In the autumn of 1883 it was seen by the housemaid about 10 p.m., she declaring that someone had got into the house, her description agreeing fairly with what I had seen; but as on searching no one was found, her story received no credit.

3. On or about December 18th, 1883, it was seen in the drawing-room by my brother and another little boy. They were playing outside on the terrace, when they saw the figure in the drawing-room close to the window, and ran in to see who it could be that was crying so bitterly. They found no one in the drawing-room, and the parlour-maid told them that no one had come into the house.

After the first time, I followed the figure several times downstairs into the drawing-room, where she remained a variable time, generally standing to the right hand side of the the bow window. From the drawing-room she went along the passage towards the garden door, where she always disappeared. . . .

On the night of August 2nd the footsteps were heard by my three sisters and by the cook, all of whom slept on the top landing—also by my married sister, Mrs. K., who was sleeping on the floor below. They all said the next morning that they had heard them very plainly pass and repass their doors. The cook was a middle-aged and very sensible person; on my asking her the following morning if any of the servants had been out of their rooms the night before, after coming up to bed, she told me that she had heard these footsteps before, and that she had seen the figure on the stairs one night when going down to the kitchen to fetch hot water after the servants had come up to bed. She described it as a lady in widow's dress, tall and slight, with her face hidden in a handkerchief held in her right hand. Unfortunately we have since lost sight of this servant; she left us about a year afterwards on her mother's death, and we cannot now trace her. She also saw the figure outside the kitchen windows on the terrace-walk, she herself being in the kitchen; it was then about 11 in the morning, but having no note of the occurrence, I cannot now remember whether this appearance was subsequent to the one above mentioned.

These footsteps are very characteristic, and are not at all like those of any of the people in the house; they are soft and rather slow, though decided and even. My sisters would not go out on the landing after hearing them pass, nor would the servants, but each time when I have gone out after hearing them, I have seen the figure there.

On August 5th I told my father about her and what we had seen and heard. He was much astonished, not having seen or heard anything himself at that time—neither then had my mother, but she is slightly deaf, and is an invalid.

He made inquiries of the landlord (who then lived close by) as to whether he knew of anything unusual about the house, as he had himself lived in it for a short time, but he replied that he had only been there for three months, and had never seen anything unusual.

On August 6th, a neighbour, General A., who lived opposite, sent his son to inquire after my married sister, as he had seen a lady crying in our orchard, which is visible from the road. He had described her to his son, and afterwards to us, as a tall lady in black, and a bonnet with a long veil, crying, with a handkerchief held up to her face. He did not know my sister by sight, as she had only been with us a few days, and had been out very little, but he knew that she was in mourning for her baby son. My sister was not in the orchard that day at all, is rather short, and wore no veil. . . .

During this year, at Mr. Myers's suggestion, I kept a photographic camera constantly ready to try to photograph the figure, but on the few occasions I was able to do so, I got no result; at night, usually only by candle-light, a long exposure would be necessary for so dark a figure, and this I could not obtain. I also tried to communicate with the figure, constantly speaking to it and asking it to make signs, if not able to speak, but with no results. I also tried especially to *touch* her, but did not succeed. On cornering her, as I did once or twice, she disappeared.

Some time in the summer of this year (1886), Mrs. Twining, our regular charwoman, saw the figure, while waiting in the hall at the door leading to the kitchen stairs, for her payment. Until it suddenly vanished from her sight, as no real figure could have done, she thought it was a lady visitor who had mistaken her way. Mr. Myers interviewed her on December 29th, 1889, and has her separate account.

On one night in July, 1886 (my father and I being away from home), my mother and her maid heard a loud noise in an unoccupied room over their heads. They went up, but seeing nothing and the noise ceasing, they went back to my mother's room on the first storey. They then heard loud noises from the morning-room on the ground floor. They then went half way downstairs, when they saw a bright light in the hall beneath. Being alarmed, they went up to my sister E., who then came down, and they all three examined the doors, windows, &c., and found them all fastened as usual. My mother and her maid then went to bed. My sister E. went up to her room on the second storey, but as she passed the room where my two sisters L. and M. were sleeping, they opened their door to say that they had heard noises, and also seen what they described as the *flame* of a candle, without candle or hand visible, cross the room diagonally from corner to door. Two of the maids opened the doors of their two bedrooms, and said that they had also heard noises; they all 5 stood at their doors with their lighted candles for some little time. They all heard steps walking up and down the landing between them; as they passed they felt a sensation which they described as "a cold wind," though their candles were not blown about. They *saw* nothing. The steps then descended the stairs, re-ascended, again descended, and did not return. . . .

The figure has been connected with the second Mrs. S.; the grounds for which are:—

1. The complete history of the house is known, and if we are to connect the figure with any of the previous occupants, she is the only person who in any way resembled the figure.

2. The widow's garb excludes the first Mrs. S.

3. Although none of us had ever seen the second Mrs. S., several people who *had* known her identified her from our description. On being shown a photo-album containing a number of portraits, I picked out one of her sister as being most like that of the figure, and was afterwards told that the sisters were much alike.

4. Her step-daughter and others told us that she especially used the front drawing-room in which she continually appeared, and that her habitual seat was on a couch placed in a similar position to ours.

5. The figure is undoubtedly connected with the house, none of the percipients having seen it anywhere else, nor had any other hallucination. . . .

In conclusion, as to the *feelings* aroused by the presence of the figure, it is very difficult to describe them; on the first few occasions, I think the feeling of awe at something unknown, mixed with a strong desire to know more about it, predominated. Later, when I was able to analyse my feelings more closely, and the first novelty had gone off, I felt conscious of a feeling of *loss*, as if I had lost power to the figure.

Most of the other percipients speak of feeling a cold wind, but I myself have not experienced this. ("Miss Morton and the Widow in Black")

My eighth narrative is really the first of a pair of connected narratives, written by women who did not know each other but who occupied the same house at different times. The first of these is by a Miss Morris, who occupied the house in question for just over four years. She tells us near the end of her narrative that she was never happy in the house because of the peculiar experiences she had while in it. She could account for those experiences only by a friend's having told her that a woman had hanged herself in the house a few years earlier. I eliminate the second half of Miss Morris's narrative, for it deals mostly with strange ringings of the doorbell and knocks on doors by invisible agents. The narrative appeared in the 1889 *Proceedings of the Society for Psychical Research*:

It was at the latter end of October, 1882, that we decided on taking a small house on a lease, looking forward to taking possession of it and furnishing it, with great expectations of future happiness, and longing for the day to come to enter it. On the day in question we arrived late in the afternoon, and occupied ourselves in arranging and putting finishing touches to the furniture, amusing ourselves, and laughing, as we were in high spirits over our luck in finding just the little house to suit us. That same evening, about a quarter to 10, I happened to be alone in the front drawing-room, when for the first time in my life I heard, without seeing anyone, heavy footsteps tramping round the drawing-room table, at which I was reading. Naturally I was surprised, as I had never read or believed in anything supernatural. A few minutes later my eldest sister comes and sits by my side, when suddenly she exclaims, turning pale, "Charlotte, there is some one who has got into the house, walking about upstairs. I heard such a noise, like a door banging to." We were alone at the time, excepting a little child sleeping above, and my sister had never fancied such a thing before. I replied, "Oh, it's fancy." "No, I heard it again; listen!" At which I said, "I will take up the poker with my lamp; you come too, and we will see." "No," she said, "I am afraid to go up, and will stop here." So saying in fun, "I will go, and not be afraid, though 10,000 men are against me!" I flew upstairs, and searched everywhere—discovered nothing—descended alone to the basement, but with the same result.

We laughed at our fears, and went to our rooms, but that night I could not sleep at all, for incessantly round and round the room, and up and down the stairs, I heard these ceaseless and unwearying footsteps. I slept, and they woke me again, making me light my candle, and look about me, and outside the room, to see if I could discover the reason for the strange sounds. Putting it down to noises in the adjacent house, I blew out my light, and again closed my eyes, but was awoke an hour after by feeling someone in the room, and again hearing the measured footsteps. I controlled my fears by not lighting my candle, and tried, though in vain, to sleep. I said nothing about the occurrence to anyone the next day, but kept what I thought must have been fancy to myself. Still, the same experience happened to me each night, till I got accustomed to it, not allowing myself to give way to fears which, because unseen, could not be explained, till an experience most unforeseen and strange occurred.

It was three weeks since we had occupied the house and it was about five o'clock one afternoon in November, and so light that I had no need of the gas to enable me to read clearly some music I was practising, and which engrossed my whole attention and thought. Having forgotten some new waltzes I had laid on the music shelf in the back drawing-room, I left the piano, and went dancing gaily along, singing a song as I went, when suddenly there stood before me, preventing me getting the music, the figure of a woman, heavily robed in deepest black from the head to her feet; her face was intensely sad and deadly pale. There she stood, gazing fixedly at me. The song died on my lips; the door, I saw, was firmly closed where she stood, and still I could not speak. At last I exclaimed, "Oh, auntie, I thought it was you!" believing at the moment she or some strange visitor stood before me, when suddenly she vanished.

Thinking it was a trick practised on me, and trembling violently, I went back, not getting the waltzes, to my piano, which I closed, and rushing upstairs, found my aunt alone in her room, my sisters and the servant being out. "Did you not come into the drawing-room?" I asked her. "No," she replied, "I have never left my room; I am coming down now, though." As we were alone, I saw no trick had been played upon me, and my strange vision was not imagination.

Not wishing to alarm my aunt, I did not communicate my strange experience to her, nor did I relate it subsequently to my sisters or any friends, thinking, as they could not account for it, they would not believe me if I did, so I kept it as a secret for three years, though I longed to disclose it to some friend who would believe me, and not make fun at what troubled me so much. ("Miss Morris and the Lady in Black")

Miss Morris's aunt died, and much to her relief Miss Morris left the house in December of 1886. The house stood empty until November of the following year, when a Mrs. G., the writer of my ninth narrative, moved in. With her were two daughters named Florence and Edith, aged nine and ten, and her maid Anne. Recently widowed, Mrs. G. needed a less expensive house than the one she had lived in when her husband was alive. She was entirely ignorant of any difficulties the previous tenant had had. Her experiences in the house, however, were so distressing that she felt compelled to break her lease and leave after only a few months. Edmund Gurney, who investigated the story of this troubled house, went to talk with Mrs. G. about her experiences. "She struck me," he wrote for the official record, "as an excellent witness. I have never received an account in which the words and manner of telling were less suggestive of exaggeration or superstition. There is no doubt that she was simply turned out of a house which otherwise exactly suited her, at very serious expense and inconvenience." Mrs. G.'s narrative was written with the aid of a diary that she had kept, excerpts of which are quoted in the 1889 *Proceedings of the Society for Psychical Research*. I quote below the whole of Mrs. G.'s narrative, but exclude the diary and corroborating testimony by other witnesses:

We had not been more than a fortnight in our new home (it was in December) when I was aroused by a deep sob and moan. "Oh," I thought, "what has happened to the children?" I rushed in, their room being at the back of mine; found them sleeping soundly. So back to bed I went, when again another sob, and such a thump of somebody or something very heavy. "What can be the matter?" I sat up in bed, looked all round the room, then to my horror a voice (and a very sweet one) said, "Oh, do forgive me!" three times. I could stand it no more; I always kept the gas burning, turned it up, and went to the maid's room. She was fast asleep, so I shook her well, and asked her to come into my room. Then in five minutes the sobs and moans recommenced, and the heavy tramping of feet, and such thumps, like heavy boxes of plate being thrown about. She suggested I should ring the big bell I always keep in my room, but I did not like to alarm the neighbourhood. "Oh, do, ma'am, I am sure there are burglars next door, and they will come to us next." Anything but pleasant, on a bitter cold night, standing bell in hand, a heavy one, too, awaiting a burglar. Well, I told her to go to bed, and hearing nothing for half-an-hour, I got into mine, nearly frozen with cold and fright. But no sooner had I got warm than the sobs, moans, and noises commenced again. I heard the policeman's steady step, and I thought of the words, "What of the night, Watchman? what of the night?" If he only could have known what we, a few paces off, were going through. Three times I called Anne in, and then in the morning it all died away in a low moan. Directly it was daylight, I looked in the glass to see if my hair had turned white from the awful night I spent. Very relieved was I to find it still brown.

Of course nothing was said to the children, and I was hoping I should never experience such a thing again. I liked the house, and the children were so bonny. I had too much furniture for that small house, so stowed it away in the room next to the kitchen, and we used the small room at the top of the kitchen stairs as a dining-room, and then I had a pretty double drawing-room, where I always stayed. Still the children had no play-room, and no place for their doves. I therefore had most of the furniture and boxes taken out and put in the back kitchen. It seems from that day our troubles commenced, for the children were often alarmed by noises and a crash of something, and did not like sleeping alone. I felt a little uncomfortable, and thought it was all rather strange, but had so much business affairs to settle, having no one else to help me, that I had not much time to think.

I was in the drawing-room deeply thinking about business matters, when I was startled by Edith giving such a scream. I ran to the door, and found her running up, followed by Florence and the servant, the child so scared and deadly white, and could hardly breathe. "Oh, Birdie dear, I have seen such a dreadful white face peeping round the door! I only saw the head. I was playing with Floss (dog), and looking up, I saw this dreadful thing. Florence and Anne rushed in at once, but saw nothing." I pacified them by saying someone was playing a trick by a magic lantern, but after that for months they would not go upstairs or down alone.

It was very tiresome, and thinking seriously over the matter, I resolved to return my neighbour's call, which she honoured me with the day after the first terrible night. I was ushered into the presence of two portly dames, and I should think they had arrived at that age not given to pranks. I looked at them, and mentally thought, "That sweet voice does not belong to either of you." They informed me that they had lived in that house 18 years, so I thought I might venture to ask whether anything had ever taken place of a disagreeable nature in my house, as we were so constantly alarmed by heavy noises, and that my eldest daughter, aged 10, had seen a dreadful white face looking round the door at her, and of course I should be glad to know; that as far as I was concerned, I feared nothing and no one, but if my children were frightened I should leave, but I liked the house very much, and thought perhaps I might buy it. They said, "Don't do that, but there is nothing to hurt you," and I saw sundry nods and winks which meant more, so in desperation I said, "Won't you tell me what has occurred?" "Well, a few years ago, the bells commenced to ring, and there was quite a commotion, but then the former tenant, a Miss M., had a wicked servant." The other dame replied, "I may say, a very wicked servant." Well, I could not get much more, but of course I imagined this very wicked servant had done something, and felt very uneasy.

On my return, Edith said, "Oh, dear, I have seen such a little woman pass, and I often hear pitter patter; what is it? Of course magic lanterns couldn't do that." So I said nothing, and said I was too tired to talk. That night I felt a very creeping feeling of shivering, and thought I would have Florence to sleep with me, so when I went to bed about 10, I carried her in wrapped up in a shawl, leaving Edith asleep with the maid. It was about 11; I had tucked my little pet in and was about to prepare to go to sleep, when it seemed as if something electric was in the room, and that the ceiling and roof were coming on the top of us. The bed was shaken, and such a thump of something very heavy. I resolved not to risk my child's life again, for whatever it was came down on me, she would be safe in the next room with the others, but I dreaded going to bed, as I never knew what might happen before the morning.

We had a dreadful night, December 29th, such heavy thumps outside the bedrooms, and went to Mr. W., the agent, intending to tell him we must leave, or we should be bereft of our senses, but I was too late; the office was shut, so I went to friends and asked them to come and sleep, as I really was too unnerved to remain alone on New Year's Eve. They kindly came. Mrs. L. said she heard knocks. They returned home the next morning, having a young family to look after. I then wrote to a sister-in-law I was fond of at Cheltenham, and she came for a week, but everything was quiet. January 18th, I heard three loud knocks at my bedroom door. I was too terrified to speak for a minute, and then called out, "Who's there? What do you want?" My terror was intense, for I thought, supposing it is a burglar! It was a great relief to hear the children call out: "Birdie, who is knocking at your door?" "I wish I could tell you." A fortnight previously I asked a policeman on duty if he would see if any one was in the empty house. He came to tell me it was securely fastened, and no one could get in. Then I suggested coiners under the houses, but he said they only go to old castles. "Well, then what is it?" He said a sad occurrence had taken place some years ago. I said, "Oh, dreadful!" but he was matter-of-fact was Policeman X., and replied, "It is an every-day thing, and no doubt most of the houses people lived in something has happened in." "But," I said, "this is such a very strange house, and we have no rest either by day or night, and why should this dreadful white face appear to my child?" Well, he didn't believe in ghosts. "Very well," I said, "will you kindly catch whoever it is frightening us, and let them be well punished?" "But, madam, I can't catch nothing!" "Right, Policeman X., I knew that was impossible, but what am I to do?" So he suggested detectives, but that wouldn't do.

I found that house very expensive, and I had to keep the gas burning downstairs and up all night. I asked a young friend from Richmond to stay, a clergyman's daughter. She laughed at such a thing as a ghost. We both went up the trap-door and explored the space over the bedroom, and next to the roof; it was very dark, but I took a candle, and then discovered three holes as large as a plate between my house and the old ladies'. The next morning I walked down to the landlord who owns both houses, and told him again what we were continually going through and that I and my children were getting ill, and that it was quite impossible to live in the house. He came up on the following day, and told me that a woman had hanged herself, he thought, in the room the children slept in. The holes were filled up, and I thought now nothing can come in to alarm us. What puzzled my friend was that the two old dames being invalids should go out in the snow and wet between 9 and 10 most nights in their garden; it certainly was odd, but, of course, they had a right to do what they liked in their own house, only they banged the back door; when Anne locked up she scarcely made a sound.

Florence was often saying to her eldest sister, "You see it was your imagination, for I never see anything." "Wait till you do, you won't forget it!" The next morning, as Florence was passing the room on the stairs, she saw a man standing by the window staring fixedly; blue eyes, dark brown hair, and freckles. She rushed up to me, looking very white and frightened; the house was searched at once, and nothing seen.

I had forgotten to mention that the night after the knocks came to my bedroom I resolved that the dog, who is very sharp, should sleep outside, but oh, that was worse than all, for at a quarter past 12 I looked at my clock. He commenced to cry, it was not exactly howling, and tore at the carpet in a frantic manner. I threw my fur cloak on, threw the door wide open, and demanded what was the matter. The poor little animal was so delighted to see me; I saw he had biscuits and water, and the children were then awake, and asked me why Floss was making that noise. I went to bed, and in 10 minutes he recommenced. I went out three times, and then made up my mind not to move again, for I felt so cold and angry.

Another night something seemed to walk to the children's door, and turn the handle, walk up to the washstand, shake the bed, and walk out. It really was enough to shake anyone's nerves. My sister and brother-in-law, Mr. B., came for a couple of nights, but that was when I first went in. They heard nothing. I then had my husband's first wife's sister, who is very fond of me, to stay over Easter. She, fortunately, did not hear anything.

The children frequently saw lights in their bedroom, generally white, and Florence one night saw a white skirt hanging from the ceiling. She was so frightened that she put her head under the clothes, and would not look again.

Then my solicitor and his wife came down for a night, for he was very kind about my business matters, as I understand so little about money matters, so he came to advise me. Mrs. C. could not go to sleep until four, as she heard such a heavy fall outside her bedroom door.

One Sunday I was reading by the fire in the drawing-room, and thinking it was very cosy, when I heard a cry, and thinking it one of the children ill, was going upstairs. Edith called out, "Birdie, come quickly; something has opened and shut our door three times, and some one is crying." I went up, and we all heard someone sobbing, but where it came from we could not tell, but seemed near the wall.

One day, when I was out, the children were playing with Anne in the room downstairs; they all distinctly heard a very heavy footfall walk across the drawing-room, play two notes on the piano, and walk out. I came in shortly after, astonished to see them, candle in hand, looking under the beds. It was a dreadful time.

March 3rd I was writing in the drawing-room, when the front door bell rang violently. I asked who it was; "No one, ma'am." I thought I would stand by the window, and presently it rang again; down the servant came, no one there, and after the third time I told her not to go to the door unless she heard a knock as well. I knew no one had pulled the bell, as I was standing by the window.

I then had an interview with Miss M., the former tenant, who told me she had gone through precisely what I had, but had said very little about it, for fear of being laughed at. I was far too angry to take notice whether anyone laughed or not. Miss M. said one afternoon between four and five she was in very good spirits, and was playing the piano, and as she crossed the room a figure enveloped in black, with a very white face, and such a forlorn look, stood before her, and then it faded away. She was so terrified, but did not tell anyone about it. For some time after she was ill from fright on two occasions, but her aunt being old did not care to move, and she was too much attached to her to leave. It was satisfactory to find some one else had gone through what we were daily experiencing. March 20th. I was resting in the drawing-room, when as I thought, I heard Edith's voice say three times, "Darling!" I ran downstairs, much to their astonishment, and said, "Well, what is it now?" They replied, "We were coming directly, why did you come down?" "Well, that is cool; why did you call me?" "But we didn't; you called to us to put on our hats at once as you were going into the town." Anne said she distinctly heard me say it when I had not even spoken. I believe it was that same night as they were going upstairs to bed, they saw a white figure standing by the little room. How I hated that room!

Well, then friends suggested I should have the floors up, the chimneys taken out to see if there was any communication to the other house, and the door taken away, and a new one put. One friend offered to lend me a mastiff which flew at everything; another offered me his savage bull-dog, which was always chained up when I called there, and then last, but not least, I was to have two detectives. "Well," I thought, "it is time to move; in this bitter weather to have no floors, no grates, no door, a ferocious mastiff, and still worse a bull-dog and two detectives, a pretty state of affairs for any one!" I asked my landlord to release me, but he would not unless I paid my rent up to Christmas.

Having had very heavy expenses all the year, I thought I would if possible stay till September, as the evenings would be light, and we should be out all day, but even that I was not allowed to do, for coming home from paying visits, I found Florence looking deathly white, and in a very nervous state, and in breathless haste she said she had seen the same face, but the figure was crawling in the little room as if it would spring on her. I at once called on my doctor, who advised me to take the children away as soon as possible, and let them be amused, so I left my servant and her father in charge, locked my bedroom door, and took the key, went to London, where Edith was so ill that I had to call in Dr. F., and as soon as she was better I thought I would remain a week longer, making three weeks, so that she might go to a circus and be amused, and forget the frights; but even that I wasn't allowed to do, for on Monday I received a letter from my servant to say they could not stay in the house any longer, for since her father left, her mother and sister had slept with her, and they were all startled one night by hearing someone walk upstairs, throw paper down, and run after it, and the next night some one knocked loudly at my bedroom door, walked and moved all the furniture about, and nothing was moved, and that in consequence they had locked up the house, taking the doves and Floss with them, and leaving food enough for the two cats for three days. I got up early, very much annoyed about the horrid house, packed and came back with the children, May the 8th. Fortunately, Edith kept well. My banker's wife kindly met me at the station, and made me go back with the children to lunch. I telegraphed to my servant to meet me at the house, and Mrs. L. and I went to look at my present abode, and that afternoon agreed to take it from the 10th inst. Mrs. L. came up to sleep, and says she heard such thumps and bumps in the little room underneath, and a hissing sound round the top of the bed. I paid my rent and left; I asked Mr. C. to write and tell the landlord he must let me off a quarter, as I had been put to a great expense through his house, as we could not possibly live in it, and we cleared out on the following Thursday. Such a relief to be free from alarms and noises!

And so ended my sojourn of five months in that very extraordinary house. All is quite true that I have stated, whether mortal or immortal I know not. I am glad to say my children are recovering, though Edith is still very weak, and I am suffering dreadfully from neuralgia, the result of the anxiety and worry I have gone through. ("Mrs. G. and the Two Ghosts")

One small footnote to this narrative is worth mentioning. Frank Podmore, another Society for Psychical Research investigator, found a newspaper record of the death by hanging of an earlier occupant of that same house. Here is the article, from an April 5, 1879, newspaper, as reprinted in the 1889 *Proceedings of the Society for Psychical Research*:

SINGULAR CASE OF SUICIDE.—The Coroner held an inquest on Saturday at the —— Inn, on the body of Mrs. M. F., aged 42 years, who committed suicide by hanging herself on the previous day. Deceased, a lodging-house keeper in —— road, had more than once threatened to destroy herself, but no importance was attached to what she said. On Friday, however, she sent a letter to a friend saying that she would never be seen alive again in this world; but this, like her previous assertions, was regarded as an empty threat, and it was not until Mr. B., lodging at her house, missed her, and mentioned the fact to a relative, that any notice was taken of the letter. The house was then searched, and deceased was discovered hanging by a skipping-rope to a peg behind the door of the top back bedroom, quite dead. The jury returned a verdict, "Suicide whilst in a state of unsound mind."

Mrs. G.'s narrative might have provided Henry James with suggestions for a large number of the motifs we find in *The Turn of the Screw*: a woman with two young children and a servant in a delightful house that turns out to fill her with terror; the strange noises heard; the appearance of two ghosts, one male and one female; the suggestion of a suicide of the female; the white face; the woman's reluctance to speak to the children of what she has seen; the fruitless search for a man at a window; the "wicked" former servant of a previous occupant; the shaking room; the presence of skeptics who think the woman must be imagining things; the relief at discovering that the ghosts are real; the child made sick by the strange goings on and sent away from the house for her health; the children's father having been a military man killed in India; one of the children's voices saying strange things; and so on. Although we cannot fail to be impressed with how

Henry James weaves out of such motifs a far different narrative, we must also be impressed with how much the fictional *The Turn of the Screw* owes to the motifs its author could have learned by reading this and other ghost narratives.

Certainly I do not suggest that James was familiar with all nine of these particular narratives; it is as unlikely that he knew them all as that he knew none of them. I do urge, however, that these nine narratives suggest a context or tradition out of which James wrote *The Turn of the Screw.* In any event, they pave the way for my next chapter, in which I shall show, in much more detail, how most of the narrative motifs associated with the ghosts in James's story were part of a tradition of the ghost narrative.

3
MOTIFS OF THE
GHOST-CASE TRADITION

Having established that Henry James was familiar with the work of the prime movers behind the Society for Psychical Research, and having presented nine complete (or nearly complete) ghost narratives by women about their encounters with ghostly manifestations, I now want to call attention to a number of parallels between fourteen specific motifs in *The Turn of the Screw* and similar motifs in some of the ghost cases that would have been available to Henry James. I do not suggest that James had read the two-thousand-odd ghost cases that I have read in preparation for writing this chapter, or even that he had read the nearly one hundred case narratives from which I draw below. There can be no question, however, that he was familiar with some of these cases. To think otherwise is to be left with a multitude of coincidental similarities between these cases and James's story.

We will never be sure exactly which of the published cases I cite below Henry James might have read. Although all of my selections are worth presenting because they are interesting to read in their own right, they are especially valuable because they help to prove that as the number of published ghost cases grew, a kind of standard gradually emerged against which to measure the authenticity of other attested ghosts. The similarities between the description and actions of the "standard ghost" and those of the Peter Quint and Miss Jessel ghosts suggest that Henry James knew that if he wanted his Christmas-season ghost story to be taken seriously by a contemporary adult audience, he had better make his ghosts as accurate as he could. Whether he wanted to terrify, to entertain, or to instruct his readers, James must have known that he could do none of these if his ghosts were not at least superficially authentic, according to the ghost traditions prevalent in the 1880s and 1890s.

My purpose in this chapter is to establish, first, that there were motifs associated with psychical ghosts and, second, that James was not only aware of those motifs, but also consciously wrote *The Turn of the Screw* in conformance with many of them. If I succeed in establishing those two principles, then of course it will be difficult to avoid the conclusion that, for Henry James at least, Peter Quint and Miss Jessel are ghosts rather than the imaginings of a mad governess. Why, after all, would a mad woman imagine ghosts that turn out, upon careful investigation, to be so "accurate," so close to the "standard ghost" which the scientists of the day had been at such pains to identify and describe? The more true to the standard Peter Quint and Miss Jessel are, the less deluded the governess will turn out to have been.

I have identified the following fourteen motifs, or patterns, that emerged as key identifying features:

1. Ghosts appearing to two children
2. Noises in the night
3. The face at the window
4. The upper part of the figure
5. The fixed stare
6. Precise description of ghosts
7. Identifying the ghost
8. The sad face
9. The felt presence of ghosts
10. Ponds, tables, and stairs
11. A feeling of cold
12. Cold winds
13. Extinguished lights
14. Selective seeing of ghosts

In the pages below I will gather together excerpts from various ghost cases that exemplify each motif.

Because all of the cases I cite below were in print before James began writing his story late in 1897, he could have read any of them. I present only excerpts from the narratives, only those portions that focus on the specific motif I am discussing in each section. Many of my citations, then, are only a sentence or two long, and most give only the vaguest suggestion of the full narrative. For readers who may wish to consider those narratives in more detail, full bibliographical information, including dates, for each case is given in the Bibliography of Cases at the end of this book.

As in the previous chapter, the titles of all cases are my own. In the various books, journals, newspapers, and proceedings from which the cases are drawn no titles are given. Sometimes the cases are given a now meaningless code or file number, such as "G 27," but even this practice is irregular and inconsistent.

In my titles, the first person mentioned is almost always the percipient—the person who sees or hears the ghost. The second is almost always the apparition or ghost of some agent—a person who has died. The names I give are taken from the cases, though many of those names were made up at the time to protect the privacy or reputation of an informant, or to protect the financial interests of a property owner who did not want word to get out that his house was haunted. When only an initial is given in the report, I use that. When neither a name nor an initial is given in the report, I resort to using a name like "Mrs. Blank." Many of the fourteen motifs are represented in the nine narratives quoted at length in the previous chapter. I do not, however, quote again here from any of those nine. I have indicated omissions with ellipses and have inserted information within square brackets. I have made a few silent emendations of obvious typographical errors or arbitrary paragraph divisions, of inconsistent punctuation, of italicization, and of capitalization at the start and punctuation at the end of certain passages.

GHOSTS APPEARING TO TWO CHILDREN

In the opening chapter of *The Turn of the Screw,* Douglas says that, though he knows of several instances in which ghosts have appeared to a child of tender age, it is unusual for ghosts to have appeared to two children. Indeed, the appearance of ghosts to two children gives the governess's narrative an additional "turn of the screw" (p. 1). The record of psychical ghost cases very much reinforces those statements. There are so many recorded cases in which ghosts appear to a child that I need not make special reference to them here. Cases involving two children are far less frequent, though by no means unheard of. In the previous chapter I presented a number of complete narratives involving two or more children. Here are excerpts from some additional cases:

Our household consisted of my husband and myself, my step-daughter, and two little boys, aged 9 and 6, and two female servants. . . . We had been there about three weeks, when, about 11 o'clock one morning . . . I was suddenly aware of a figure peeping round the corner of the folding-doors to my left; thinking it must be a visitor, I jumped up and went into the passage, but no one was there, and the hall door, which was half glass, was shut. . . . [Later on her stepdaughter (no age is given for her, though she was apparently somewhat older than the boys) and one of the boys see what afterward proved to be the same figure.] I was upstairs playing battledore and shuttlecock with my eldest brother in his bedroom. The door was open. Stepping back in the course of the game, I got out on the landing; I looked sideways over my shoulder, in order to strike the shuttlecock, and suddenly saw the same face as before, and my brother called out at the same moment, "There's a man on the landing." ("Mrs. W. and the Man with the Pale Face")

On the 26th of 10th mo., 1841, about 9 a.m., Joseph and Henry were playing at the foot of the stairs; they both saw a white face looking down upon them over the stair rails leading to the garret. ("Joseph and the Willington Mill Ghosts")

About the year 1875, I and my sister (we were about 13 years old then) were driving home in the tax-cart one summer afternoon about 4 o'clock, when there suddenly appeared, floating over the hedge, a female figure moving noiselessly across the road; the figure was in white, and the body in a slanting position, some 10 feet above the ground. The horse suddenly stopped and shook with fright, so much so that we could not get it on. I called out to my sister: "Did you see that?" and she said she had, and so did the boy Caffrey, who was in the cart. ("Miss Montgomery and the Figure in White")

One day Mrs. Harrison was receiving a call from another lady in the drawing-room, which on one side opened on the veranda. Mrs. Harrison's little daughter and the little daughter of her visitor were in one of the windows looking out upon the veranda while their mothers were talking. Suddenly the children uttered an exclamation, and the ladies, looking up, saw this same strange visitor passing the window at which their daughters were sitting. She appeared to be coming from the street, and to be going towards the other end of the veranda, at which there was only a window. All four looked into the gallery after her, but she was gone. ("Mrs. Harrison and the Lady on the Veranda")

On the same evening I and my brother (aged about six and five years) were in bed, watching the bright moonlight, when suddenly we saw a figure, a lady with her hands folded on her breast, walking slowly, between the bed and the window. ("Mr. Colchester and the Ghost of His Grandmother")

NOISES IN THE NIGHT

Just before dawn at the end of her first night at Bly, the governess hears "faint and far, the cry of a child" and "a light footstep" just outside her door (p. 8). The records of psychical ghost cases abound with strange noises, especially the sounds of footsteps. I give only a few of the many examples of these. The sound of a crying child is rarer, though I have discovered examples of this also:

The governess used to complain of . . . footsteps, which had passed along the corridor past her door. ("Mr. Bruggeling and the Ghosts at Silverton Abbey")

About 1.15 a.m., Monday, October 9th, Mrs. Claughton was in bed with one of her children, the other sleeping in the room. . . . She had been asleep, and was awakened by the footsteps of a person coming downstairs, whom she supposed to be a servant. . . . The steps stopped at the door. The sounds were repeated twice more at the interval of a few moments. Mrs. Claughton rose, lit the candle, and opened the door. There was no one there. ("Mrs. Claughton and the Lady in White")

The house was very disturbed on Saturday night, voices and footsteps distinctly heard. ("Rev. Ware and the Boarding-School Spirits")

On the night of the 26th J. P. heard the sound of footsteps in the attic. . . . One evening J. P. heard a very peculiar moan or cry in the same room; also J. and E. P. and Jane C. heard footsteps and noises. . . . A voice by the foot of the bed said, "Chuck" twice, and then made a noise like a child sucking. ("Joseph and the Willington Mill Ghosts")

A few years since, she took a furnished house in Stevenson Street, North Shields, and she had been in it a very few hours, before she was perplexed by hearing feet in the passage, though, whenever she opened the door, she could see nobody. . . . Then there were sounds of feet and of a child crying, and a woman sobbing. ("Mrs. L. and the Dead Child")

Several of the girls, and one of the teachers, at different times have seen the figure of a child of three or four years old appearing about the house in an unaccountable way, and girls have frequently declared that they have lain awake during the night listening to the wailing of a child's voice, for which no reasonable account could be given. ("Miss P. and the Wailing Child")

THE FACE AT THE WINDOW

We find frequent references in the psychical cases to faces looking in at windows, faces that turn out to have been those of ghosts. Here are just a few that recall the governess's seeing the frightening face of Peter Quint "close to the glass" (p. 20). The last citation below is particularly relevant to James's story in that it suggests that the figure at the window, like Quint, is looking for someone:

All of a sudden a white face—a face most awful in its pallid aspect and miserable imploring look—was pressed from outside against the glass of the window and stared at us wildly. ("Mr. Eustace and the White Face")

That evening he was sitting in the parlour, the better to enjoy his pipe, when he was startled by the face of a man looking in at the window. He did not know the face. ("Mr. Butler and the Face of His Friend")

He suddenly heard three taps upon the window pane, and, looking up, saw what he describes as the upper portion of a female face, encased in an old eighteenth century bonnet. He naturally thought it exceedingly strange to see a female in such a lonely spot at midnight. . . . He hurriedly pulled on his coat and rushed out, only to find that there was no one about. ("Mr. Canning and the Face at the Window")

One afternoon, a few years ago, I was sitting in my chambers in the Temple, working at some papers. . . . Suddenly I became aware that I was looking at the bottom window-pane, which was about on a level with my eyes, and there I saw the figure of the head and face of my wife, in a reclining position, with the eyes closed and the face quite white and bloodless, as if she were dead. I pulled myself together, and got up and looked out of the window, where I saw nothing but the houses opposite. ("Mr. Searle and the Face of His Wife")

Suddenly Mr. B. said, "Who is that looking in at the window?" pointing to the furthest of the two windows. We laughed, knowing that no one could look in, as there was nothing there for them to stand on. Mr. B. persisted in his assertion, saying that it was a woman with a pale face and black hair. ("Mr. B. and the Face Looking In")

The other two maids, with myself, were sitting at supper in the kitchen, close to the window, when we all became conscious of being watched by a woman from the outside, whom the other two immediately recognized as a person whom they both knew as Mrs. Robinson. Before her marriage, she lived at the parsonage for some time as housemaid. She looked intently upon each one, and then turned her face quite to the cook, looking slightly reproachful, then pleadingly. . . . One was just about to go and ask her in, when we saw a great change come over the face, and it looked like that of a corpse, then disappeared altogether. ("Miss Farrand and the Face of Mrs. Robinson")

In the evening I was writing, and, wanting to refer to a book, went into another room where my books were. I placed the candle on a ledge of the bookcase, took down a book and found the passage I wanted, when, happening to look towards the window, which was opposite to the bookcase, I saw through the window the face of an old friend whom I had known well at Cambridge, but had not seen for 10 years or more, Canon Robinson. . . . I saw the face clearly and distinctly, ghastly pale, but with the features so marked and so distinct that I recognized it at once. . . . I was so sure I saw him that I went out to look for him, but could find no trace of him. I went back into the house and thought I would take a look at my newspaper. I tore off the wrapper, unfolded the paper, and the first piece of news that I saw was the death of Canon Robinson! ("Mr. Tandy and the Face of Canon Robinson")

They had been some considerable time in the house without the occurrence of anything remarkable, when one evening, towards dusk, Mrs. Chapman, on going into what was called the oak bed-room, saw a female figure near one of the windows; it was apparently a young woman with dark hair hanging over her shoulders, a silk petticoat, and a short white robe, and she appeared to be looking eagerly through the window, as if expecting somebody. ("Mrs. Chapman and the Woman at the Window")

THE UPPER PART OF THE FIGURE

The first two times the governess sees Quint, she sees only the upper half of him. The rest is obscured by some physical object or obstruction—the tower wall, or the wall below the window. In the ghost cases, the figures of ghosts are often seen only, or more prominently, from the waist up:

I was suddenly aware of a figure peeping round the corner of the folding-doors to my left; thinking it must be a visitor, I jumped up and went into the passage, but no one was there, and the hall door, which was half glass, was shut. I only saw the upper half of the figure, which was that of a tall man, with a very pale face and dark hair and moustache. . . . In the following August, one evening about 8.30, I had occasion to go into the drawing-room to get something out of the cupboard, when, on turning round, I saw the same face in the bay-window. . . . I again saw only the upper part of the figure. ("Mrs. W. and the Man with the Pale Face")

The lower part of the apparition grew indistinct. ("Miss T. and the Sad Man")

I started up, and then saw Mrs. B. From the head to the waist the figure was distinct, clear, and well-defined: but from the waist downwards it was all misty and the lower part transparent. ("Mr. B. and the Ghost of His Wife")

THE FIXED STARE

One of Peter Quint's more remarkable features is that he stares so much, both at the governess and at objects: he "seemed to fix me . . . never took his eyes from me . . . and even as he turned away still markedly fixed me" (p. 17); "his stare into my face, through the glass and across the room, was as deep and hard as then, but it quitted me for a moment during which I could still watch it, see it fix successively several other things" (p. 20); "it stopped short and fixed me exactly as it had fixed me from the tower and from the garden" (p. 41). Miss Jessel, similarly, stares fixedly: she "fixed the child . . . with such awful eyes" (p. 32). The ghosts of the psychical cases routinely indulge in similar fixed stares:

Suddenly a "phantom" stood before me, so close that had it been a human being it must have touched me; blotting out for a moment the landscape and surrounding objects; itself indistinct in outline, but with lips that seemed to move and murmur something, and with eyes fearfully distinct that fixed and followed and glared into mine, with a look so intense and deeply earnest that I fairly recoiled from the spot and started backwards. ("Mr. Garling and His Friend's Visit")

Suddenly, however, he advanced to that part of the area which was immediately below where I was standing, fixed on me a wide, dilated, winkless sort of stare, and halted. ("Rev. Louis and the Ghost in the Sunlight")

I distinctly heard the door open and saw the tall thin figure of a man cautiously and lurkingly enter the room and look with his small piercing eyes . . . fixedly at me. ("Mr. Potocnik and the Staring Man")

A green baize door opposite me slowly opened, and there stood a gentleman in evening dress, who holding the handle of the door gazed steadily at me for what seemed a long time. ("Mrs. Pickering and the Man at the Door")

The figure stood still for two or three minutes gazing steadfastly at him and then suddenly disappeared. ("Mr. Horlock and the Lady in His Room")

Soon after I had put out the light the door opened, a woman came in with a lighted candle, and kept on looking at me; she came up to the table which stood facing the bed, and over which hung a large mirror. I could see in the mirror the face of the woman, who continued to look fixedly at me. ("Mrs. C. and the Staring Woman")

He looked with a fixed regard at N. J. S., and then passed away. ("Mr. S. and the Ghost of Mr. L.")

The phantom turned round, approached the bed, and fixed her eyes upon him. ("Col. D. and the Cadaverous Lady")

He found her standing at the foot of the bed, and apparently looking fixedly down at him. ("Mr. Hill and the Ghost in Jamaica")

Fixing his dark piercing gaze upon me. . . . For a full minute was I exposed to the fixed gaze of the phantom. ("Mr. Blank and the Phantom Cavalier")

Then the figure moved towards me, still gazing at me fixedly. ("Miss T. and the Sad Man")

PRECISE DESCRIPTION OF GHOSTS

Those of us who think of ghosts as shadowy, indistinct, featureless figures covered by a white sheet may be surprised to read about those very distinct features of Peter Quint: "red hair, very red, close-curling . . . pale face, long in shape . . . little rather queer whiskers that are as red as his hair . . . eyebrows are somewhat darker . . . eyes are sharp . . . rather small . . . mouth is wide . . . never—no, never!—a gentleman." Then too there are the clothes: "no hat . . . dressed . . . in somebody's clothes . . . not his own" (pp. 23–24). The ghost cases abound in such descriptions, a number of which will appear in the next section. I give in this section a few of those with details particularly relevant to the governess's description of Peter Quint:

I was awe-struck by the sudden appearance of a figure gliding noiselessly towards me from the outer room. The appearance was that of a young man, of middle height, dressed in dark clothes, and wearing a peaked cap. His face was very pale, and his eyes downcast as though deep in thought. His mouth was shaded by a dark moustache. ("Miss Du Cane and the Pale Visitor")

He was middle-sized, broad-shouldered, with shoulders thrown back, had a florid complexion, reddish-brown hair (bare headed) and beard, and wore a brown sack overcoat, which was unbuttoned. His expression was grave, neither stern nor pleasant, and he seemed to look straight at Mrs. Wilson, and then at Mrs. Rogers without moving. Mrs. Wilson supposed, of course, that it was a real man, and tried to think how he could have got into the house. ("Mrs. Wilson and the Ghost of Mr. Tisdale")

I now clearly saw the features and general appearance. It was apparently a tall, well-built, rather good-looking man, in a frock coat, and with a long reddish beard. ("Mrs. Blank and the Man at Her Bedside")

The rider was in full dinner dress, with white waistcoat, and wearing a tall chimney-pot hat. . . . I at once recognized the rider as Lieutenant B., whom I had formerly known. The face, however, was different from what it used to be; in the place of being clean shaven, as when I used to know it, it was now surrounded by a fringe (what used to be known as a Newgate fringe). ("Gen. Barter and the Ghost of Lieutenant B.")

A young man of middle height, clad in dark clothes, with long black hair, a very pale face, a high white forehead. . . . The nose was long, but not high, and on each side of it there curled up a long thin black moustache. ("Miss T. and the Sad Man")

The man's face was turned away from me, but I saw his closely cut reddish-brown hair, his ear and shaved cheek, the eyebrow, the corner of his right eye, the side of the forehead, and the large high cheekbone. ("Rev. Jessopp and the Man at His Desk")

Young, and ghastly pale, he was dressed in evening clothes, evidently made by a foreign tailor. Tall and slim, he walked with long measured strides, noiselessly, without a sound—a tall white hat, covered thickly with black crape, and an eye-glass, completed the costume of this strange form. ("Dr. Leslie and the Friend at Tavistock")

I knew the face quite well, but could not say whose it was, but the suit of clothes impressed me strongly as being exactly like one which my husband had given to a servant named Ramsay the previous year. . . . As far as appearances went, the man was a gentleman . . . and, moreover, was dressed in a suit of clothes of which no gentleman need have been ashamed. ("Mrs. Bolland and the Ghost of Ramsay")

IDENTIFYING THE GHOST

After the governess describes the man she has seen, the horrified Mrs. Grose identifies him: "Quint! . . . Peter Quint—his own man, his valet" (p. 24). Modern critics, of course, make much of this scene. Those who read the story as a ghost story cite this scene as proof that Peter Quint must be the apparition of a dead man. Those who read it as a psychological case study must explain this scene away. Stanley Renner—one of the latter—puts it this way: "For readers and critics for whom the true—and clearly the richer—story of James's *The Turn of the Screw* is its dramatization of a woman's psychosexual problem and the damage it does to the children in her charge, the immovable stumbling block has always been the governess's detailed description of Peter Quint, a man dead and buried whom she has never seen. If James does not mean for readers to take Quint (and subsequently Miss Jessel) as a bona fide ghost, so the argument runs, why does he arrange things so that the only way to account for her description of him is that she has seen a supernatural manifestation?"[1] There have been many attempts to avoid this stumbling block, but the nonapparitionists—including Renner himself—continue to stumble.

1. Stanley Renner, "Sexual Hysteria, Psysiognomical Bogeymen, and the 'Ghosts' in *The Turn of the Screw*," 175.

Actually, the scene presents a double stumbling block. First, if the figure the governess describes is not the ghost of a man who had once lived, why does Mrs. Grose identify him so readily? Second, if the governess's vision of this figure arises from a "psychosexual problem," why does her insane vision sound so much like the figure described in so many of the nonfiction ghost cases that were in print before Henry James wrote *The Turn of the Screw*? I have little to say about the first stumbling block. Portions of this chapter, of course, attempt to demonstrate the massiveness of that second stumbling block.

It is important to note that the scene in which the governess describes Peter Quint accurately enough for Mrs. Grose to identify him fulfills one of Gurney's three tests (referred to in my first chapter) for the validity of ghosts: that the apparition be of someone the percipient has never seen but who is later identified by another person from the specific and definite description given by the percipient. Because this test is so crucial, both in James's story and in the ghost cases, I shall cite several variations on this test, including the recognition of the agent by the percipient from a painting or photograph seen after the appearance of the ghost. It should be noted that James provides his governess with more specific and convincing details for the identification of Peter Quint than are available in many of the ghost cases:

The apparition seemed to have a morning gown of a darkish colour, no hat nor cap, short black hair, a thin meagre visage, of a pale swarthy colour; seemed to be of about five and forty or fifty years old; the eyes half shut, the arms hanging down, the hands visible beneath the sleeve; of a middle stature. I related this description to Mr. John Lardner, rector of Havant, and to Major Batten, of Langstone, in Havant parish; they both said the description agreed very well to Mr. P. a former rector of the place, who had been dead above twenty years. ("Mr. Wilkins and the Ghost of Mr. P.")

Next morning Mr. Drury remarked to Lady Lyttleton that it was a very odd thing, but a stable-man had walked into his room in the middle of the night, and would not go away for some long time, adding, "I suppose the man was drunk, but he did not look so"; and he then proceeded to describe his dress and general appearance. Lady Lyttleton turned pale.

"You have described," she said, "my father's favourite groom, who died a fortnight ago." ("Mr. Drury and the Groom")

It was a female figure, in soft, clinging drapery, greyish whitish,—some sort of shawl or kerchief crossed over the bosom; the features, well-cut, delicate, and of an aquiline type; but what struck me most was the head-dress or coif, which had lace lappets or strings which, passing under the chin, were tied in a bow on the top of the head. . . . Many years afterwards I was in Paris after my marriage, and I used to see a cousin of my mother's, who had married abroad, and I told her once what I have above narrated. Madame de Valmer at once said to me, "My dear, you have described your great aunt to the minutest item of her dress and appearance." ("Mrs. de Gilibert and Her Great Aunt")

I suddenly awoke, and saw a lady sitting by the side of the bed where my wife was sleeping soundly. At once I sat up in the bed, and gazed so intently that even now I can recall her form and features. Had I the pencil and the brush of a Millais, I could transfer to canvas an exact likeness of the ghostly visitant. I remember that I was much struck, as I looked intently at her, with the careful arrangement of her coiffure, every single hair being most carefully brushed down. . . . I lay till my wife some hours after awoke and then I gave her an account of [our visitor]. I described her colour, form, &c., all of which exactly tallied with my wife's recollection of Miss W. Finally I asked, "But was there any special point to strike one in her appearance?" "Yes," my wife promptly replied; "we girls used to tease her at school for devoting so much time to the arrangement of her hair." This was the very thing which I have said so much struck me. ("Rev. Bellamy and the Apparition of Miss W.")

We asked her to describe the figure; and with her eyes fixed on the bed and with motion of the finger, she went on to tell us how that the old wife was not lying under the blankets, but on top, with her clothes and boots on, and her legs drawn up as though she were cold; her face was turned to the wall, and she had on what is known in the Highlands as a "sow-backed mutch," that is, a white cap which only old women wear; it has a frill round the front, and sticks out at the back. She also wore a drab-colored petticoat, and a checked shawl round her shoulders drawn tight. . . . Her right hand was hugging her left arm, and she saw that the hand was yellow and thin, and wrinkled like the hands of old people who have done a lot of hard work in their day. . . . Later they learned from a neighbor, Mrs. McP., that the description exactly fitted the wife of the previous tenant. ("Miss L. and the Lady on the Bed")

The next morning I related the circumstances to my landlady, and described the figure to her. She was visibly agitated, and at last told me that my description corresponded exactly with the previous tenant of the farm, who had shot himself in that very room. ("Mr. A. and the Ghost in His Bed")

One of the lads who saw the apparition was quite twelve years of age, and was a quiet sedate lad for his age; he entered the school after the deceased boy had left it (on account of illness about a fortnight before his death), and had never seen Daniel in his life-time. This lad, on examination, gave an exact description of the person of the deceased, and took especial notice of one thing about the apparition which the other boys had not observed, and that was, it had a white cloth or rag round one of its hands. ("The Beaminster Boys and the Ghost of Daniel")

Almost on a level with my own face I saw that of an old man, over every feature of which the putty-colored skin was drawn tightly, except the forehead, which was lined with deep wrinkles. The lips were extremely thin, and appeared perfectly bloodless. The toothless mouth stood half open. The cheeks were hollow and sunken like those of a corpse, and the eyes, which seemed far back in the middle of the head, were unnaturally luminous and piercing. This terrible object was wrapped in two bands of old yellow calico. . . . The strangest part of my story yet remains to be told. My host, after questioning me closely in regard to the features of the face, the place I had first seen it, and the spot where it disappeared, told me that fifteen years before that time an old recluse, answering in every detail to my description (calicoes, bands, and all), lived in a house whose ruins still stand close by where I first saw it, that he was buried in the exact spot in the churchyard where I saw the face disappearing, and that he was a very strange character altogether. I should like to add that I had not heard a syllable about this old man before the night in question. ("Rev. Thomas and the Old Beggar")

As the family had frequently lost their servants through terror of the mysterious disturbances, they took measures to prevent the report of these from reaching this woman's ears. She heard, however, at various times, disturbing noises at night, and declared that on several occasions she had distinctly seen move silently across the floor a form, her description of which tallied exactly with the usual appearance of poor Louise, whom in life she had never seen. . . . In taking up one of Louise's dresses, she dropped it in sudden terror, declaring that in exactly such a dress had the figure been clothed that bent over her when she swooned away. ("Mrs. F.'s Maid and the Ghost of Louise")

There he stood looking at me, and a curious smile came over his countenance. He had a stand-up collar and a cut-away coat with gilt buttons and a Scotch cap. . . . What increased the excitement was the fact that a man a number of years before, who was employed in the office of the station, had committed suicide, and his body had been carried into this very cellar. I knew nothing of this circumstance, nor of the body of the man, but Mr. Pease and others who had known him, told me my description exactly corresponded to his appearance and the way he dressed. ("Mr. Durham and the Coal-Yard Man")

I could have painted her likeness had I been an artist. She was pale, of the thick pallor of age, cold grey eyes, straight nose, thick bands of yellowish grey hair crossing her forehead. She wore a lace cap with the border closely quilted all round, a white handkerchief crossed over her chest, and a long white apron. Her face was expressionless, but fixed and sad. . . . A fortnight afterwards we had a visit from the parish priest. . . . At a loss for conversation, I told him of my visitor. . . . The padre listened to me with the greatest gravity, and said, after a pause:—"Madam, you have accurately described the old mistress of this house, who died, six months before you came, in the room over yours." . . . I ought to mention that I had no knowledge of there having been such a person in existence until her likeness stood at my bedroom door. ("Mrs. Clerke and the Old Padrona")

Mrs. Hildreth said that Mrs. Wilson's description agreed exactly with Mr. Tisdale, Mrs. Rogers' first husband. ("Mrs. Wilson and the Ghost of Mr. Tisdale")

I suddenly looked up, and saw most distinctly a tall, thin old gentleman enter the room and walk to the table. He wore a peculiar old-fashioned cloak. . . . My mother and an uncle . . . agreed that it could not be imagination, as I described my uncle so exactly. ("Miss L. and the Ghost of Her Great Uncle")

The clerk of the parish of "Meresby" states that Mrs. Claughton correctly described one of their local ghosts as he was when alive, though nobody knows how she even knew of his existence. Neither this latter ghost nor Mrs. Blackburn seems to have been known to Mrs. Claughton. ("Mrs. Claughton and the Lady in White")

Captain Ayre proceeded to describe him. He was a man of short stature, with a stoop, and wore knee breeches, a red-fronted waistcoat with sleeves, and a little black hat. Hunt instantly identified the description as answering exactly to his own father. Captain Ayre . . . had never seen Hunt's father. ("Capt. Ayre and the Ghost of Hunt's Father")

I saw a face looking round one of the bookcases. . . . The face was pallid and hairless, and the orbits of the eyes were very deep. I advanced towards it, and as I did so I saw an old man with high shoulders . . . walk rather quickly from the bookcase to the door of a small lavatory, which opened from the library and had no other access. . . . To my extreme surprise I found no one there. . . . Next morning I mentioned what I had seen to a local clergyman, who, on hearing my description, said, "Why that's old Q.!" ("Mr. J. and the Face in the Library")

He was next led to a gallery of pictures. . . . Among the oldest there was one of a lady. Col. D. had no sooner got a glimpse of it, than he cried out, "May I never leave this spot, if that is not . . . the detestable phantom that stared me out of my senses last night": and he related every particular that had occurred. Mr. N., overwhelmed with astonishment, confessed that to the room where his guest had slept there attached a certain tradition, pointing it out as having been, at a remote period, the scene of murder and incest. It had long obtained the repute of being haunted by the spirit of the lady whose picture was before him. ("Col. D. and the Cadaverous Lady")

I saw his features so plainly that I recognized them in a photograph which was shown me some days after. . . . [Another resident of the hotel where Mr. Husbands saw the figure writes:] Curiously enough, Mr. H. had never heard of him or his death. He told me the story the morning after he had seen the figure, and I recognized the young fellow from the description. It impressed me very much, but I did not mention it to him or anyone. I loitered about until I heard Mr. Husbands tell the same tale to my brother; we left Mr. H. and said simultaneously, "He has seen Mr. D." No more was said on the subject for days; then I abruptly showed the photograph. Mr. Husbands said at once, "That is the young fellow who appeared to me the other night." ("Mr. Husbands and the Ghost in His Room")

A gentleman in C., hearing of the supposed appearances and of my wife's having seen the apparition, brought over half a dozen photos, amongst others one of what is supposed to be the spirit, to test my wife. She was not present in the room when he arrived, but came in about a quarter of an hour later. We purposely refrained from mentioning the subject at all. Taking up the photos I asked her if any of them reminded her of a friend, all the pictures being twenty years old. She looked them through, and thought one an early one of a friend who was present. I took up one and tossed it across the tea-table, and only uttered the words "Who's that?" and she, after looking at it for a moment, said, "Oh, that's the ghost—where on earth did it come from?" ("Mr. Z. and the Ghost in His House")

I related the strange adventures to my host, who was remarkably upset at my narrative. He said there was a family secret he could not reveal, and contented himself by asking me to inspect a certain picture in his possession. I was astonished to find the ghost and this portrait to exactly tally. The latter must have been at least seventy years old. I await an "explanation" from those scientists and conjurers who laugh at spiritualism. I know that my experience is real. ("Mr. Smith and the Sad Woman")

THE SAD FACE

Miss Jessel is "a woman in black, . . . in mourning" (pp. 31–32). There are many, many cases of female ghosts dressed in black— apparently a favorite color of female ghosts. Rather than cite any of the scores of examples of these, however, I shall give examples that show how common was Miss Jessel's sadness. She sits on the stairs, we recall, with "her head, in an attitude of woe, in her hands" (p. 43). Later, in the schoolroom, she displays "an indescribable grand melancholy" and an "unutterable woe" (p. 59). One encounters sad and despairing ghosts in surprising number as one reads through the ghost cases. Here are just a few of them:

She stood motionless, silent, immovable, framed by the doorway, with an expression of despairing sadness . . . melancholy. . . . Her face was expressionless, but fixed and sad. ("Mrs. Clerke and the Old Padrona")

Eyes that looked at me with unutterable sadness. . . . But those eyes! Oh, the sadness that filled them! ("Miss T. and the Sad Man")

She was gazing earnestly into the grounds through the window, with a very sad expression on her face. ("Mr. Smith and the Sad Woman")

Her face appeared extremely sad. As he was going up stairs she was on the staircase before him, and turned round, looking earnestly at him. . . . She turned her head a little round and gave the same long wistful glance as before, and faded out of his sight. . . . It was a tall, long, thin face, [and] looked as if it had seen a great deal of sorrow. ("Mrs. Oliver and the Lady in Blue")

That night I awoke suddenly, and saw facing the window of my room, by my bedside, . . . my brother kneeling, . . . looking lovingly, imploringly, and sadly at me. ("Capt. Colt and the Ghost of His Brother")

Her countenance was grave and rather sad. ("Mr. B. and the Ghost of His Wife")

The lady, with a look of terrible despair in her face, ceased wringing her hands, seemed to be absorbed in the moonlight, and disappeared through the window. ("Mr. Frith and the Woman in His Room")

It was the face and figure of quite a young girl, and I saw her as clearly and distinctly as the paper I am now writing upon. She sat in an attitude of dejection, her hands clasped tightly together in her lap, and on her face an expression of sorrow such as is seldom seen on one so young. ("Mrs. Davies and the Ghost of Lillias Muir")

THE FELT PRESENCE OF GHOSTS

One of the strange "facts" of *The Turn of the Screw* that plays most directly into the hands of those who would prove the governess to be insane is that she is aware of the presence of Miss Jessel before she sees the ghost and even knows before she looks up from her work what she will see across the pond: "I became aware that on the other side of the Sea of Azof we had an interested spectator. . . . I began to take in with certitude and yet without direct vision the presence, a good way off, of a third person. . . . There was no ambiguity in . . . the conviction I from one moment to another found myself forming as to what I should see straight before me and across the lake as a consequence of raising my eyes" (p. 29). Reading a few ghost cases, however, shows us that it was not unusual for certain sensitive people to feel the presence of a ghost. The first citation below would have been particularly interesting to psychical researchers because two people independently feel the presence of a ghostly visitor before they see it:

About 20 minutes past 11 o'clock on the night of the 20th of April last, I was engaged with my wife's mother in playing a selection from "La Figlia del Reggimento" for the flute and piano. . . . I was thoroughly intent upon the music, . . . when suddenly, in the midst of the performance, a strange feeling of mingled awe and fear came over me, and I distinctly felt the approach of someone, or rather of something, coming behind me. . . . As it approached nearer, I turned my head to the right, and distinctly perceived a shade of a greyish colour standing by me upon my right, a little in advance of me. I did not see the whole figure, but what I saw was part of a shadowy face, the outline of the forehead, nose, mouth, chin, and a part of the neck being visible. . . . I did not cease playing, . . .

nor did I mention the matter to my wife's mother. . . . At or about 11.30 a.m. on the following day, my wife's mother came into the private room, and suddenly said, "Did you see something when you turned your head last night? . . . I felt that someone had come in. . . . I saw the back and shoulders of the form of a man; it passed across like a shadow behind you, stood to your right hand." She said she felt the presence of the visitor in her mind before she saw it; and this is my experience of it. I felt its presence before I saw it. ("Mr. Smith and the Music-Room Visitor")

There was a woman in the room, but I could not look up till she had gone. I considered this to be a species of nightmare, till last August. I was, as before, lying awake, when the same feeling came over me; this time far more strongly. I heard a dress rustle, and *felt* a short, dark woman was coming towards my bed. . . . I told my maid what I had seen, saying it must be a nightmare, when she said, "Why, that is what B. used to say. A short, sallow woman used to come into his room, and pass by him to the window." This B. was our late man-servant, and his room was over mine. . . . Her face seemed in darkness, and yet I *could* see it. You will laugh, because it was all at my back. I am curious to know if anyone will believe in a *non*-seeing sight. ("Mrs. Blank and the Sallow Woman")

I woke up with a feeling of some one being in the room with me, and looking across the room I saw Mrs. X. sitting upon the rocking-chair in the window. . . . About a fortnight after that I again woke at 4 a.m. with the same feeling, and there was Mrs. X. sitting in the same chair. ("Mr. X. and the Woman in Night Attire")

I felt someone in my room. On opening my eyes, I saw a young fellow about twenty-five, dressed in flannels, standing at the side of my bed and pointing with the first finger of his right hand to the place where I was lying. ("Mr. Husbands and the Ghost in His Room")

I was lying down in my drawing-room on a bright sunshiny afternoon, reading a chapter on Chalk Streams in "Kingsley's Miscellanies," when I suddenly felt that some one was waiting to speak to me. I looked up from my book and saw a man standing beside an arm-chair, which was about six feet from me. He was looking most intently at me, with an extraordinary earnest expression in his eyes. ("Mrs. Bolland and the Ghost of Ramsay")

I felt someone was behind me. I turned round sharply, and there again stood the same old man! He quickly vanished. ("Mrs. Wilson and the Old Man in Her Bedroom")

No sooner was I in bed than I became possessed of the feeling that someone was near me, that other persons were in the room. . . . The feeling came over me that here there was something out of the common and very uncomfortable. . . . I could not throw off the feeling that there was someone moving about my room. ("Mrs. Davies and the Ghost of Mary Jeffs")

One night I awoke with a feeling some one was in the room. . . . I looked about, and presently saw something behind the little table. ("Miss R. and the Face in Her Room")

Being asleep, I was awakened with or by a sudden feeling of terror. I stared through the darkness of my bedroom, but could not see anything, but felt overcome by an unnatural horror or dread. ("Mr. Matthews and the Reappearance of Susan")

She saw nothing, and indeed dared not look round the rooms again, but burying her head in her pillow, she lay trembling violently, but utterly powerless to move. She at the same time was perfectly conscious of the movements of the ghostly intruder, knew one moment that it stood in the vicinity of the front window, then felt it was standing by the fire-place, then she knew that it moved again, and was now pausing at the head of the couch on which she was lying. ("Miss Blank and the Dining Room Ghost")

That same intense, indescribable feeling passed over me—that horrid, creepy dread, but I resolutely turned from the side on which the embrasure lay, and reproached myself for being a fool. Nor would I look, and yet I felt assured of her presence. ("Mr. Hernaman and the Little Old Woman")

I suddenly awoke . . . with a sort of certainty that a tall, thin old man, in a long flowered dressing-gown, was seated and writing at the table in the middle of the room. I cannot say what gave me this certainty, or this distinct picture, for I did not once turn my eyes to the place where I felt that the intruder was seated. It did not, in fact, occur to me at the time how odd it was that I thus knew of his appearance without seeing him. ("Mrs. Pittar and the Man at the Desk")

PONDS, TABLES, AND STAIRS

The ghost in the last case sits at a desk, just as Miss Jessel does in the governess's schoolroom. We tend not to find cases in which ghosts appear on the tops of towers, presumably because the distances involved would be so great as to rob any identifications of evidential significance. We do, however, find cases in which ghosts appear near ponds, seated at tables, and on stairs. The first case cited below is particularly interesting because of its association with a 1690 murder trial. It seems that a William Barwick murdered his pregnant wife, threw her body into a pond, then later retrieved the body and buried it near the pond. The subsequent appearance of the murdered woman's ghost to Thomas Lofthouse, her brother-in-law, led to the arrest of Barwick, his confession, the digging-up of the body (dressed, incidentally, in clothes similar to those in which the ghost had been attired), the trial and conviction of Barwick, and his execution. I quote not from the original legal record, but from a report of a haunting associated with Cawood Castle, in Yorkshire. This report appeared in an 1890 book by John Ingram, *The Haunted Homes and Family Traditions of Great Britain*, which would have been readily available to Henry James:

About half an hour after twelve of the clock, in the day-time, he was watering quickwood, and as he was going for the second pail, there appeared, walking before him, an apparition in the shape of a woman. Soon after she sat down over against the pond, on a green hill. ("Mr. Lofthouse and the Woman by the Pond")

Mr. A. W. Hall, of St. Thomas's House, Oxford, tells us how he saw a venerable old man "sitting writing at the table in the centre of the room in which I was," the room being one in which there had, in fact, been previous rumours (unknown to Mr. Hall) of the appearance of Lord Hood, Mr. Hall's great-grandfather, whom he had never seen. ("Mr. Hall and the Man at the Desk")

There sat a figure of a somewhat large man, with his back to the fire, bending slightly over the table, and apparently examining the pile of books that I had been at work upon. ("Rev. Jessopp and the Man at His Desk")

I saw the grey outline of a big form, huddled together in the chair near to my writing table. ("Mrs. Davies and the Ghost of Mary Jeffs")

After I put the children to bed I sat down in the nursery to my work, when I heard someone coming up the stairs. I went to the door, and on the first landing . . . I saw, as I thought, Madame N. carrying something heavy. I felt that she ought not to be out of her bed, and I called to her in French: "Je viendrai vous aider," running down the stairs to where I supposed she was. When I got there it gave me a queer sensation to find no one. However, I said to myself, it was a shadow, and made myself go back to my work. I had scarcely seated myself when a voice called: "May, May, May" (the name my children called her). I got up, went to the door, and seeing someone, ran halfway down the stairs to meet the woman, when a terrible dread came upon me. ("Miss M. and the Lady on the Stairs")

I then heard a sound on the stairs, as if somebody was going down without boots on, thud, thud; so I called out "Who's there? Do speak, you have frightened us." Not receiving an answer I waited awhile, then softly opened the door and looked out. All was quiet; the gas was burning on the lower landing. By its light I saw a woman standing at the foot of the stairs. ("Mrs. H.'s Nurse and the Lady at the Partition")

She satisfied herself that the animal was all right, and was at the foot of the stairs preparing to go up again when she saw an old man standing above her at the top and gazing directly at her. ("Mrs. Wilson and the Old Man in Her Bedroom")

A FEELING OF COLD

The appearance of Peter Quint at the window makes the governess "catch my breath and turn cold" (p. 20). In feeling that cold in the presence of a ghost, she was feeling something many other percipients had felt:

Suddenly a "phantom" stood before me. . . . In probably a few seconds, which seemed to me far longer, it vanished, leaving me rooted to the spot for a few moments, and sensible of the reality of the vision by the curious physical effect it left upon me. This was as if the blood was like ice in my veins; no flutter of the nerves, but a deadly chill feeling that lasted more or less for nearly an hour. . . . I have never felt any similar sensation before or since. ("Mr. Garling and His Friend's Visit")

Is it usual for persons, whilst sitting at the table, to experience a sensation of a shivering, or cold chills, causing one to shake? I have felt this each time, but more than usual last evening. ("Rev. Ware and the Boarding-School Spirits")

I appeared to be quite paralysed, and quite cold. . . . The apparition had vanished. I remained still very cold (which appeared to me a few minutes) before I felt a glow of warmth. . . . My brother then told me he had (during my absence at home) been awakened one night with a cold feeling, and there was a white figure standing by his side. ("Mr. X. and the Woman in Night Attire")

The same icy chill . . . crept over me. . . . I felt an icy chill all over me. ("Mrs. Davies and the Ghost of Lillias Muir")

A kind of shudder passed through me, accompanied by a most extraordinary feeling, which I can only compare to that of a jug of cold water poured on the nape of the neck, and running down the spine. ("Rev. Blank and His Friend")

On Thursday evening, 14th November, 1867, I was sitting in the Birmingham Town Hall with my husband at a concert, when there came over me the icy chill which usually accompanies these occurrences. ("Mrs. Taunton and the Ghost of Her Uncle")

I found myself very cold from my feet as high as my middle, though I was not in great fear: I went into the bed betwixt the tenant and his man, and they complained of my being exceedingly cold. ("Mr. Wilkins and the Ghost of Mr. P.")

At that moment an icy chill passed through him. ("Mr. S. and the Ghost of Mr. L.")

I was awakened by the opening of my bedroom door, and saw, to my horror, Susan enter in her night-dress. She came straight towards my bed, turned down the clothes, and laid herself beside me, and I felt a cold chill all down my side where she seemed to touch me. . . . We heard by the village woman on her return the Sunday evening, that Susan died in the middle of the night. ("Mr. Matthews and the Reappearance of Susan")

I . . . felt myself grow perfectly cold. ("Miss R. and the Face in Her Room")

COLD WINDS

Near the end of her story, when she tries to persuade Miles to talk about what had happened to him before she came to Bly, the governess feels a cold wind in the room: "The answer to my appeal was instantaneous, but it came in the form of an extraordinary blast and chill, a gust of frozen air and a shake in the room as great as if, in the wild wind, the casement had crashed in" (p. 65). Such icy winds are common enough in the ghost cases:

In the autumn of 1876 I was awoke one night, and felt an icy wind blowing through my room, and heard loud sobs; the curtains of the bed were pulled back, and my hair was pulled. ("Mrs. R. and the Sobbing Lady")

This much I know for a fact, that often when taking my notes or watching quietly by my patient, with a good fire, and a light burning, I have suddenly felt as if a cool wind was blowing me about so that I could not help shivering. ("Mrs. H.'s Nurse and the Lady at the Partition")

A cold draught of air seemed to fill the whole passage . . . and I felt as if I was being frozen up. ("Miss X. and the East Riding Ghosts")

The apparition glided onwards towards my sisters, who were standing inside the room, quite close to the outer door, and who had just caught sight of it, reflected in the mirror. When within a few inches from them it vanished as suddenly as it appeared. As the figure passed we distinctly felt a cold air which seemed to accompany it. . . . One of my sisters did not see the apparition, as she was looking the other way at the moment, but felt a cold air. ("Miss Du Cane and the Pale Visitor")

EXTINGUISHED LIGHTS

Sometimes those winds have a way of extinguishing candles and lamps. Just before the governess sees Peter Quint on the stairs, a "bold flourish" blows out her candle (p. 40). Later, when she asks Miles about delicate subjects, her candle again is blown out, even though the window is closed and the curtains are "unstirred" (p. 65). This time Miles claims to have blown out the candle himself, but we cannot be so sure, and there is reason to doubt him. In any case, extinguished candles and lamps are frequent occurrences in the presence of ghosts, who often do not seem to like the light. The first quotation below may be of particular interest in that it involves a woman and a young girl sharing an apartment when the experience described takes place:

On one occasion a lady and her child were staying for a few days at the castle. The child was asleep in an adjoining dressing-room, and the lady, having gone to bed, lay awake for awhile. Suddenly a cold blast stole into the room, extinguishing the night-light by her bedside, but not affecting the one in the dressing-room beyond, in which her child had its cot. By that light she saw a tall mailed figure pass into the dressing-room from that in which she was lying. ("Mrs. Blank and the Mailed Figure")

The next moment, as from a strong wind, the light was extinguished, while knocks and raps and a rushing sound passed round the apartment. ("Mr. L. and His Tormentor")

"Every time that I struck a match, Miss Mary," added the frightened girl, "something would blow it out." ("Miss Anderson and the Invisible Attackers")

About 1.15 a.m., Monday, October 9th, Mrs. Claughton was in bed with one of her children, the other sleeping in the room. . . . Woke up, finding the candle spluttering out. Heard a sound like a sigh. Saw a woman standing by the bed. ("Mrs. Claughton and the Lady in White")

My sister L. went up into the garrets or attics about 9 o'clock one evening with a candle in her hand, to get something from an old chest. Water was thrown obliquely across the room, nearly extinguishing the candle, wetting her hand, and leaving an oblique splash on the wall. There was a pool of water on the floor as well. My sister was alarmed at this, as she knew no one was in the room or on that story with her. ("Miss L. and the Wet Candle")

During the night I became aware of a draped figure passing across the foot of the bed towards the fire-place. I had the impression that the arm was raised, pointing with the hand towards the mantel-piece, on which a night-light was burning . . . and the light was extinguished. . . . I need hardly say that Mrs. Gwynne was in a very nervous state. She asked me what I had seen, and I told her. She had seen the same figure. [Mrs. Gwynne's statement follows:] I distinctly saw the hand of the phantom placed over the night-light, which was at once extinguished. ("Dr. Gwynne and the Draped Figure")

The lady, now my wife . . . went, candle in hand, to the larder for something for the supper table, and as she descended some steps leading to it she seemed to lose her hold of the candlestick and it went to the ground. She felt for the dish she went for and brought it away. Next night she went again. This time she was careful to hold the candlestick firmly, but at the same spot she felt it forcibly drawn from her hold and thrown into a corner. ("Mr. C. and the Ghostly Man")

On one occasion when he was standing in the dining-room with a candle in his hand, comparing the clock with his watch about midnight, all doors and windows closed and a perfectly still night, he felt a distinct breath on his neck behind, and the next moment the candle was violently blown out, and the room left in utter darkness. ("Mr. Horlock and the Lady in His Room")

On one occasion his mother saw through the bed curtain a figure cross the room to the table on which the light was burning, take up the snuffers and snuff the candle, then cross the room towards the bed. ("Dr. Proctor and the Willington Mill Ghost")

I went in with my candle, and as soon as I had got inside the door saw, to my horror, the form with the huge head coming towards me. There was a puff, and I was in darkness. ("Miss X. and the East Riding Ghosts")

The house was lighted by small oil lamps, hung or standing in various places, and it now became exceedingly difficult to keep these lamps alight. They were in no draught, oil was abundant, wicks perfect, but they went out every few minutes, and on going to them it was discovered that the screw of the wick had been turned down! No human hand had been near them. ("Rev. A. and the Parsonage Imp")

Shortly after nightfall he endeavoured to kindle a fire in one of the rooms and to light the lamp with which he had provided himself, but to his surprise and consternation, found it impossible to do either. An icy breath, which seemed to proceed from some invisible person at his side, extinguished each match as he lighted it. ("Mr. Gunn and the Match-Blower")

SELECTIVE SEEING OF GHOSTS

The starting point and ending point for critics who question the reality of the ghosts of Peter Quint and Miss Jessel is the fact that we can be sure only that the governess herself sees them. She wishes Mrs. Grose could see them, but Mrs. Grose never does. She believes Miles and Flora see them, but there is no firm evidence that they do and some reason to believe that they do not. The general logic of critics who doubt that the ghosts are real is that because the governess alone sees the ghosts, she must be imagining them, or else others also would see them. Actually, the governess herself is not vastly puzzled by her seeing the ghosts when Mrs. Grose does not. She refers to her "dreadful liability" to see such things and to her "questionable privilege" (p. 25). She almost envies Mrs. Grose's "exemption" from the responsibility of being able to see them (p. 25) and wishes at one point that she might "lose my power" to see them (p. 52). She seems to accept it as quite natural—if at times terribly frustrating—for some people to have their eyes unsealed to such sights, whereas the eyes of others remain sealed. Such experiences were common to those interested in psychical research. Thistleton Dyer opened a chapter on "Ghost Seers" in his book *The Ghost World* (1893) with the statement: "Some persons have the peculiar faculty of seeing ghosts, a privilege which, it would seem, is denied to others."[2] And Frederic Myers, having done some statistical research on the cases reported in *Phantasms of the Living,* tells us that in approximately a third of the cases in which two or more persons are present when a phantasm is noticed, "it is perceived by only one of the persons present."[3] Whether or not James read such statements, or others like them, he could have found case after case of recorded sightings in which ghosts were not visible to everyone in their presence but were visible only to those people with a special faculty or privilege. It will be noted that the governess's apparent frustration when others do not see—even when she points and tells them, "there, *there!*" (pp. 71, 88)—is anticipated by the last several citations given below:

One fact seems to be satisfactorily established, and that is, two or three people out of a room full can see a spirit, and the others remain in ignorance of its presence. I have tried on four occasions to see it when it has appeared. My wife, a lady friend, and the butler could see it, but four other people present failed to do so. ("Mr. Z. and the Ghost in His House")

There it was that I saw the figure of a man on the right-hand side, walking, or rather gliding, at the head of the horse. . . . My cousin and the man-servant saw it distinctly, but my friend was unable to do so, though the figure stood out plainly against the evening light. ("Mrs. Stone and the Horseman")

I got up after some time to go into the house, not having noticed anything at all—when this black woman said to me, "Missis, who was that gentleman that was talking to you just now?" "There was no one talking to me," I said. "Oh, yes, dere was, Missis—a very pale gentleman, very tall, and he talked to you, and you was very rude, for you never answered him." I repeated there was no one, and got rather cross with the woman, and she begged me to write down the day, for she knew she had seen

2. T. F. Thistleton Dyer, *The Ghost World*, 214.
3. Gurney, Myers, and Podmore, *Phantasms*, 2:278.

someone. I did, and in a few days I heard of the death of my brother in Tobago [on that day]. Now, the curious part is this, that I did not see him, but she—a stranger to him—did; and she said that he seemed very anxious for me to notice him. ("Mrs. Clerke and Her Brother's Appearance")

On a summer evening, about 9 o'clock, Captain Ayre and his companion went to their bedroom, when they both heard a noise at the side of the house, and both went to the window to see what was the matter. The captain distinctly saw a man walking outside, but Hunt could see nothing there, though he had heard the tramp of feet as well as the captain. ("Capt. Ayre and the Ghost of Hunt's Father")

Then Mrs. W. became aware of a figure standing on the other side of the bed—the figure of a woman completely dressed, and looking at him earnestly, with one finger raised and pointing towards her, as if in warning. She did not feel alarmed, but said to her husband, "Look round this way, there is some one in the room." He looked but saw nothing. ("Mrs. W. and the Pointing Lady")

The nursemaid told me, next day, that Muriel (a child of three years) had woke her in the night, saying, without any fear in her voice, "Clara, Clara, there is an old woman in the room." The nurse herself saw nothing. ("Mrs. Bettany and the Night Visitor")

On the morning of my father's death, between 4 and 5 o'clock, I saw a sort of shadowy light at the foot of my bed, and half arose to look at it. I distinctly saw my father's face, smiling at me. I drew the curtains apart, and still saw him looking fixedly at me. I awoke the girl who was sleeping with me, and asked her to draw up the window blind. I then asked her if she saw anything. She said, "Nothing. It is too dark." ("Mrs. Clarke and Her Father's Face")

While yet very young, she one day began to cry out that there was a young woman looking at her, and wanting to come to her, and, according to her description of the person, it must have been her mother. . . . No one else saw the apparition. ("Miss Blank and the Visit of Her Mother")

About the year 1834 or 1835, I was in a boarding school . . . where, amongst other pupils, there were two sisters with whom I was very intimate. . . . We slept in a large dormitory in which were several beds, the two sisters occupying a double bed. On a certain night, most of the girls were asleep, and myself in the next bed to one of the sisters, who was already in bed, and, like myself, anxious to be quiet and allowed to go to sleep. . . . As the elder sister was urging her to be quiet and to get into bed, the younger one suddenly exclaimed, and putting her hands over her face, seemed greatly agitated. As there seemed no cause for this sudden excitement, we, thinking it was only another form of her non-sense, and fearing the noise would bring up the governess, who also slept in the room, scolded her well, upon which she got into bed. Turning again to look towards the door, she uttered another cry, directing her sister's attention to the door; but she saw nothing, and still thought the younger one was joking. ("Mrs. Richards' Friend and Her Mother")

Annie (a girl of 12 at the time), along with another girl, was sent home to fetch something that had been forgotten. On entering the kitchen, Annie said to the other girl, "See, there's a man sitting by the fireside." The other girl said there was nobody there. The two went upstairs to get what they had been sent for, when Annie said, "There's the man again." The other girl persisted that there was nobody there. Having got what they wanted, they returned to the friend's house. On coming home late at night, Mrs. Adams said to her husband—"There's my brother standing beside that house; don't you see him, all in white?" Mr. Adams did not see him. ("Miss Adams and the Man by the Fireside")

My younger sister L., going in first, said, on going into the kitchen: "There she is," pointing to the bed, and turned to us, expecting that we would wake her up and ask what she was there for. I looked in the bed, and so did my elder sister, but the clothes were flat and unruffled, and when we said that there was nothing there she was quite surprised, and, pointing with her finger, said: "Look, why there's the old wife with her clothes on and lying with her head towards the window"; but we could not see anything. ("Miss L. and the Lady on the Bed")

Mrs. H. was with me. We were walking home together, and had joked about not meeting anyone on the road. . . . We walked on, talking about various things, and then I saw someone coming. I said, "Here we meet someone at last." She said, "I don't see anyone." "*There*," I said; "look, *there* comes an old woman, and she is twisting her shawl round her neck." My wife, however, could see nothing. ("Rev. H. and the Apparition of Mrs. B.")

Suddenly the girl exclaimed: "Oh, mamma, there's Mr. B!" "Where?" cried the scandalized mother, clutching and pulling up the bed-clothes. "There, mamma! Do you not see him? There." ("Miss Blank and the Ghost of Mr. B.")

A party of children, sons and daughters of the officers of Artillery stationed at Woolwich, were playing in the garden. Suddenly a little girl screamed, and stood staring with an aspect of terror at a willow tree there. Her companions gathered round, asking what ailed her. "Oh!" she said, "there—there. Don't you see. There's papa lying on the ground, and the blood running from a big wound." All assured her that they could see nothing of the kind. ("Mr. Cox and the Little Girl's Father")

I might point out that in this last section we have been dealing only with human beings who see ghosts. It is not entirely irrelevant to consider the nonhumans that see them. Nearly all previous scholars have ignored the implications of the unnatural silence that falls on Bly just when the governess sees the ghost of Peter Quint: "All the rest of the scene had been stricken with death. I can hear again, as I write, the intense hush in which the sounds of evening dropped. The rooks stopped cawing in the golden sky and the friendly hour lost for the unspeakable minute all its voice" (p. 16). In no small number of ghost cases we find references to animals being frightened by ghosts. Usually (as in "Mrs. G. and the Two Ghosts," cited in Chapter 2) the animal is a pet, most commonly a dog. Sometimes (as in the citation from "Miss Montgomery and the Figure in White" in the first section of this chapter) it is a horse. Sometimes, indeed, there are more animals than one:

As she entered, her son's favorite pointer rushed out of the room. "So," he said, "the dog's gone! I have not been able to keep a dog in my room at night for years; but under your roof, mother, I fancied, I hoped, I might escape a persecution that I see now pursues me even here. I am sorry for Kate's canary-bird that hung behind the curtain. I heard it fluttering after the first round. Of course it is dead!" The old lady got up, all trembling, to look at poor Kate's bird. It *was* dead. ("Mr. L. and His Tormentor")

I could cite many more cases, but because they almost all involve pets, they offer at best only an inexact parallel with the wild rooks at Bly.[4] It may, however, be instructive here to quote a few sentences published in 1872 in a journal called *Human Nature*. They were written by a barrister and anthropologist named George Harris. In an article on how to separate mistaken or delusionary ghost-sightings from authentic ones, Harris specifically mentions

4. Readers interested in seeing some typical examples are referred to *Light* 11 (1891): 250 (dog and horse), 261–62 (dog and canary), 278–79 (horse and cat), and 244 (mule).

terror-stricken animals as worthy of notice in determining which reports of ghosts are likely to be reliable:

> If, moreover, an animal, a dog for instance, accompanying the person who sees the apparition, gives token of the presence of some supernatural being, either by its cries, or by exhibiting unusual symptoms of terror, as is alleged to have happened in some avowedly well-authenticated cases of apparitions, these must undoubtedly be regarded as a strong additional proof of the reality of its appearance, and that no mere illusion of the senses of the person witnessing the apparition occasioned a belief in its existence.[5]

When Henry James has the governess tell us that the rooks at Bly, which are normally active and noisy on a late sunny afternoon, fall into an unnatural and prolonged silence, is it not possible that he is really telling us that the rooks see, from the treetops and from the sky, what the governess sees from the ground? And if so, may he not have given us an early indication that the ghost of Peter Quint is, in Harris's words, "no mere illusion of the senses of the person witnessing the apparition"? Of course, some readers will decide that the governess is deluded in her perception that the rooks are silent.

I could continue to add, as the governess puts it, "stroke to stroke" to make a more complete listing of the motifs associated with ghost cases. For example, there are numerous parallels in the ghost cases with the governess's reading, her discovering a ghost on returning to pick up an item accidentally left behind, her attempt to speak to the ghost of Miss Jessel, the violent shaking of the room in the presence of Peter Quint's ghost in the final scene, the movement of curtains in the presence of a ghost, the sudden appearance and disappearance of ghosts, the governess's inability to determine the exact duration of a ghost's visit, and so on. I shall leave the work—and the fun—of finding such parallels to others, who will have their own reasons for seeking them. My reason for citing the fourteen motifs listed above and for calling attention to certain parallels between James's story and the psy-

5. George Harris, "Supernatural Visitations," 172.

chical cases is that I wish to show that James created in Peter Quint and Miss Jessel two ghosts that would have been recognized as "realistic" by an audience familiar with psychical cases. Had James not been interested in telling a ghost story about "real" ghosts, he would not have gone to such trouble to make Peter Quint and Miss Jessel so true to traditional form. Had he wanted to give encouragement to readers who might suspect that the governess was crazy or was merely imagining those ghosts, he would not have gone to such lengths in describing the ghosts, for if the ghosts were merely the imaginings of a mad woman, why would she have imagined such *accurate* ghosts, ghosts that might have passed muster before almost any psychical research panel on either side of the Atlantic?

Would Peter Quint and Miss Jessel have passed muster as genuine ghosts before such a panel? We cannot know the answer for sure because, of course, no panel was ever convened to pass judgment on them. We are fortunate, however, to know what one serious psychical researcher said to another about Peter Quint and Miss Jessel. Shortly after *The Turn of the Screw* was published in book form in *The Two Magics* on October 5, 1898, no less a psychical researcher than Frederic Myers wrote a letter to his friend and fellow researcher Sir Oliver J. Lodge. I quote here only the relevant paragraph of the letter, dated October 28, 1898:

Henry James has written a forceful story of country-home life,—"The Turn of the Screw," in a book called "The Two Magics." The hero and heroine are two sweet and lovely children,—a boy of 9 and a girl of 6. The little girl feels lesbian love for the partially-materialized ghost of a harlot-governess; and the little boy (who is expelled from school for obscenity) feels pederastic passion for the partially-materialized ghost of a corrupt manservant. The story is told by a governess (a good and virtuous one) with much force and dignity. The man-servant seduces the first governess, who kills herself in pregnancy; he is himself killed by some apparently male victim of his lust. On this simple groundwork some striking and even tragic scenes are inwrought;—the main *motif* being the natural desire of the ghosts to carry off the children to hell.[6]

6. Frederic Myers to Sir Oliver J. Lodge, October 28, 1898, Letter No. 1520, Lodge Collection, Society for Psychical Research Archives, London, England.

This letter raises a number of interesting questions, some of which are outside the scope of this book. I will, however, comment briefly on a few of those questions before getting to the primary issue, the nature of the ghosts. First, what about the ages of the children? James tells us that Flora is eight and Miles is ten, whereas Myers puts them at six and nine, respectively. The confusion is understandable. In *Collier's Weekly,* which had concluded its extended serialization of *The Turn of the Screw* the previous April, Flora is only six. Myers might have read the earlier version and only skimmed the book version, in which James had raised Flora's age. Indeed, although James did alter the age of Flora in the book version, he did not change certain expressions that seem to refer to a younger Flora: her eating supper "in a high chair and a bib" (p. 8); her very basic penmanship exercises consisting of copying "nice 'round *O*'s'" (p. 11); the governess's calling her "a scrap of an infant" (p. 32). For Myers to name Flora's age as six, then, seems an honest enough mistake. As for Miles's age, the only reference to it is Mrs. Grose's comment that he is "scarce ten years old" (p. 11), a phrase that Myers might easily have interpreted as "not quite ten" rather than "just past ten."

As for Myers's speculation that Flora feels a "lesbian love" for Miss Jessel, that Miles feels a "pederastic passion" for Peter Quint, and that Peter Quint is murdered by a "male victim of his lust," I have little more to say than that I do not think it is necessary to read the story that way. Indeed, unless we attribute to Peter Quint and Miss Jessel an omnivorous bisexuality, such a view seems to be contradicted by Myers's own suggestion that there was a quite heterosexual affair between the two which resulted in Miss Jessel's pregnancy and eventual suicide. Although it is possible that Myers may have been joking about the homosexual interpretation of James's story, there is independent evidence that he was serious. He asked Edward Marsh, another friend, whether Marsh believed there could be "the Lesbian vice between the ghost of a governess and a little girl of six."[7] I think it is more likely that Myers was wrong than that he was merely joking.

7. Christopher Hassall, *A Biography of Edward Marsh,* 89.

I shall have more to say in later chapters about Myers's view that Miles is expelled from school for "obscenity" and that Peter Quint and Miss Jessel have a "natural" desire to carry the children off to hell. More relevant to our immediate concern is that Myers finds the governess to be "good and virtuous." Myers's judgment here must carry more than a little weight, for the first task of any experienced psychical researcher was to assess the character of the person who claimed to have had supernatural experiences. Myers apparently saw no reason not to share the views of his fellow Trinity graduate, the fictional narrator Douglas, that the governess was "clever" and "worthy" of any position whatever (p. 2). Myers, a poet and a literary scholar in his own right as well as an experienced investigator of psychical phenomena, might have been expected to be sensitive to ambiguities of character in fictional governesses who said they saw ghosts. Myers found James's governess to be a reliable witness.

Of particular relevance to the thesis of this and the previous chapter is Myers's judgment that Peter Quint and Miss Jessel are ghosts. It apparently never occurred to Myers to doubt that James wrote a ghost story, and a most effective one at that—a "forceful story" with "striking and even tragic scenes." This is not to say that Myers thought James's ghosts were entirely convincing as realistic ghosts. Indeed, Myers's characterization of the ghosts as "partially-materialized" indicates that in his view they were somewhat different from the realistic ghosts that he and Gurney theorized about. Let me explain what I mean.

Edmund Gurney did the lion's share of the work of collecting, investigating, categorizing, and discussing the many hundreds of cases that went into the two-volume 1886 *Phantasms of the Living*. Frederic Myers and Frank Podmore did little, relatively speaking, though they were listed as joint authors on the title page. Podmore investigated a few cases. Myers investigated even fewer and wrote the introduction and a lengthy "Note on a Suggested Mode of Psychical Interaction."[8] Although Myers and Gurney disagreed on many of the finer theoretical points concerning the manifestation of "phantasms" (that is, ghosts seen, felt, or heard),

---

8. Gurney, Myers, and Podmore, *Phantasms*, 2:277–316.

they agreed that ghosts were *not* "material." Rather than being in any sense made up of matter or endowed with any physical properties, ghosts were essentially "telepathic"—a term invented by Myers. By that term they meant that ghosts did not actually become manifest in any physical sense but that they were some-how mental projections from the mind of one being (an "agent," whether living or dead) to another (a "percipient"). In some cases, the agent and the percipient might be essentially the same being, which meant that the person "seeing" the ghost was seeing some-thing actually in his or her own mind and thus was having a subjective, though not necessarily insane, experience. In other cases, the agent really did in some sense convey by means of his or her personal "energy" an impression that was picked up or perceived by a percipient, who thus was experiencing a "ve-ridical," or true, perception of something or someone transmit-ting rays or reserves of energy.

Now, Gurney tended to think about ghosts in ways that mini-mized the energizing role of the agent, whereas Myers was inclined to think about them in ways that minimized the creative role of the percipient. For example, if John and Mary at the same time saw what they perceived as the same phantasm, Gurney thought that the mind of only one of them—say, John—actually picked up telepathic rays from an agent. John, having formed in his own mind an "externalized" impression of a phantasm, then telepathically conveyed it to Mary, who perceived from John, not directly from the agent, her own impression or mental picture. Myers, on the other hand, thought that in such a situation the agent must be generating sufficient energy that both John and Mary independently formed a telepathic image.

In his "Note on a Suggested Mode of Psychical Interaction" Myers discusses at great length why he differs with Gurney about what causes two or more people to see the same phantasm. Myers makes it clear, however, that he and Gurney stand firmly united against the mundane view that two or more people see the same ghost because the ghost is a materialized embodiment of the agent's physical self. Early in the note, for example, Myers speaks with some contempt of the "crude popular credence which attributed to 'ghosts' some sort of tenuous materiality." He immediately dismisses such credence:

The popular view—to take that first—lies so far outside the pale of any recognised scientific conceptions that strong evidence indeed would be needed to reconcile us to it. We are sometimes asked to believe that this body of ours—with its digestive system, &c., and all its traces of physical evolution—is interpenetrated with a "meta-organism" of identical shape and structure, and capable sometimes of detaching itself from the solid flesh and producing measurable effects on the material world. Now that material effects should be produced by something which (like our own will) is only cognisable by us on its psychical side is not in itself an absurd supposition, though we have little evidence which goes to support it. But this hypothesis of a connate molecular "meta-organism" is at once grotesque and entirely insufficient.[9]

Later in the note Myers somewhat tones down his attack, though he still makes it clear that he does not support the notion that ghosts have a material existence:

At the cost of some cumbrousness of language, I have been careful to express my hypothesis in exclusively psychical—as opposed to physical—terms. I desire that the reader should clearly distinguish it from any view which implies a material or objective presence, of however tenuous a kind. I shall not, indeed, commit myself to the assertion that any such presence is impossible; or that there may not be some intermediate view between what seems to me the gross conception of a molecular *meta-organism*, already alluded to, and the purely psychical agency which is all that I postulate here. The line between the "material" and the "immaterial," as these words are commonly used, means little more than the line between the phenomena which our senses or our instruments can detect or register, and the phenomena which they can *not*.[10]

I go into so much detail for two reasons. First, it is important that we understand what Myers meant by "partially-materialized ghost": a ghost with sufficient physical existence that it is capable of "producing measurable effects on the material world." Myers views Peter Quint and Miss Jessel as being not merely telepathic,

9. Ibid., 2:278–79.
10. Ibid., 2:290.

that is, not entirely dependent for their existence on the mental processes of the governess. Their existence is independent of the governess's ability to see or telepathically receive them. Myers appears to think that only by means of their partial materialization could the ghosts, acting independently of the governess, constitute any kind of palpable threat to the living Miles and Flora.

Second, we must understand that though Myers unquestionably thinks of Peter Quint and Miss Jessel as ghosts rather than as subjective phenomena arising solely out of the governess's own psychic energy, he does not therefore conclude that *The Turn of the Screw* is factually accurate in all particulars in its portrayal of those ghosts. For Myers, James's ghost story was clearly just that: a ghost story, a piece of fiction about made-up ghosts that were more material than the telepathic ghosts of the factual narratives. The ghosts considered most convincingly factual by members of the Society for Psychical Research did not go around materially threatening little children—or anyone else for that matter.

We are left with something of a paradox. On the one hand, Henry James's two ghosts are sufficiently realistic to be clearly and unmistakably ghosts in the view of one of the most experienced investigators in the Society for Psychical Research. On the other hand, those same ghosts, because they are material enough to be independent threats to the living, are sufficiently unrealistic to be unmistakably fictional in that same investigator's view.

We can resolve the paradox, I believe, by trying to look at it from Henry James's point of view. It seems clear that James wanted his two ghosts to behave, for the most part, like the ghosts in the many, many reports published by the more conservative and cautious central management of the Society for Psychical Research. In addition, he wanted to tell an effective story, and to do that he needed ghosts who were more palpably and purposefully evil than the ghosts in the fully investigated and approved narratives of psychical research. In the end Henry James acceded to the needs of fiction by giving his ghosts a power for malevolence not entirely consistent with the tradition of the best-attested psychical cases. In breaking with that tradition, however, he did not separate himself entirely from psychical research. Rather, he aligned himself with a more liberal branch of psychical research led by William T. Stead.

4
PURPOSEFUL GHOSTS
AND EVIL SPIRITS

The ghosts investigated and authenticated by what I have called the central management of the Society for Psychical Research tended to be a boring lot. They glided in, looked around, and promptly disappeared. They had no clear purpose for making themselves manifest to living persons. Most often, indeed, they seemed unaware that they might be audible or visible to human beings. Narratives about these ghosts were, as Frederic Myers and Edmund Gurney were to write in the very first volume (1882) of the *Proceedings of the Society for Psychical Research*, "far more likely to provoke sleep in the course of perusal than to banish it afterwards."[1] One of the arguments sometimes advanced in favor of the authenticity of a particular narrative is that none of the percipients in the narrative could have any imaginable motive for *inventing* stories about having seen or heard such boringly purposeless ghosts. The author of one narrative, for example, opens his report by suggesting that the very ordinariness of his account is substantial proof that it must be true:

I wish to give an account of what I call "a well authenticated apparition." I wish to give it, not because it is any better attested than a hundred others, nor because it is in the least startling, for a quieter ghost never was; but because there is so little in it that is unique, and it is therefore an excellent type of the better sort of such accounts, and because the facts are such as cannot possibly be strained into an explanation that treats them as the effects of one or two excited imaginations, and also because their entire want of purpose or dramatic effect makes them more credible. ("Mr. Hill and the Ghost in Jamaica")

It seems that true ghosts were, almost by definition, purposeless. Indeed, Frederic Myers found it necessary to eliminate from his definition of "ghost" any notion of purpose. He put it this way in the 1889 *Proceedings of the Society for Psychical Research*:

1. *PSPR* 1 (1882): 117–18.

114

Just as we cease to say that the phantom *is* the decedent, so also must we cease to ascribe to the phantom the motives by which we imagine that the decedent might be swayed. We must therefore exclude from our definition of a ghost any words which assume its intention to communicate with the living. . . . Let us attempt, then, a truer definition. Instead of describing a "ghost" as a dead person permitted to communicate with the living, let us define it as *a manifestation of persistent personal energy,*—or as an indication that some kind of force is being exercised after death which is in some way connected with a person previously known on earth. In this definition we have eliminated, as will be seen, a great mass of popular assumptions. . . . For they [ghosts] are not like what any man would have imagined. What man's mind tends to fancy on such topics may be seen in the endless crop of fictitious ghost-stories;—which furnish, indeed, a curious proof of the persistence of preconceived notions. For they go on being framed according to canons of their own, and deal with a set of imaginary phenomena quite different from those which actually occur. The actual phenomena, I may add, could scarcely be made romantic. One true "ghost-story" is apt to be very like another;—and all to be fragmentary and apparently meaningless. Their meaning, that is to say, lies in their conformity, not to the mythopoeic instinct of mankind, which fabricates and enjoys the fictitious tales, but to some unknown law, not based on human sentiment or convenience at all.[2]

Five years later, Andrew Lang referred to that same lack of purpose in what he called—with a hint of nostalgia for the good *old* kind—the "modern ghost." I quote from his *Cock Lane and Common-Sense*:

A change, an observed change, has come over the ghost of the nineteenth century. Readers of the *Proceedings* [of the Society for Psychical Research] will see that the modern ghost is a purposeless creature. He appears nobody knows why; he has no message to deliver, no secret crime to reveal, no appointment to keep, no treasure to disclose, no commissions to be executed.[3]

What were fiction writers at the end of the nineteenth century to do with such ghosts? Had not the Society for Psychical Research effectively eliminated the ghost as a useful character in

2. *PSPR* 6 (1889): 15–16.
3. Andrew Lang, *Cock Lane and Common-Sense*, 95.

fiction? If the dead became such purposeless ghosts, were not ghosts henceforth dead for the purposes of fiction?

Well, not quite. Some fiction writers attempted to use "modern ghosts" in their fiction. We will be in a better position to understand why Henry James took the approach he did in *The Turn of the Screw* if we consider the approaches taken by two other writers who attempted to write more or less fictional adaptations of the "modern ghost" narrative. One of these was a woman named Mary L. Molesworth. (She usually wrote under the name "Mrs. Molesworth," eliminating her own given name and initial.) She wrote a great many books. Only two of them concern us here. In 1888 Macmillan published her *Four Ghost Stories*, and in 1896 Hutchinson published her *Uncanny Tales*. Although most of the stories in these two books are of no interest to us, three of them are worth describing briefly as examples of the kind of story that resulted when lesser fiction writers than Henry James set their hands to writing ghost fiction for a turn-of-the-century readership.

Molesworth's "Mrs. Farquhar's Old Lady" is about a ghost who frightens Lady Farquhar by appearing in her room and on the stairs. The ghost does nothing frightening and appears to no clear purpose. Mrs. Farquhar later learns that it is apparently the ghost of a Miss Fitzgerald, one of three maiden sisters who had died destitute some years earlier. Descendants of a once rich family, these three sisters had finally yielded to the demands of poverty and had sold the family estate, including the contents of the family house, and went away. Why the one Miss Fitzgerald returns in ghostly form is never discovered, though Mrs. Farquhar thinks that perhaps the ghost is seeking some possession she had left behind after the sale of the house: "Family papers of importance, perhaps; possibly some ancient love-letters, forgotten in the confusion of their leave-taking; a lock of hair, or a withered flower, perhaps, that she, my poor old lady, would fain have clasped in her hand when dying, or have had buried with her. Ah, yes; there must be many a pitiful old story that is never told." The story never is told, and we are left to agree with Mrs. Farquhar, if we are so inclined, that "genuine ghost stories are generally abrupt and inconsequent in the extreme, but on this very account all the more impressive."[4] Mrs. Farquhar's logic here seems to be that because there is so little to the story, it must be true-to-life and therefore impressive. This story, in which there is nothing to tell, runs to some forty pages.

Appropriately entitled is Molesworth's story "Unexplained," though this one takes 140 pages not to explain anything. It is a first-person narrative about a woman who travels to Germany with her two children, a daughter of twelve and a son of nine. Traveling through remote forest regions, they stop one day to visit a pottery shop, where the mother purchases a pretty teacup and saucer. Not long after, they spend a little time in a substandard peasant village in which the only available accommodation is with a surly peasant. The second day little Nora, the daughter, stays alone in the house while her mother and brother are away on an errand. Nora leaves her room for a moment at one point, then returns to get her shoe. In her room she sees a ghost. Here is the brief passage in which Nora describes the incident to her mother:

"The door was not closed, but I think I had half drawn it to as I came out. I pushed it open and went in, and then—I seemed to feel there was something that had not been there before, and I looked up; and just beside the stove—the door opens *against* the stove, you know, and so it had hidden it for a moment as it were—there, mamma, *stood a man!* I saw him as plainly as I see you. He was staring at the stove, afterwards I saw it must have been at your little blue paper parcel. He was a gentleman, mamma—quite young. I saw his coat, it was cut like George Norman's. I think he must have been an Englishman. His coat was dark, and bound with a little very narrow ribbon binding. I have seen coats like that. He had a dark blue necktie, his dress all looked neat and careful—like what all gentlemen are; I saw all that, mamma, before I clearly saw his face. He was tall and had fair hair—I saw that at once. But I was not frightened; just at first I did not even wonder how he *could* have got into the room— now I see he *couldn't* without my knowing. My first thought, it seems so silly," and Nora here smiled a little, "my first thought was, 'Oh, he will see I have no boot on,'"—which was very characteristic of the child, for Nora was a very "proper" little girl,—"and just as I thought that, *he* seemed to know I was there, for he slowly turned his head from the stove and looked at me, and then I saw his face. Oh, mamma!"

"Was there anything frightening about it?" I said.

4. Mrs. Molesworth, *Four Ghost Stories*, 41, 3.

"I don't know," the child went on. "It was not like any face I ever saw, and yet it does not *sound* strange. He had nice, rather wavy fair hair, and I think he must *have been* nice-looking. His eyes were blue, and he had a little fair moustache. But he was so *fearfully* pale, and a look over all that I can't describe. And his eyes when he looked at me *seemed not to see me*, and yet they turned on me. They looked dreadfully sad, and though they were so close to me, as if they were miles and miles away. Then his lips parted slightly, very slightly, as if he were going to speak. Mamma," Nora went on impressively, "they would have spoken if *I* had said the least word—I felt they would. But just then—and remember, mamma, it couldn't have been yet two seconds since I came in, I hadn't yet had *time* to get frightened—just then there came over me the most awful feeling. I *knew* it was not a real man, and I seemed to hear myself saying inside my mind, 'It is a ghost,' and while I seemed to be saying it—I had not moved my eyes—while I looked at him—"

"He disappeared?"

"No, mamma, he did not even disappear. He was just *no longer there*. I was staring at nothing!"[5]

This account is in some ways similar to the governess's account to Mrs. Grose of her seeing the ghost of Peter Quint. But the ghost in "Unexplained" comes to no purpose and in no way poses a danger to Nora or to anyone else in the story. The ghost never again appears, and the mother and children soon leave. Years later the mother learns that the ghost Nora had seen was probably that of an Englishman who had been struck and killed by lightning in the forest; he had, however, no connection with Nora or her family except that he too had purchased from the same pottery shop a teacup and saucer similar to the one Nora's mother had bought. What does this unexplained fiction add up to? Very little, it seems. As one of the characters in the story says: "But that is always the way with modern ghost stories—there is no sense or meaning in them. The ghosts appear to people who never knew them, who take no interest in them, as it were, and then they have nothing to say—there is no *dénouement*, it is all purposeless."[6]

In Molesworth's "The Shadow in the Moonlight," published just a year before Henry James wrote *The Turn of the Screw*, the ghost has only slightly more purpose. This story is interesting to

5. Ibid., 162–66.
6. Ibid., 201.

us in part because of a few superficial parallels with James's story: a character named Miles; a nineteen-year-old narrator, who moves with her parents and siblings to a lovely house with a worrisome ghost; a little brother who still takes lessons with a governess who lives in the house with them; an older brother who is usually away at school; a feeling of intense cold when the ghost is about. The ghost is that of a gambler who "resides" in an old tapestry the family has bought from a used-furniture dealer. They hang the tapestry in the gallery of their new home, only to discover that on moonlit nights a strange presence comes out of the tapestry and into the room. They eventually discover a deck of cards and a valuable ring hidden behind a secret panel in a certain room in the house where the tapestry had once hung. When the ring is sold and the money donated to a good cause, the tapestry is purged of its haunting spirit. Molesworth was aware of the many puzzling features in her story. She even has one of her characters list "three inconsistencies about the thing which will probably never be explained": why the ghost moved with the tapestry rather than staying with the jeweled ring, why the ghost appeared only in the moonlight, and why the ring had been concealed in the first place. In the last line of the eighty-page story the narrator notes: "We feel rather proud of having been the actual witnesses of a ghostly drama."[7]

An author with no story to tell, ghosts with no purpose to reveal, characters with no stake in the ghostly drama to which they are the puzzled witnesses—is it any wonder that no one reads Molesworth's ghost stories today? Her stories did, however, receive some positive publicity in their own time. This last one, for example, "The Shadow in the Moonlight," was praised in 1897 in William T. Stead's *Borderland* as a story "which makes your flesh creep after the approved orthodox fashion" and as "a very clever little story, almost good enough to be true."[8] To us, however, it seems distressingly unexciting.

I quote below the opening five paragraphs in another fiction-alized story about a "modern ghost." This one is especially inter-

---

7. Mrs. Molesworth, *Uncanny Tales*, 78, 81.
8. *Borderland* 4 (1897): 103, 105.

esting because it shows an attempt to make a more lively and interesting ghost narrative and because it is one with which Henry James was almost certainly familiar and from which he probably picked up certain suggestions for his own story. Readers will recognize it immediately as a retelling of the narrative first printed in Chapter 2: "Mrs. Vatas-Simpson and the Two Ghosts." This second version, written by Arthur Morrison, was published in 1891 in his *The Shadows Around Us: Authentic Tales of the Supernatural.* Morrison entitled the story "No. 15 St. Swithin's Lane":

The difference which thirty years will make in the appearance of a London street is well exemplified in St. Swithin's Lane. Brand new stone-fronted shops and offices stand where, a generation ago and less, were the old houses once inhabited by city merchants—houses which had stood since the Great Fire of 1666.

The stranger who walks down St. Swithin's Lane to-day from the Bank will find No. 15, if he looks for it, on the right hand side, some little way past New Court and Salter's Hall. It is a substantial stone and glazed-brick fronted new building, and is used as a bank—quite a different structure to the one which it replaced. The old No. 15—or Nos. 14 and 15 as the one building was called at the time of this story—was a very large, dark, old-fashioned place, built after the Great Fire, and having underneath many extensive cellars, as well as, it was rumoured, many secret passages which had remained unexplored for generations.

In the year 1854, before the practice of city men to live in the city had quite died out, the upper floors of this strange old house were occupied by a Mr. John Simpson and his family. Mr. Simpson was a general agent in a fairly extensive way of business, and his family was a large one. Their part of the house was separated from that below by a strong gate of ornamental iron on the stairs. This gave them practically a separate house, for the gate was kept shut, visitors having to ring before being admitted, just as would have happened at an ordinary front door.

On the top floor was a large dining-room facing the street, with three windows. At each end of this room there was a fireplace, and on the side opposite the windows was one door leading to the stairs and another leading into a bed-room. Immediately below the dining-room was the drawing-room, and on this floor also was the kitchen; below these again were Mr. John Simpson's offices, and all this part of the house, including other rooms, bed-rooms, etc.—which are not connected with the story—was cut off from all below by the gate previously alluded to. The rooms below the gate were used as offices, Mr. Marshall, a builder, and Mr. John Scott, a solicitor, being the occupants.

One evening, soon after taking up residence, Mrs. Simpson heard the prolonged cry of a baby proceeding from the kitchen.[9]

The rest of the story follows Mrs. Vatas-Simpson's diary very closely, and even contains quotations from that diary. Altogether it is pretty tiresome stuff.

If ever proof was needed that good ghosts make bad fiction, a story like this provides it. The two ghosts appear for no purpose to living persons who, though perhaps initially frightened, are in no way threatened by them. The characters do not grow, unless we take as a sign of growth, at the end of the story, Mr. Simpson's more tolerant view of the possibility that ghosts exist. What limited suspense the story has is not answered by any revelation about the history of the ghosts or their relationship with any past or present inhabitants of the house at St. Swithin's Lane. It is true that a reviewer in the 1895 *Borderland* speaks highly of Arthur Morrison's attempt to turn ghostly facts into ghostly fiction:

One can't help wondering why no one ever did before what Mr. Arthur Morrison has done for us now, namely, put into story form some of the marvellously dramatic tales which writers on the supernatural have collected as evidence, and which at present are regarded only as "cases." So long as the real gist of the story is not "doctored," they are very fair game for the story-teller. . . . Mr. Morrison seems to have done his work conscientiously enough. They have already reached a second edition, and deserve the popularity they have acquired.[10]

Again, however, few modern readers will concur with this judgment. Our hesitation comes partly in the designation of attested ghost cases as "marvellously dramatic" and partly in the stricture that fictional retellings must refrain from "doctoring" the cases to make them more dramatic.

Had Henry James read either Morrison's story or the *Borderland* review of the volume in which the story appeared, he must have been encouraged about writing his own ghost story. If *that* kind of

9. Arthur Morrison, *The Shadows Around Us: Authentic Tales of the Supernatural,* 94–103.
10. *Borderland* 2 (1895): 86.

story made for second editions, think what his own might do, provided James could free himself somewhat from the stipulations that cases must not be "doctored" and that storytellers must not depart from the "real gist" of the basic factual narratives. James knew he could do better than the likes of Morrison and Molesworth. To do so, however, he needed either to do extensive "doctoring" of a case or else to find a case that really was, in its original state, dramatic enough that he could simply retell it. He needed ghosts different from those we have been considering in the previous two chapters. He needed ghosts that appeared to the living not merely to frighten them for a moment or puzzle them for a week and then disappear forever. He needed ghosts that came to the living for a definite purpose, ghosts that came to the living with a desire to do evil.

To find models for such ghosts, was James to forget entirely the modern factual cases and return to the purely fictional ghost tales of an earlier age? Indeed not, for he discovered that there were some exceptions to the boringly purposeless ghosts found in such devastating abundance in the reports of the Society for Psychical Research. These exceptions were to be found especially in the publications of researchers who were less rigorously selective than were the editors of the society's *Proceedings* and of Gurney's *Phantasms of the Living.* They were to be found, particularly, in publications written or edited by William T. Stead.

Stead, for example, devotes a chapter of *Real Ghost Stories* to "Ghosts of the Dead with a Practical Object." In this chapter, however, nearly all the ghosts are "good" ones: dead persons who return to the living to clear their names of some false accusation, to pay a debt, to look after a widow or loved one, to bless a lovers' union, to console, to escort or "fetch" a loved one into death, and so on. Far more interesting, at least from a literary point of view, are those rare cases—perhaps one in one hundred—involving "bad" ghosts. It will be useful to take a look at some of these cases, if only to see some of the options for evil that Henry James might have had if he had decided to search out factual antecedents for the kinds of ghosts he wanted to put into his story.

In a discussion of evil ghosts, it is helpful to note a distinction between harmless ghosts of people who did evil while they were still alive and evil ghosts of people who did only good while alive. There are precious few published cases involving either kind of ghost, and the few that can be found tend to involve either one or the other. That is, people who have done bad things in life tend to be quite benign and purposeless as ghosts. Those few ghosts who appear to desire to do evil as ghosts are generally not clearly associated with evil deeds done during their lifetimes.

A few cases involve ghosts of people who had been less good than they might have been in life. In one case, for example, a woman named Mrs. Bolland, wife of Lieutenant-Colonel G. H. Bolland, guardedly reported that she had had to dismiss Ramsay, a former servant, who later died and appeared to her as a ghost:

This man was a discharged soldier whom I had found in a dying state in Inverness, and who had been taken into our service after leaving the infirmary. He turned out badly and I had to send him away before we went to Gibraltar. ("Mrs. Bolland and the Ghost of Ramsay")

Mrs. Bolland does not tell us why or how this Ramsay had "turned out badly," and James could have picked up no usable information from this case except that the dead servant, like Peter Quint, appeared as a ghost wearing gentleman's clothes that had formerly belonged to the master of the house.

In another case a woman who later appears as a ghost was known to have murdered a young relative:

Our friends are sometimes terrified by the apparition of the dreadful woman who committed a murder in that room. No, she is no ancestor of ours, but she became possessed of this property by the murder of the heir to it—a child who was the only obstacle to her inheriting the estates. This she managed by sending the child's nurse on a fictitious errand, and during her absence she strangled the heir, but so skilfully that no traces of foul play were discernible, and nothing would have been known of the crime if she had not confessed it on her deathbed. ("Mr. Frith and the Woman in His Room")

Several ghost cases suggest—though seldom in any detail or

with much explicitness—that a certain "badness" of a sexual nature had been associated with people who later appear as ghosts:

One night, on retiring to my bedroom about 11 o'clock, I thought I heard a peculiar moaning sound, and someone sobbing as if in great distress of mind. . . . There on the grass was a very beautiful young girl in a kneeling posture before a soldier, in a general's uniform, sobbing, and clasping her hands together, entreating for pardon. . . . The youngest daughter of this very old, proud family had had an illegitimate child; and her parents and relatives would not recognize her again, and she died broken-hearted. ("Mrs. M. and the Sobbing Girl")

Five or six years afterward, a person who had bought [the house] having taken up the floor of that upper room to repair it, there was found . . . the skeleton of a child. It was then remembered, that some years before, a gentleman of somewhat dissolute habits had resided there, and that he was supposed to have been on very intimate terms with a young woman servant, who lived with him. ("Mrs. L. and the Dead Child")

Mr. P., the former incumbent, whom the apparition represented, was a man of very ill report, supposed to have got children of his maid, and to have murdered them. ("Mr. Wilkins and the Ghost of Mr. P.")

The figure which you saw is supposed to represent the daughter of a former baron of Berry Pomeroy, who bore a child to her own father. In that chamber above us the fruit of their incestuous intercourse was strangled by its guilty mother; and whenever death is about to visit the inmates of the castle, she is seen wending her way to the scene of her crimes with the frenzied gestures you describe. ("Dr. Farquhar and the Castle Ghost")

The current tradition, explanatory of all this, was that a young woman and her infant child had been murdered in the house and buried in the walk by the Squire, who subsequently made away with himself, being haunted by his victim. This tradition certainly has truth for its foundation, and is generally accepted. ("Squire Theed and the Ghost of His Victim")

There is nothing particularly striking in any of these cases, perhaps, but one of them might have suggested to James the notion that, as Mrs. Grose cautiously puts it, there was "everything" between Peter Quint and Miss Jessel and that he "did what he liked" with her. Mrs. Grose goes on to hint that Miss Jessel had "paid for" her association with Quint by getting pregnant. She speaks darkly of Miss Jessel's "real reason" for leaving Bly: "She could n't have stayed. Fancy it here—for a governess!" (p. 33). The new governess, having learned more about the relationship between Peter Quint and Miss Jessel, later refers to Miss Jessel as "dishonored and tragic" (p. 59). The details of the dishonor and the tragedy are never made entirely explicit, though James gives us enough hints to fuel speculation. Did Miss Jessel murder her baby? Perhaps, for she appears dressed "in mourning" (p. 32), and there are those strange cries of a child that the new governess hears just at dawn after her first night at Bly. Did Miss Jessel then drown herself? Perhaps, for she appears twice near water, and suicides and victims of violent death were known to be more apt to reappear as ghosts than were people who died peacefully and of natural causes. If James is giving hints at such events in the lives of Peter Quint and Miss Jessel, it is quite possible that some of the germs of those hints can be traced to one or another of the cases cited above. It is more likely, however, that those germs derived from the more explicit case cited below, which appeared just a year before James wrote *The Turn of the Screw.*

The case I refer to involved Bessie Russell Davies, an old friend of William T. Stead. Davies (earlier referred to as Bessie Williams or Bessie Fitzgerald in publications about her mediumship experiences) had certain psychic powers. It was she who introduced Stead to the mysteries of spiritualism and aroused in him a curiosity about ghosts and spirit communication. In February of 1896 she was invited to spend a week at the home of her friend "Lady B." At Stead's suggestion, and after securing Lady B.'s permission, Davies wrote about her experiences for publication in *Borderland* that same year. Lady B. had given her permission only on condition that nothing would be published that gave clues to the identity of the persons or places involved. Davies prefaced her remarks by stating that she had experienced the events described because of certain "gifts of mediumship which place me in direct communication with what I know to be the living spirits of those who once lived, loved, suffered and passed out of this planet."[11]

---

11. *Borderland* 4 (1897): 207.

The full narrative does not concern us. What is of interest is the part where Davies, during a seance, receives a message from Doris D., a young noblewoman from the time of Queen Elizabeth. Doris D. recounts her unfortunate experiences with a diabolical young chaplain. This chaplain is described, like Peter Quint, as a "hound" (p. 33) and a "devil" (p. 88):

I lived here with my parents, who adored me. My father adored me. My father had a Chaplain, who resided in the house, young and handsome, and I was only a country girl. One night, here in this room, a child was born, and in my madness and agony, I strangled it. For three awful days and nights I lay in my bed with the cold, dead little form beside me. Oh, those awful days, will they never fade from my memory! On the 4th night, when all the house was sleeping, I crept out of my bed, with my dead baby in my arms, and down to the river, into its cold and rushing waters, I threw my fearsome burthen; then back to the house, it was four in the morning, as nearly as I could judge. Back to my bed, to lie and think, and rage against the false scheming devil, who had brought all this woe and sin upon me. But thought of revenge gave me no help or comfort. How I lived through those days which followed, those terrible days, but worse nights; when the sound of the river running past my windows, bore only the cry of my murdered baby. . . . When I had appealed to him, he had long before denied ever having been other than my spiritual adviser, and swore that if ever I permitted his name to be brought in question, he would produce evidence of my wickedness, with one of my father's lowest servants. This was my lover, the Chaplain; this, the hound, who had betrayed me. . . . I bore as long as possible my terrible position, until one day a hunting party of ladies and gentlemen rode through these, my father's woods. I would have joined them, but their cold repellent looks drove me from their midst, and I rode away alone. I crossed the border into Somersetshire, and then in the same river wherein I had thrown my dead child, I laid down my own wretched life. ("Mrs. Davies and the Seduction of Doris D.")

The elements of plot in this case might have particularly interested Henry James: the love, the betrayal, the murder, the suicide.

Such features are all too rare in the traditional ghost narrative. The next narrative suggests an illicit affair between a monk and a nun. It is of special interest to us not only because it appeared in the July 1897 *Borderland*, just two months before James set seriously to work on *The Turn of the Screw,* and not only because it tells of two ghosts who in life had had, like Peter Quint and Miss Jessel, an illicit and forbidden affair. It interests us also because of additional features of the narrative that remind us of similar features in James's story: the old house in the country; the reference to ghost stories told on Christmas Eve; the rooks, the body of water, and the old boat; the narrator's feeling the presence of ghosts before she sees them; the cold drafts of wind and the extinguished candle; the narrator's feeling almost "possessed" and strangely compelled to follow a ghost (recall James's governess's statement on p. 40 that she is not sure "what determined or what guided me" the night she follows Peter Quint out of the room and down the stairs); the narrator's "superhuman strength" in moving the wardrobe (recall Flora's strength in rowing the boat); and the narrator's finding herself outside the house in the cold night air (recall Miles's mysterious nocturnal excursion). I quote the narrative in full, omitting only the editorial subheadings inserted every few paragraphs in the *Borderland* version. The narrator, Miss X., who was later identified as Ada Goodrich Freer, was William T. Stead's editorial assistant on *Borderland.* She wrote many of the articles that went into the quarterly. She was also personally involved in several investigations of houses suspected of being haunted, among them Silverton Abbey, in 1896, and the Ballechin House, which was so much in the news after she and several other investigators occupied it in the first months of 1897. The narrative given below recounts her first personal experience with ghosts:

The first time I ever remember seeing a ghost was in a curious old-fashioned house in a remote part of East Riding in Yorkshire. I had gone to stay for three weeks with some cousins during the month of September.

It was, I suppose, a pretty place, but the surrounding country was too flat to please me, and I had heard so much about the house that I was bitterly disappointed to see a large, bleak, and very straight white house. There were no gables, no creepers, or anything to relieve the ugly whiteness. A rookery on the left-hand side as you went up the drive was the only really redeeming point. There was also on the left a small "beck," as they call it in these parts, in other words, a running stream with an old punt on it. At the right were a few trees, and beyond these stretched large kitchen gardens, hidden from view by high walls. In front of the house, and running also to the left, was a large rookery, beyond was a sunk fence and a green field, neither of these at all took from the bare look of the house.

Before going there I had heard that there was an old well not far from the house, and that the place was reputed to be haunted.

This rather pleased me than otherwise, as I never thought I should be the one to see the ghosts.

The inside of the house was charming; a lovely oak staircase went up from a big hall. All round the gallery at the top of the stairs were rooms. These were nearly all called after some colour, such as "the blue room," "red room," &c. But there were heaps of passages, in the middle of which were three or sometimes two little steps leading to other passages, which branched off to different parts of the house.

But there were two rooms which pleased me very much indeed. One was downstairs, and was called "the justice room"; it had curious figures all round the walls, and was a very uncanny looking room; the other was an old garret, which went by the name of the "crocodile garret." How it came by the name I do not know, but it was the joy and terror of my heart. It had great chests in it, which we were told were full of old dresses, lovely brocades, all hand embroidered, and jackets slashed and lined with satin, hats with long feathers, silk stockings, complete costumes of the old-fashioned day for men and women. It was also full of all the rubbish which was not wanted anywhere else. The window of the garret had been barricaded up since the time of the window tax, and the only light there was came from the door or was made artificially.

The door was usually kept locked, but whenever I could get the key I loved to go there, as I wanted very much to find out, if possible, why it felt so uncanny. I never told anyone why I loved it, or what I wanted to find out. Ghosts were rarely spoken of except on Christmas Eve, when with bated breath, and the lamps turned low, our hair was made to stand on end by some blood-curdling tale.

After I had been about three days in the house, it was arranged that there should be a fancy ball, and we were to use the old dresses. Great was the turning out, and immense fun it was trying to fit the old-fashioned clothes on to young-fashioned shoulders. The men's things seemed to be much too narrow for the back, and yet they were supposed to be such big men.

Everyone was fitted at last, and a grand time we had.

That evening I went as usual to my room, and went to sleep. After having been asleep some hours, I woke feeling something in my room. I was too frightened to cry out, and I lay still staring at the darkness, when a form gradually appeared out of the darkness, and a person with a huge head appeared at the foot of my bed. Presently the form began to move, and then my courage began to return, but my body remained in a sort of frozen condition, though my mind was clear, and I was able to follow every movement accurately. It moved rather slowly towards my wardrobe, and finally disappeared behind it. As soon as the form had gone, I got up, lighted my candle, and determined to follow it.

I had to pull out the wardrobe, and certainly must have had superhuman strength as it has been perfectly impossible for me to move it again. I squeezed myself behind, and in the panel of the wall was a little door. I went in with my candle, and as soon as I had got inside the door saw, to my horror, the form with the huge head coming towards me. There was a puff, and I was in the darkness. Just as the puff came, I saw a very strange thing, that the body had no end to it, below the waist was mist.

But my candle was out, and I was in the strange little place with that horrible head not far from me, and even now I hardly know how I managed to get back through the little door into my room. Of course I tried to push back the wardrobe, but it refused to go, and after many unsuccessful attempts, I was forced to leave it, and get into bed. I had been there some little while trying to sleep, when I heard a shoving noise, I struck a match quickly, and saw, to my astonishment, that the wardrobe was in its place, but I saw nothing more.

In the morning it seemed to me as if I must have dreamt it, except that my muscles ached with the vain attempts I had made to put the wardrobe back in its place. I decided not to say anything about it to my cousins, as they would be sure to say that it was the excitement of the dance, and I had a great horror of ridicule in any way.

Nothing occurred for about a week, and I was beginning to think it really was a dream, when one afternoon as I was going upstairs in broad daylight, I saw the same thing. A huge head and the same peculiar finishing off of mist. This time I followed it, determined to find out, if possible, what it was, and where it was going to. It led me down the gallery along a passage in which were two or three little steps, up a flight of stairs into the "crocodile garret." The door was shut when we arrived, but it opened apparently easily, and we both passed through. Then the door shut, and I was horrified, so much so that I hardly dare breathe. There was I alone in the place with this creature; for as I explained before, the only scrap of light there was came through the door, so that if I had wanted to move, it would have been almost impossible for me to do so, as the garret was so full of old furniture and everything else that was old or disabled; but as I stood there a light appeared. I could not at first make out where it came from, as I did not know then that everybody, whether alive or not, gives out his own peculiar light.

It grew clear enough for me to see that the apparition was opening one of the old chests and was robing himself in the dress of a monk. Very slowly, but very surely one garment was put on over the other, and the monk's cowl completed it. The light seemed to die out, and I could feel the apparition was quite close to me. He opened the door, from which I shrank back in horror, but some unknown force compelled me to follow. Down the little passage and stairs we went until we reached a small flight of stairs with a door at the top. This appeared to me to take a long time to open. A cold draught of air seemed to fill the whole passage while we waited; it was so strong that once it blew back the monk's cloak, which was a very wide one, and I was afraid it was going to touch me, and I felt as if I was being frozen up. The door opened finally and he turned and looked at me with eyes which shone and dilated as though with inward fire.

Though horrified, I was again compelled to follow; and as soon as I had reached the top stair the door shut, leaving me once more all alone with the terrible phantom.

At first it seemed to me absolutely dark, but soon my eyes became accustomed to the dimness. The darker it was the better I could see the strange luminous light which he threw from him. At last a ray of real light appeared, and we went through another door, which led us into the garden near the old well. I had inspected the well by daylight, and had found out that there were two sets of steps to it: one led to the water, another to a long passage, into which I did not go. Down these steps we went. They were green and slimy, and I found it extremely difficult to keep my footing. I would have given worlds to have turned back, but whenever I tried to do so he turned and looked at me, and it seemed to me as if I was mesmerised and could not help myself. We stopped once for a few moments, till he pulled out from under his cloak a lantern, which I had not seen before. On he went again, faster than ever; and I saw another curious thing. The light he gave out was changing colour. Was it the effect of the lantern, or what? I looked and looked, when, to my utter horror, I saw another figure approaching.

Such a lovely woman, with short hair curling all over her head, and a long white drapery on. Her skin was very fair, but her eyes were dark. She was walking along with her head down, but a slight noise from the monk made her look up, and she blushed such a lovely colour, while her eyes shone like stars. Apparently she did not see me. The monk rushed forward, caught the woman in his arms, and kissed her. Then they walked up and down the passage, while I paced behind like a sentinel. I could not hear what words they said, as they spoke very, very low. They must have gone up and down for a long time before they decided to part, and then each went their own way. I was standing irresolute, not knowing which to follow, when the monk looked at me again, and pointed to the woman, and I at once began to move after her. To do this I had to pass him, and a shiver ran over me as I did so, and a cold wind blew over me as I passed. But again a look propelled me forward. The passage, as I said before, was quite dark, except for the light she gave out. This did not appear to be visible to herself, for, while it helped me, she stumbled and fell, and groped, as if in the dark, for the side of the passage. Sometimes I heard a great sob come from her, as if she was heart-broken; still she went on, and in time we arrived at the end of the passage.

Then I understood how it was the door opened, for I saw her look at this one fixedly, and as she looked her eyes grew larger and more luminous, until the door opened very slowly. Still she kept on looking at it, until we were able to go through. As soon as she took her eyes off, the door closed.

We were in the open air at last, and I drew it in, thankful to breathe it again. But I had not seen the end yet. She went on, crossed a courtyard, up some more small steps, and into a very bare-looking room. I saw she was a nun, and that I was in a huge nunnery. She laid down on her bed, and cried her heart out. Presently she stopped, and I went out, but as I went I could still hear her crying and sobbing. So this was their story: the monk and the nun were meeting, and I had been a witness to the fact.

I was left alone to find myself some five miles from home. I hunted about for the passage, but could not find it anywhere, so I had to trudge as best I could, in dread and terror, lest I should meet anyone I knew so far from home, and so weary that I did not know how to walk back; and not being very sure of the way made me feel more tired than ever. However, I gained my own room at last, and was glad enough to do so, but found it was impossible to rest.

The following day I tried hard to make people talk on the subject, but in those days they were very reticent on such subjects; so I got no definite news at all.

For about a week I saw nothing more, when one evening, going upstairs, I saw the same apparition at the top. He looked at me with the same strange luminous eyes, but though I had determined not to follow him any more, I found it impossible to keep those resolutions, when he looked at me, and when I got to bed my heart beat so fast that I knew something was going to happen. True enough it did, and I went once more through the scene I have just described, only there were more actors in it, for I saw to my horror that there were two other on-lookers. They had been found out, and I concluded that the end was near.

After the interview, which lasted an unconscionable time, an old nun showed herself, and also another old monk, and they were taken back in custody. This time I had to follow the monk. He was led to the justice room, where all the monks were assembled, and they sat in judgment upon him. Though I did not hear their words, I knew by their actions that he would not be spared. He was evidently found guilty, and was marched off to a place that looked almost like a dungeon, where he was put on the rack. It was awful, and though several years have passed by, I shudder all over with horror when I recall it. But enough. His legs were torn from their sockets, and he died.

How I got back to my room I do not know, but for several days I was unable to leave it; but one evening I was passing the old well, when I saw the nun. Her draperies were the same, but she carried her head under her arm; so I concluded that was her end.

I have never been to the house since, and I do not think I should wish to go there. The old house has passed into alien hands, but still exists, and only last year I was informed that the present inhabitants had seen the figure of a man at the head of the stairs in broad daylight, and that below the waist was mist.

Also it is a fact that a white lady walks by the old well, and is a well-known apparition to the family. If either the owners of the house or the present inhabitants see this story, they will recognise the ghosts, and will also hear the true story which connects both of them. ("Miss X. and the East Riding Ghosts")

The spirits referred to in these last several cases were "bad" only in their living states, not in their ghostly ones. Doris D. returns not to harm anyone but rather to seek amendment for her sins by offering to help and comfort Lady B. The disgraced monk and nun do seem to beckon or to entice Miss X. into potentially dangerous places, but to no particular evil purpose or unfortunate consequence. Because Peter Quint and Miss Jessel in *The Turn of the Screw* are bad both in their earthly and in their spiritual states, to find meaningful antecedents for them we must seek out those infrequent psychical cases where ghosts also do, or try to do, evil to the living.

Stead gives an account, for example, of a maritime ghost who seeks revenge against a fisherman with whom he had quarreled in life. The fisherman one day found that his boat was stopped in the water by a mysterious force:

In vain he strained at the oars; it would not move a foot. He looked over the prow, thinking he might have got entangled in seaweed, but the water was clear. He thought he might have struck on a hidden shoal, and rocked the boat. She rocked freely, showing there was water under her keel. Grey then looked over the stern, and to his horror he saw a man, whom he knew had been dead for six months, holding on to the stern post. This man was one with whom he had had some little quarrel, and Grey besought him to free the boat, saying that he had hoped that death would have cancelled all enmity between them. Without replying, the man still held on, and at last, in despair, Grey took his axe and hacked off the stern post, when the boat at once shot forward. The man, however, cried out that he and Grey should meet again in six weeks. Grey, in great fear, hastened home and told his family and friends of the occurrence. In six weeks, at the exact time the dead man had named, Grey was found in the morning dead in bed. ("Mr. Grey and the Swimming Ghost")

In the next case, both the White Lady's attempt to entice the boy to "go with" her and the boy's feverish sweating recall certain elements in the final scene of James's story. I cite it, however, primarily to show one kind of purpose a supposedly realistic ghost might have: to seek to recover a chest of gold. Part of the narrative relates to Thomas de Blenkinsopp and his wealthy foreign wife, but I quote below only that portion of the narrative dealing with the White Lady's appearance to the frightened son of a laborer at Blenkinsopp many years later:

One night, after retiring to rest, the parents were alarmed by loud, reiterated screams, issuing from the adjoining apartment. Rushing in, they found one of their children, a boy, sitting up in bed, trembling, bathed in perspiration, and evidently in extreme terror. "The White Lady! the White Lady!" screamed the lad, holding his hands before his eyes as if to shut out some frightful object. "What lady?" cried the astonished parents, looking around the room, which, to all appearance, was entirely untenanted; "there is no lady here." "She is gone," replied the boy, "and she looked so angry at me because I would not go with her. She was a fine lady—and she sat down on my bedside, and wrung her hands and cried sore; then she kissed me and asked me to go with her, and she would make me a rich man, as she had buried a large box of gold, many hundred years since, down in the vault, and she would give it me, as she could not rest as long as it was there. When I told her I durst not go, she said she would carry me, and was lifting me up when I cried out and frightened her away." ("Mr. Blank and the White Lady")

This ghost may, of course, have had an entirely noble motive in beckoning the boy, though reason for wanting to make him rich is uncertain. The exact motives of the ghostly lady in the next narrative are equally uncertain, though this narrative is particularly interesting in connection with *The Turn of the Screw* because of the narrator's feeling that she is, like the governess in Henry James's story, struggling with an evil foe for the life of a child. The narrator was an itinerant nurse. I quote her account in full:

I never feel nervous about my nursing capacity, or the recovery of my patients, except I am nursing in the place where I am writing this.

The house is old, and like most old houses has its haunted room, in addition to a subterranean passage, which was blocked up 50 years ago, and from which, it is reported, strange sounds have come, like the blows from a mallet, and the sound of somebody digging. I have never heard anything of the sort, but this much I know for a fact, that often when taking my notes or watching quietly by my patient, with a good fire, and a light burning, I have suddenly felt as if a cool wind was blowing about me so that I could not help shivering, and as if fingers were lightly touching my shoulders, and more than once feeling positive that somebody passed quickly through the room. Now I have never experienced these strange sensations when nursing in any other house, but I always feel when called here to nurse that I am about to do battle for the life of my patient, with a foe whose exact power I do not understand, and have always striven to defeat an influence which I felt was evil, by soliciting the protection of One Who is Almighty.

About four years ago I came here to nurse a little girl, five years of age, suffering with whooping cough and inflammation of the lungs.

My patient was isolated as much as possible, as there were other children in the house. The room in which I was to nurse seemed in all respects suitable for nursing—large, lofty, properly heated and ventilated. There was only one arrangement I did not like, and that I did not notice until I saw my little patient more than once look anxiously towards it, being a large window or partition, partly of glass, which had been recently added to make the room lighter. The door, also partly of glass, was at the side of the partition and opened directly on to the stairs. One day, shortly after my arrival, I was informed that the baby, only a few months old, was dangerously ill. The doctor did not think it would recover. Consequently the person who had charge of my patient while I was off duty could not be spared, so when night came I was rather tired. After giving my patient her medicine, making her comfortable and attending to the fire, I rested for a short time on a spare bed which was in the room. When I arose I looked at my watch; it was just 10 minutes to 1.

At that moment the child, who had been sleeping quietly, sat up, looked wildly at the partition, gave one piercing scream, then hid her face in the bed clothes. I dared not look at the partition, but turning my head went quickly to the child saying, "Did anything hurt or frighten you?" She would neither answer nor look up. I then heard a sound on the stairs, as if somebody was going down without boots on, thud, thud; so I called out "Who's there? Do speak, you have frightened us. Is it you, Mrs. ——?" meaning the person who waited on us. Not receiving an answer I waited awhile, then softly opened the door and looked out. All was quiet; the gas was burning on the lower landing. By its light I saw a woman standing at the foot of the stairs. Her face was turned up towards me. It was perfectly colourless, the eyes and mouth were closed; her hair was of a drabbish colour and her neck appeared to be slightly twisted. I drew back instantly, for the face I had seen shocked me; it resembled the face of a corpse. For a moment I thought, is it possible that anybody would attempt to frighten us? I looked again—the woman had disappeared.

There was a bell communicating with the housekeeper's room. I rang it violently, waited a few minutes, then heard the well-known footstep of Mrs. —— on the stairs. As she came into the room, she said, "Is anything the matter, nurse?" Before I could answer, she said, "The dear baby's gone. She died just 10 minutes to 1." "Well," I remarked, "that is strange." Then I told her what had occurred, and concluded by asking her if she had heard or seen either of the servants about the house. "Oh, it's not the girls," she said. "They are all in bed, except the nurse that has been with the baby. It is not the first time, I can tell you, that strange things have been seen and heard; to tell you the truth, nurse, I wouldn't sit in this room alone, no, not for a pension. One nurse that was here declared that her patient's medicine and spoon were thrown across the room, and I myself once went through the nursery and saw a woman in a dark dress looking into one of the drawers. I went into the next room and said to the nurse, 'Who's that person at the drawers?' She answered, 'You must be mistaken, there isn't anybody in the nursery.' I went back to see and the woman had disappeared. Yes, it's strange, but it's true, before trouble, sickness or death, that woman is always seen, but there," she said, "it does not do to talk about such things. You know what people are, and there wouldn't be a servant got that would stay in the house if they knew all." Then looking at my patient she said, "I think she seems worse than when I last saw her." "Well," I said, "she has been dreadfully frightened," and I thought, but did not say, if she dies, it will be as much from fright as any other cause. A few days after, I was called away to a very important case. My little patient lived only two or three days after my departure. More than once since then I have asked myself this question, "Was she frightened to death?" ("Mrs. H.'s Nurse and the Lady at the Partition")

The notion of a struggle between the living and the dead is almost unheard of in ghost narratives, though scattered examples can be found. In the next case, for instance, Mr. Addison nearly comes to grips—or thinks he does—with a dark specter in his bedroom. I quote only that portion of his narrative in which he describes his attempt to overpower the elusive ghost:

Whatever it was, it was advancing straight towards me, and in another moment retreat to the door would be cut off. It was not a comfortable idea to cope with the unknown in the dark, and in an instant I had seized the bed-clothes, and grasping a corner of them in each hand and holding them up before me, I charged straight at the figure. (I suppose I thought that by smothering the head of my supposed assailant I could best repel the coming attack.) The next moment I had landed on my knees on a sofa by the window with my arms on the window-sill, and with the consciousness that 'it' was now behind me, I have passed through it. With a bound I faced round, and was immediately immersed in a darkness impalpable to the touch, but so dense that it seemed to be weighing me down and squeezing me from all sides. I could not stir; the bed-clothes which I had seized as described hung over my left arm, the other was free, but seemed pressed down by a benumbing weight. I essayed to cry for help, but realised for the first time in my life what it means for the tongue to cleave to the roof of the mouth; my tongue seemed to have become dry and to have swelled to a thickness of some inches; it stuck to the roof of my mouth, and I could not ejaculate a syllable. At last, after an appalling struggle, I succeeded in uttering, and I knew that disjointed words, half prayer, half execrations of fear, left my lips, then my mind seemed to make one frantic effort, there seemed to come a wrench like an electric shock, and my limbs were free; it was as if I tore myself out of something. In a few seconds I had reached and opened the door and was in the passage listening to the hammerings of my heart-beats. ("Mr. Addison and the Dark Specter")

Another reported struggle involves the actress Mary Anderson, who reported having been frightened by an unknown ghostly visitant while she stayed overnight in the manor house of writer Bulwer Lytton. The case, quoted in full below, suggests several parallels with James's story: the feeling of cold, the candle blown out by a ghostly intruder, and the housekeeper who evidently knows more than she wants to reveal about strange doings in an elegant country mansion. Perhaps particular attention should be called to the invisibility of the attackers, reminding us that Miles and Flora, though they apparently never see the ghosts of Peter Quint and Miss Jessel, may nevertheless be endangered by them:

One of the best authenticated of modern ghost stories that I ever heard was told me lately by an English lady, who had it from the lips of the heroine of the adventure, the fair and famous American actress, Mary Anderson. At one time during a former visit to England Miss Anderson was invited to pay a visit to Lord and Lady Lytton (the former best known as Owen Meredith), who were then at the ancestral seat of the Bulwers, the well-known manor of Knebworth. The fair actress was a great favourite with the host and hostess, and had more than once before been their guest at their historical country home, a certain apartment there, called the White and Gold Room, having been placed at her disposal. On her arrival on this last occasion another apartment was allotted to her, her usual quarters having been taken by an earlier comer. Her new room was equally spacious and handsome, though somewhat gloomy on account of the massive antique furniture, while a large picture of Queen Elizabeth, evidently a contemporary likeness, hung upon the wall, and its faded hues and imperious aspect lent an impression of weird mystery to the surroundings. But these ideas only occurred to Miss Anderson after the incident I am about to relate. She found her room on first entering it very pleasant, and every arrangement had been made for her comfort, her maid having been installed in a small room just beside her own and communicating with it by a door.

Miss Anderson arrived in the afternoon. Dinner was served at eight o'clock, and the evening passed off in a very agreeable manner. No ghost stories were told, the conversation taking an animated and merry tone, and the party did not separate until nearly one o'clock, "so you see," remarked Miss Anderson, parenthetically, when she first narrated the history, "it is not at all likely that I could have been suffering from indigestion." She retired to rest, the door between her bedroom and that of her maid being wide open, and that leading to the corridor having been securely bolted. No sooner had Miss Anderson put out the light and laid her head on the pillow than she became conscious of a singular and unpleasant change in the atmosphere of the room, which became at once intensely cold and damp and overwhelmingly oppressive, so as to be scarcely respirable. "I could compare it," she afterwards said, "to nothing except a blanket saturated with ice water, and pressing upon my mouth and nostrils so as almost to stop my breath." She tried to cry out, but strength and power of speech seemed to have alike forsaken her.

Then she became aware of something clutching at the bedclothes: a strong grasp fastened at intervals on the coverlets and blankets she had drawn over her. In the extremity of her alarm she contrived, by putting forth all her strength, to raise herself in a sitting posture, supported by her hands, and she was instantly dashed back against the headboard of her bed by a fierce grasp fastened upon her neck and shoulders. During this mute and terrible struggle, Miss Anderson could see a light in her maid's room flashing up and going out, this process being repeated several times. She tried in vain to reach her own match-box, which was placed beside her bed; but, failing in that attempt, she finally broke loose from the hold of her invisible persecutor and sprang from the bed, uttering a piercing shriek. Her maid rushed into the room, exclaiming in terror, "Oh, Miss Mary, did you see it?" "See what?" asked Miss Anderson, in renewed alarm. "Something—I cannot tell what—that caught me by the throat and tried to choke me as soon as I got into bed." On comparing their experiences, the mistress and the maid found that they had suffered in precisely the same manner, but the latter had contrived to get hold of the match-box. "But every time that I struck a match, Miss Mary," added the frightened girl, "something would blow it out." The two terrified girls lighted their lamps and sat down together on Miss Anderson's bed, wrapped in blankets, to await the dawn of day, having first investigated the fastenings of the outer doors of their rooms, and having found them secure and in good order.

As soon as it was light they dressed themselves and went downstairs, exciting a great deal of attention and comment on the part of the early risers among the servants by their extreme paleness and evident agitation. Finally the housekeeper came to ask Miss Anderson if anything was the matter, and the first exclamation of that functionary on hearing her story was: "What!—again?" This remark she tried to explain away, assuring Miss Anderson that she must have been suffering from nightmare, though she failed to account for the fact that this dreadful form of nightmare had attacked both the mistress and the maid at the same moment. ("Miss Anderson and the Invisible Attackers")

The next narrative appeared in the July 1897 issue of Stead's *Borderland*, just after the narrative of "Miss X. and the East Riding Ghosts." Its narrator is the same Bessie Davies who related the story of the seduction of Doris D. Worth special notice are elements that might have supplied Henry James with ideas for his own story: the charming but previously occupied bedroom; the strange voices and footsteps; the feeling of a ghostly presence; the mention of drawbacks associated with the ability to perceive ghosts; the need for secrecy about such perceptions; the novel read late at night; the presence of two young children, a boy and a younger sister, one of whom has an encounter with a ghostly lady; the opening of a bedroom door after noises are heard in the hall, only to reveal an empty hallway; the attempt to speak to a ghost, after which it disappears. Of particular interest for our present purposes are the final two paragraphs, where Davies tells of her frightening experience with "evil spirits" and her struggle, almost for her life, to escape from them. I call special attention to the fact that the spirits do not attack or become violent until Davies speaks and offers to "help," recalling the violent reaction in the room when James's governess offers to "help" Miles (p. 65). I quote the narrative in full, excluding once again the editorial sub-headings within the narrative. The Mr. Stead mentioned at the end of the tenth paragraph is, of course, Davies's friend, the editor of *Borderland*. To the best of my knowledge, nothing more about Mary Jeffs was ever learned beyond what appears here in Mrs. Davies's narrative:

Auchin's Brae, as I propose to call it, is not the real name of the haunted house I propose giving an account of. Ayrshire, however, is the true name of the county wherein the house and estate are situated, and the exact locality is just thirty miles as the crow flies from the old "Brig o' Ayr," and is, I think, as pretty as any part Ayrshire can boast of.

The house is not an ancient one, and is in an excellent state of order and condition, but the site on which it stands was in the long ago occupied by a genuine feudal castle, and a few minutes' walk from the house through the park there is to be seen an enormous cairn or cromlech, almost hidden now by the large dark Scotch firs which have grown around and upon it.

I have visited my friend Mrs. Carre many times during the past few years, perhaps eight or nine visits have been made, each one for not less than a couple of weeks, and during my first stay the ghostly powers of the house had scarcely manifested themselves, and I had only been disturbed on the last two nights of my stay by noises and movements which might have been caused by mice. On the morning of October 18th, 1893, I started by an express from St. Pancras to Edinburgh, and arrived at my destination at 9 p.m. same day, and met with my usual hearty reception from my friends, Mrs. Carre and her sister, Miss Gilbert. My hostess showed me to my room, remarking as she led the way, "You are rather far away from Freda and me, but we thought you would be warmer in the west wing now that the weather has set in so very cold, and you have the Blue room, which faces south-west."

I found my room looking cosy and charming, an enormous fire burnt in the grate, and many candles lighted up every part. Curtains to the windows, and bed of chintz, bright with garlands of flowers. A pretty light blue carpet, and the same shade of colour was in the wall-paper. "One of the cosiest rooms I ever saw," was my remark. "I shall sleep here like a top."

This is an early household, and all retired before 11 p.m. In my room I drew up a comfortable armchair in front of the blazing fire, and sat for about half-an-hour before getting into bed. On the right side of the fireplace I noticed a doorway covered by curtains, and thinking it might lead into a dressing-room, or be another entrance into mine, drew them aside, and found that wherever it had originally led to, the doorway was quite closed by a handsome oak cupboard being built up in it. I closed the curtains and retired for the night. I like a fire in my bedroom, and had taken care to see that mine would last for some time. My armchair was before it just as when I had sat there, and my night-light made a soft glow where I had placed it near my bed. There was nothing weird or likely to suggest the idea of ghosts in connection with this bright little room. But no sooner was I in bed than I became possessed of the feeling that someone was near me, that other persons were in the room.

Suddenly my attention was attracted by a sound near the curtained doorway, which I have described as having been converted into a cupboard. I sat up in bed listening intently and plainly heard voices whispering, but was unable to distinguish words or one voice from another. Then came movements as of a person walking in large, ill-fitting slippers. Whoever they were, the persons causing the noises were on the other side of the doorway cupboard, in what I supposed to be another bedroom, and I came to the conclusion (as it was now nearly 2 a.m.) that someone must be taken ill, and wondered who it could be, as there had been no mention made of other visitors staying in the house, and only we three ladies had dined together.

Certainly there was a very large staff of servants, but they were in quite another part of the house, and none would be likely to be near the west wing apartments.

Once or twice it occurred to me to get up and offer my services, but knowing that if my friends desired my presence, we were on such intimate terms that either Mrs. Carre or Miss Gilbert would not hesitate to send a maid for me. I lay quietly until 4 a.m., not for one moment had I slept up to this hour. But now the sounds died away, and I fell asleep, not waking until the maid arrived with my breakfast (which I always take in my own room) at 8:30. The maid was a disagreeable sulky girl, whom I had never liked, and therefore I did not ask her who had been ill during the night, although feeling very curious on the subject.

Leaving my room later on, I found Mrs. Carre and her sister in the drawing-room, and in response to the question as to how I had slept, answered that after the sick person in the next room had quieted down, I had slept well. While saying this, I saw a look of surprise in the faces of my friends, and both exclaimed at once, "Sick person, why there is no one ill, *neither is there a room next to yours.*" "Oh, yes, the room to which the door near my fireplace led into formerly!" "But there is no room, that door is an old way cut through the wall on to the great landing; not requiring it we had it made into a cupboard or wardrobe, and the depth through the wall is five feet; ours, I think, was a house built to withstand a siege, surely you were dreaming and restless in the strange bed!" "Not at all! I slept quietly enough when I did go off, but it was 4 a.m. before this happened, and it was the noise of people whispering and shuffling about in loose slippers which hindered my going to sleep." I could see my hostess was becoming alarmed, and when she said, "Oh dear, I do hope you are not going to find we have ghosts!" I wished I had not spoken of the disturbances, and determined upon not mentioning in future anything which might occur, as doubtless there would be a repetition of the previous night's noises. Events proved that this resolve was a wise one, for I found Miss G. was even more excitable and nervous than her sister, and being physically very delicate, she could not, without suffering, bear any excitement or emotion. So the experiences which came to me I kept in my secret heart, with the exception of one or two incidents, which I wrote of to Mr. Stead, and these were simply by the way, and not for publication.

On the second night I found a goodly supply of books had been put into my room, and the hour still early, I stirred up my fire, popped my toes on the fender, and seated in my easy chair, settled down to my book. I had read for some time, being deeply interested in my story, when a sound, like a loud sigh close by my side, disturbed me. I looked up. No one near me! and then, although there was nothing to be seen, I heard the sound of a person breathing hard, and it came from the direction of the opposite side of the fireplace on my right. Here there was another chair on which I had thrown a heavy shawl I had worn over my shoulder when coming through the cold corridors from the drawing-room to my own apartments. I now laid my book softly on to my lap and listened intently. That the chair near me was occupied I felt quite sure, though I could discern no form, but a sound, as of a person breathing heavily and with difficulty was very distinct, and to say the least of it, there was something exceptionally uncanny going on. It would be useless to pretend that I did not feel just a tiny bit nervous, for I am no braver than other women, beyond the fact that from many and long experiences I had grown more or less familiar with what is called the supernatural. But this was distinctly uncanny, and as I sat and listened, without seeing, the feeling came over me, that here there was something out of the common and very uncomfortable. How I sneaked into bed I don't know, all I can tell is that when once the bed-clothes were over me I got under, and never moved until it was time to get up.

Not one word did I breathe to my two friends in regard to what I had heard; but as the day wore on and night was near, it was not without a feeling of creepiness, "to say the least of it," that I thought of bed-time. Time flies when least desired, and 10 o'clock p.m. came all too quickly. No sooner had I opened my book (let me now mention that my reading was a very frivolous novel), not a book likely to induce nervous attacks or hysterical imaginations or to lead one's thoughts towards the supernatural. As I have said, no sooner had I opened the book than the usual sound, half sigh and half moan, disturbed the stillness round me. But it was louder and stronger than ever before it had been, and I saw the grey outline of a big form, huddled together in the chair near to my writing table which was about three feet from me. It was only a glimpse I caught, and then all disappeared, and no further disturbance occurred that night; but what I had seen and heard had been quite sufficient for me, and I wished with all my heart that my friend could give me some other room, not quite so isolated and a little less haunted. I would cheerfully sacrifice all the stray gleams of sunshine my window reflected, for the blessing of a peaceful night's sleep. I do not object to ghosts by day, but in the still small hours of the night, I prefer their room to their company. It would have been a great relief if it had been possible for me to have talked over my experiences with Mrs. Carre and her sister; but the least allusion to the subject would I know terrify both, and in all probability make them ill, for both were nervous highly-strung women. I could not ask for another room without appearing fidgety or giving a good reason for my wish to leave the Blue room. So for a fortnight I bore the frequent disagreeable sounds and occasional glimpses of the ghostly forms who seemed never far away. Night after night they came, sometimes softly sighing, at others making a distinct sound of groaning, while once or twice I heard a sound like to that of people whispering. I found that in a strong light the manifestations were weaker, so my only chance of obtaining rest and sleep was by brilliantly illuminat-ing my room, and I have frequently slept under the "protecting" influence of the light from six candles and a pyramid night light. The possession of the "gift of discerning of spirits," is not without its drawbacks, and I have had many shocks during the thirty years I have been in possession of my strange faculty.

At the end of a fortnight I bade my friends farewell, and returned to London.

It was in 1894 that I once more became an occupant of the sunny room in Auchin's Brae, to which my friends thought I was so devoted. It was ten months since my former visit, and I had had time to recover from the frights of that time; and as the house was to have many other visitors besides myself, I hoped that some of them would be placed near to me in the west wing; here, however, I was disappointed, for all the rooms on the same floor as mine were unoccupied, only those above were to be used, and these by two little children and their nurses. I arrived on the 1st of August, and until the 8th not a sound or movement came to disturb me, and I had ceased to expect anything uncanny to occur. But, alas! before I had been many minutes in bed on this night the old sighs reached my ears, distinct, even loud whispers came from several parts of the room. I felt hands on my head and face stroking gently, and in what appeared to me a caressing manner. But this I could not lie still and endure, and trembling violently sat up in bed, exclaiming aloud as I did so: "Who are you, why do you disturb me?"

To my astonishment a voice answered distinctly: "I am Mary Jeffs." I saw a woman's form run swiftly across my room, the dress making a loud rustling sound as she passed. The woman was *running,* not merely walking quickly, and she disappeared in the recess I have previously described as being filled up by a cupboard, and covered by a curtain. In a few seconds I heard a crash in the room above me, and felt certain one of the little children had fallen out of bed, seriously hurting itself. I listened for some time, but nothing further happening I lay down, and while thinking of the wonderful appearance, the voice, and the crash overhead, fell off to sleep, and did not wake until called by the maid at eight in the morning.

My friend and hostess always comes to have a chat with me in my room before going down to her own breakfast, and I was not long before telling her that I had heard one of her little visitors fall heavily out of bed during the night; she was much concerned, for both the little ones are delicate children and easily made ill. Mrs. Carre hastened to see and question the head nurse, in whose room the children slept. The woman declared that nothing of the kind had happened. The boy slept in a cot at her side, and the girl, four years of age, had a small bed, out of which there was no reason she should fall.

Mrs. Carre returned to my room to tell me this, adding, "You were dreaming, my dear." I knew this had not been the case, but did not further discuss the matter, preferring to wait and make enquiries personally. Later in the day, meeting the nurses and children, I said, "Nurse, I hope Miss Margaret was not hurt by her fall out of bed last night." "Oh, no, ma'am, she did not fall, and I told Mrs. Carre so this morning." "Oh, but she did, I heard distinctly." The nurse again denied, when suddenly the little girl exclaimed, "Yes I did, nurse, I fell out of bed; you were asleep, and the *lady picked me up*." Mrs. Carre, who had stood by listening, here spoke, saying: "Margaret, what do you mean? who put you back into bed?" The child hesitated, and then answered, "I don't know, a lady. I was sleepy." "Were you hurt?" I asked. "No, not a bit. I was sleepy." This was all we could get the child to say; she is naturally a stupid child, but all the same I knew that it was "Mary Jeffs" who had gone to her aid.

On the night of August 11th I retired to my room at the usual hour whenever staying in this delightful house, viz., ten. By the time I was ready to get into bed it would be about eleven, or a few minutes past. Not feeling inclined to sleep, I placed two candles on a small table by my bedside, and opening an interesting book began to read. The room I always occupied was reached by a long narrow passage leading to the west wing of the house. This passage terminated with a glass panelled door, which stood at the head of a very steep staircase. At the time of my present visit no other person than myself occupied any rooms on this floor, and even if there had been thus, this staircase is never used, excepting when the two bedrooms—mine called the "Blue" and the other the "Yellow" room—were occupied by gentlemen, whose servants would require to go up and down to their own apartments.

Not a sound could be heard as I lay reading, and my astonishment was great when I heard the handle of my door turned as though a person intended entering. I was not at all surprised that no sound of footsteps had reached me, because the carpets were very thick and soft, preventing even the sounds being heard a person with a heavy tread would make. My only idea was immediately: "Oh, Mrs. Carre wants something," and calling out: "Wait a moment, the door is bolted!" I got out of bed and opened the door. There was no one there! The lamps were all out and the passage very dark. I called: "What is it; who wants me?" Not a sound of any kind disturbed the stillness, and fastening the door again returned to my bed, where I lay thinking over the strange occurrence. I did not want to read any longer, but could not go to sleep, so lay thinking until close upon 2 a.m., then putting out my candles turned on my left side and composed myself to sleep. But sleep refused to come, and I could not throw off the feeling that there was someone moving about my room.

I heard the sound of voices whispering, but could not what I call "locate" them. They were near me one instant, almost close to my face, but before I could move or speak, the sounds would be in quite a different direction, near the ceiling, the door, or the fireplace. Beyond the disturbing effect of the voices and movements, no attempt had ever been made to injure or hurt me, and I had grown comparatively fearless, and on this night sat up very boldly in my bed, and drawing back the curtains, looked round the room, fully expecting to see a number of ghosts lurking in my neighbourhood, but there were none, not even a very small one. I spoke, saying, "If there is an unhappy soul here who wants mortal help, will he or she speak to me now and tell me what troubles them, or how I can help them." The voices ceased, not a sound broke the stillness now; I waited, expecting every instant to see some form near me; none came, and after sitting up for between ten and fifteen minutes, lay down, satisfied that I had stopped the ghosts for this night, at all events.

I was wide awake, my night-light and fire both bright, when suddenly I saw hovering over me and near the ceiling, what I can only describe as a large shapeless *black mass* falling towards me. I felt myself seized by a *number* of arms, every part of my body seemed gripped in a vice by this evil spirit or spirits. I felt that "it" was trying to lift me up from the bed, and the feeling of horror which possessed me is beyond description. I was paralyzed with terror, when seemingly from afar off I heard a voice call my name twice; it seemed to rouse me and to restore my strength. I tried to move, I struggled, again the voice came, but in tones of agony, thus: "Oh, my Medie! struggle, save yourself, save yourself!" I did struggle. I fought, and at last freed my right arm, which I lifted up and struck out with. I felt it pass through some soft resisting substance, and heard a sound as though I had *slapped* flesh, and I was free. I saw the "mass" roll, as it were, off the bed and sink through the floor of the room. How I lived through that night I cannot tell, my terror was so great, I felt as if my life hung by the merest thread. I know that many people reading this will say at once, "Oh, this was nightmare." It was not nightmare, it was no dream. I had dined as usual at 8 p.m., and as mine is a very small appetite, had taken very little food and nothing later.

This manifestation was not my only experience, it was the climax of a regular systematic haunting by evil or earth-bound spirits, and only one of the many forms of annoyance caused by these unholy beings. ("Mrs. Davies and the Ghost of Mary Jeffs")

I do not insist that these cases involving purposeful ghosts and evil spirits provided James with the kernel of *The Turn of the Screw*. Indeed, James himself has provided us with quite a satisfactory account of how he first got the idea for his story. He wrote in his notebook on January 12, 1895, that two nights earlier, on January 10, he had been told a ghost story by Edward White Benson, the archbishop of Canterbury. I quote from *The Complete Notebooks of Henry James*:

The story of the young children (indefinite number and age) left to the care of servants in an old country-house, through the death, presumably, of parents. The servants, wicked and depraved, corrupt and deprave the children; the children are bad, full of evil, to a sinister degree. The servants *die* (the story vague about the way of it) and their apparitions, figures, return to haunt the house *and* children, to whom they seem to beckon, whom they invite and solicit, from across dangerous places, the deep ditch of a sunk fence, etc.—so that the children may destroy themselves, lose themselves, by responding, by getting into their power. So long as the children are kept from them, they are not lost; but they try and try and try, these evil presences, to get hold of them. [12]

The archbishop's account, James wrote, was "vague, undetailed, faint."[13] Nearly three years later, when he set about writing a story based on this account, James apparently felt the need to make his story more concrete, detailed, and distinct by reading the reports of serious psychical researchers. In their official reports he would have come across many, many ghosts that did not quite suit him. These ghosts provided him with the details of ghostly appearance and some of the details of ghostly behavior, but they tended to be too purposeless and good. If his fictional ghosts were to be the manifestations of servants who had been "wicked and depraved" in life and then "evil presences" in death, James required cases that would serve his needs more precisely. He would have found some promising cases reported in the works of William T. Stead, particularly the *Borderland* stories cited above by Bessie Davies and by Miss X.

If James did read these, it seems clear that he did not find in them all that he wanted to flesh out the skeleton of the ghostly tale he had heard from Archbishop Benson. These ghosts, evil though some of them appeared to be, were not evil *enough*. Or, more precisely, they were not *powerful* enough to be able to intervene

12. *The Complete Notebooks of Henry James,* ed. Leon Edel and Lyall H. Powers, 109.
13. Ibid.

with sufficient effect in the affairs of the living. From the standpoint of a writer of fiction, the remarkable feature of the ghosts discussed in this chapter is not that they are—or were, when alive—evil, but that they are so utterly powerless to achieve any significant evil purpose among the living. Apart from their ability to frighten, they seem quite as incapable as their more virtuous counterparts of *doing* anything very damaging.

Henry James needed for his story "evil presences" who were more capable of doing harm to the living, who could more effectively control the lives of the living, influence their actions, and even cause their deaths. What good was a sense of purpose in these evil presences if they did not have the power to carry out their purposes? To write the kind of story he wanted to write and to avoid the kind of wilting narrative that the Molesworths and the Morrisons were writing, Henry James needed to replace the merely potential evil of traditional ghosts with a more powerful evil. But even as he moved beyond the traditions associated with the ghosts of conservative psychical researchers and with the evil spirits reported by Stead and his more liberal friends, James refused to cut himself off entirely from scientific reports. As we shall see in the next chapter, James was more than a little familiar with what was known in his own time about spirit possession, a phenomenon in which the spirits of the dead actually took control of the bodies of the living. In thus taking control, of course, the spirits gained maximum power over the affairs and the actions of the living.

5
SPIRIT MEDIUMS
AND DEMON POSSESSION

I have been proposing nothing radically new in urging that Henry James's *The Turn of the Screw* be taken seriously as a ghost story. After all, careful readers have been reading *The Turn of the Screw* as a story about realistic ghosts with evil intent ever since it was first published. I have rather been attempting to build a foundation under this time-honored, but now much neglected, interpretation by disclosing to the modern eye certain attitudes and documents long since forgotten. In proposing, as I now do, that Miles and Flora are at times possessed by the spirits of Peter Quint and Miss Jessel, however, I am proposing something that most readers will think of as revisionist. Actually, even this idea is not entirely new. Other critics have mentioned the possibility in a sentence or two, but no one before me has developed it or attempted to prove it.[1]

The reading I propose springs from my inability to answer certain questions through either the deluded-governess reading or the evil-ghost reading. Advocates of the deluded-governess reading make some sense of the character of the governess but leave unexplained why in her lunacy she would have imagined, decades before the Society for Psychical Research was even thought of, ghosts that subsequent investigations would prove to be so very accurate. Advocates of the evil-ghost reading make good sense both of the governess and of the ghosts she sees but, like their opponents in the opposite camp, leave unexplained certain puzzling, even contradictory, patterns of attitude and behavior on the part of the children.

Among the questions left unanswered or unconvincingly answered by advocates of both the deluded-governess and the evil-ghost readings are these: (1) why does Flora go across the lake? (2)

1. Anthony Curtis, Introduction to *The Aspern Papers* and *The Turn of the Screw*, 25; Ernest Tuveson, "*The Turn of the Screw*: A Palimpsest," 795; Matthiessen and Murdock, in *The Notebooks of Henry James*, 179.

how does she maneuver a boat too large and heavy for her to manage? (3) why does she suddenly become ugly? (4) why does she so vehemently turn upon the governess? (5) why does she use such shockingly vile language? (6) why was Miles expelled from his school? (7) what kills him? and (8) is he "saved" at the end?

Advocates of the deluded-governess reading either ignore such questions or else answer them by reference to the irrationality or the cruelty of the governess: she is wrong about Flora, who never took the boat but rather walked around the lake; she grossly misjudges Miles, who was sent home from school merely because he was so young; the governess suffocates Miles; and so on. Advocates of the evil-ghost reading similarly ignore the questions or else answer them by reference to some naturalistic explanation: Miles was sent home because his schoolmasters were prudishly shocked by his obscene language; little girls can, after all, learn to row big boats if they are of a mind to; Miles dies of fright or of a heart attack; and so on. There are, of course, alternative answers from individual advocates of both readings, but these answers—and nonanswers—share a common uncertainty and evasiveness. We need a new reading—at least of the end of the story—if we are to answer such questions.

This new reading is that Miles and Flora are at times not Miles and Flora but are possessed by the controlling spirits of Peter Quint and Miss Jessel. I shall in the next chapter show how this reading gives answers to those eight questions, but first I must provide some history and cite some cases relating to the phenomena of trance and possession. I shall refer only to phenomena discussed in print in the fifty years before Henry James wrote *The Turn of the Screw*. Every book, article, and case I shall cite in this chapter, then, could have been known to Henry James.

The phenomena of trance and possession are simple enough: the spirit of a dead person takes dominating control of the body and will of a living person; that spirit, having temporarily displaced the spirit of the controlled person, expresses itself using that person's voice, hands, or other organs. The term *trance* usually refers to situations in which the living person is a voluntary medium. *Possession* or *demonic possession*, on the other hand, usually refers to situations in which the mediumship is involuntary. Although there were various ways to describe possession in the last half of the nineteenth century, it may be useful here to show what Charles Beecher had to say about it in 1853. His curious term *odylic* referred to a kind of psychic glue that joined the body and soul altogether. I quote from his *Review of the "Spiritual Manifestations"*:

As to cases of possession, let Josephus indicate the popular belief: "Demons are no other than the spirits of the wicked, that enter into men and kill them unless they obtain help against them." . . . Demonic possessions, as really as eclipses, have their law. And their law is, that spirits of the departed, restless and miserable, and longing to get back into life, will thrust themselves in whenever and wherever odylic conditions will let them. . . . Forlorn, lost, they seek connection to the living to escape, not to inflict, suffering. Hence, they seek impressible subjects, those, namely, in whom the odylic bond between soul and body is less firmly fastened, and capable of partial disadjustment. Having been once incarnate, they retain vestiges of odylic adaptation. They invade, they dispossess, in part, the rightful occupant, and prey upon his odylic energy.[2]

We cannot suppose that Henry James was familiar with Beecher's description, but there can be no doubt that he knew about trance and possession. It is certain, for example, that he knew about Mrs. Leonore Piper, the most famous and most unquestionably honest medium of his time. Mrs. Piper was a Bostonian who discovered almost by accident that she had certain powers as a medium. In 1885, within a year of this discovery, she was brought to the attention of William James by his wife's mother, who had visited her. William James, though at first highly skeptical, visited her himself and then, impressed with what he found, arranged sittings for a large number of others. He discovered that in her trances Mrs. Piper became the vehicle for a "control" named "Phinuit," as well as for the spirits of certain other controls who spoke through her mouth and revealed information demonstrably inaccessible to Mrs. Piper in her normal state. William James

2. Charles Beecher, *A Review of the "Spiritual Manifestations,"* 50–53.

became very much interested in Mrs. Piper and did a systematic study of her and of the strange phenomena associated with her and her trances. In 1886 he published a report of his findings in the *Proceedings of the Society for Psychical Research.*

William James's work with Mrs. Piper soon came to the attention of the British Society for Psychical Research. In 1887 Richard Hodgson, a British researcher who was sure that there must be trickery involved, came to Boston to become secretary of the American society. While there he carried out his own investigations of Mrs. Piper. His first sitting with Mrs. Piper was anonymous. That is, she was not told even the name of this stranger from England. Yet in her trance her control, Phinuit, was able to relate detailed facts about Hodgson's family, some of whom had died very young, and about his friends and relatives living in Australia. He had several more sittings with her and arranged sittings for others who were also strangers to her. He had her and her husband watched by detectives for several weeks during these sittings to make sure she did not seek, or have brought in, information about these strangers. For many of these new sitters she was able to reveal intimate details of their lives and family relationships. Before long Hodgson became convinced that there really was something to Mrs. Piper's powers and that she was not a fraud. There was growing—and sometimes humorous—evidence that her primary control, Phinuit, was at times dishonest or self-deceived or confused about his own personal history, but of the medium herself no dishonesty was ever uncovered.

Hodgson and William James then decided it would be useful to arrange for Mrs. Piper to visit England. There she could be examined in strange surroundings where she would have no access to any familiar human or literary sources of information. Their suggestion was welcomed across the Atlantic. In 1889, accordingly, Frederic Myers and two other members of the Society for Psychical Research became a committee to invite her, to arrange her activities, and to conduct a series of carefully monitored sittings in territory unfamiliar to her. One of the members of the committee was Oliver J. Lodge, a professor of physics at Liverpool University.

Mrs. Piper was soon on her way across the sea. She stayed in London at lodgings arranged by the Society for Psychical Research and with Myers and the Sidgwicks at Cambridge. Careful precautions were taken to prevent her from getting access to information about sitters. One of those sitters was Oliver Lodge himself. At his first sitting with Mrs. Piper, Lodge was amazed to hear through Mrs. Piper's mouth what seemed to be the voice of his Aunt Anne, who had died of cancer. Lodge eventually invited Mrs. Piper to stay with him in Liverpool for additional sittings. Before she arrived he hid the family Bible, which contained detailed information about his ancestors. Having recently hired new servants, he felt that they could be relied upon not to feed Mrs. Piper information about their new employer, who was as much a stranger to them as he was to her. I shall say no more here about what transpired in Liverpool except that Mrs. Piper was again able to reveal, to Hodgson and to many of the others she sat with, detailed information about their relatives and friends living and dead. Some of the information was unknown to the sitters themselves, but subsequent investigation proved it to be true. Lodge joined the ranks of the converted, and he too came to believe that Mrs. Piper had supernatural powers as an honest medium.

So impressive was the evidence about Mrs. Piper that the Society for Psychical Research decided to include an extensive report in their *Proceedings* about "certain phenomena of trance." Myers, Hodgson, and Lodge would of course contribute reports, along with stenographic records of selected sittings with Mrs. Piper. Myers decided that a key element in the report should be a contribution by William James, who had discovered Mrs. Piper and had brought her to the attention of psychical researchers. Accordingly, Myers wrote to William James and asked that he write a statement to be included in the *Proceedings* of the society. William James agreed to do what he could and sent Myers a long letter. Myers was so impressed with the letter that he wanted to have it read at the October 1890 meeting of the society. He took the liberty—without asking William's permission—of inviting William's brother Henry, who then lived in London, to read the letter on behalf of his brother. To William's subsequent amusement, Henry James agreed.

The exchange of letters on this subject is significant for several reasons, not the least of which is that it gives some indication of the extent of Henry James's interest in such matters. In responding to Myers's request that he read William's letter, Henry James confessed his lack of knowledge about psychical research and his "aversion" to mediums:

I have waited a day just to think a little whether my complete detachment from my brother's labour and pursuits, my *outsideness*, as it were, to the S. P. R., my total ignorance of Mrs. Piper and my general aversion to her species ought not (to myself, who have the full and inner measure of these limitations) to appear to disqualify me from even such a share in your proceedings as would be represented by, and restricted to, the lending of my (barely audible) voice to his paper. But even after so much reflection I *can't* make up my mind! Therefore I don't pretend to make it up—but give *sentiment* the benefit of the doubt. If it will do the paper the least good—or do you either—I will read it, as pluckily as possible, on the day you designate. Might you very kindly let me have a look at it before that?[3]

On October 9 Henry wrote to his brother in Boston that although he was "alien" to the subject matter of the paper (which he had not yet read), he had agreed to Myers's request:

Frdk Myers has written to ask *me* to read your letter on Mrs. Piper at a meeting of the S. P. R. at the Westminster Town Hall on the 31st of this month: and I have said I would, though so alien to the whole business, in order not to seem to withhold from *you* any advantage—though what "advantage" I shall confer remains to be seen. Therefore imagine me at 4 p.m. on that day, performing in your name.[4]

On October 20 William replied to his brother, expressing both his amusement and his gratitude:

I think your reading my Piper letter (of which this very morning proof came to me from Myers) is the most comical thing I ever heard of. It

3. James, *Letters*, ed. Edel, 3:302.
4. Gay Wilson Allen, *William James: A Biography*, 326.

shows how first-rate a business man Myers is: he wants to bring variety and *éclat* into the meeting. I will *think of you* on the 31st at about 11 A.M. to make up for difference of longitude. . . . Alice says I have not *melted* enough over your reading of my paper. I *do* melt to perfect liquefaction. 'T is the most beautiful and devoted brotherly act I ever knew, and I hope it may be the beginning of a new career, on your part, of psychic apostolicism. Heaven bless you for it![5]

On October 31, 1890, Henry James did read his brother's "Piper letter" at the Society for Psychical Research. I quote below substantial sections of that letter. It is important in part because it is a personal statement by an eminent psychologist about a woman who in her trances became the vehicle by which utterances were made by the spirits of dead persons. It is especially important to our own purposes because it tells us what Henry James knew about spirit mediumship. There can be no doubt that he would have found the letter interesting and would have remembered at least those parts of it that purported to reveal information about his own family, even his own father. The aunt referred to in the eighth paragraph as having for a time taken direct control of Mrs. Piper is William James's (and, of course, Henry's) aunt, who had died the previous year. I might point out also that William James uses the term *supernormal* rather than the term *supernatural* to emphasize that there was nothing unnatural or occult about Mrs. Piper's powers. The term *paranormal* has in recent years supplanted the term *supernormal*. I quote from the letter as published in the 1890 *Proceedings of the Society for Psychical Research*:

Dear Mr. Myers,
    You ask for a record of my own experiences with Mrs. Piper, to be incorporated in the account of her to be published in your *Proceedings*. . . .
    Under the circumstances, the only thing I can do is to give you my present state of belief as to Mrs. Piper's powers, with a simple account from memory of the steps which have led me to it.
    I made Mrs. Piper's acquaintance in the autumn of 1885. My wife's mother, Mrs. Gibbens, had been told of her by a friend, during the

5. Ibid., 327.

previous summer, and never having seen a medium before, had paid her a visit out of curiosity. She returned with the statement that Mrs. P. had given her a long string of names of members of the family, mostly Christian names, together with facts about the persons mentioned and their relations to each other, the knowledge of which on her part was incomprehensible without supernormal powers. My sister-in-law went the next day, with still better results, as she related them. Amongst other things, the medium had accurately described the circumstances of the writer of a letter which she held against her forehead, after Miss G. had given it to her. The letter was in Italian, and its writer was known to but two persons in this country. . . . I remember playing the *esprit fort* on that occasion before my feminine relatives, and seeking to explain by simple considerations the marvellous character of the facts which they brought back. This did not, however, prevent me from going myself a few days later, in company with my wife, to get a direct personal impression. The names of none of us up to this meeting had been announced to Mrs. P., and Mrs. J. and I were, of course, careful to make no reference to our relatives who had preceded. The medium, however, when entranced, repeated most of the names of "spirits" whom she had announced on the two former occasions and added others. The names came with difficulty, and were only gradually made perfect. My wife's father's name of Gibbens was announced first as Niblin, then as Giblin. A child Herman (whom we had lost the previous year) had his name spelt out as Herrin. I think that in no case were both Christian and surnames given on this visit. But the *facts predicated* of the persons named made it in many instances impossible not to recognise the particular individuals who were talked about. We took particular pains on this occasion to give the Phinuit control no help over his difficulties and to ask no leading questions. . . .

My impression after this first visit was, that Mrs. P. was either possessed of supernormal powers, or knew the members of my wife's family by sight and had by some lucky coincidence become acquainted with such a multitude of their domestic circumstances as to produce the startling impression which she did. My later knowledge of her sittings and personal acquaintance with her has led me absolutely to reject the latter explanation, and to believe that she has supernormal powers. . . .

I dropped my inquiries into Mrs. Piper's mediumship for a period of about two years, having satisfied myself that there was a genuine mystery there, but being over-freighted with time-consuming duties, and feeling that any adequate circumnavigation of the phenomena would be too protracted a task for me to aspire just then to undertake. I saw her once, half-accidentally, however, during that interval, and in the spring of 1889 saw her four times again. In the fall of 1889 she paid us a visit of a week at our country house in New Hampshire, and I then learned to know her personally better than ever before, and had confirmed in me the belief that she is an absolutely simple and genuine person. No one, when challenged, can give "evidence" to others for such beliefs as this. Yet we all live by them from day to day, and practically I should be willing now to stake as much money on Mrs. Piper's honesty as on that of anyone I know, and am quite satisfied to leave my reputation for wisdom or folly, so far as human nature is concerned, to stand or fall by this declaration.

As for the explanation of her trance-phenomena, I have none to offer. The *prima facie* theory, which is that of spirit-control, is hard to reconcile with the extreme triviality of most of the communications. What real spirit, at last able to revisit his wife on this earth, but would find something better to say than that she had changed the place of his photograph? And yet that is the sort of remark to which the spirits introduced by the mysterious Phinuit are apt to confine themselves. I must admit, however, that Phinuit has other moods. He has several times, when my wife and myself were sitting together with him, suddenly started off on long lectures to us about our inward defects and outward shortcomings, which were very earnest, as well as subtile morally and psychologically, and impressive in a high degree. These discourses, though given in Phinuit's own person, were very different in style from his more usual talk, and probably superior to anything that the medium could produce in the same line in her natural state. . . . Phinuit himself, however, bears every appearance of being a fictitious being. His French, so far as he has been able to display it to me, has been limited to a few phrases of salutation, which may easily have had their rise in the medium's "unconscious" memory; he has never been able to understand *my* French; and the crumbs of information which he gives about his earthly career are, as you know, so few, vague, and unlikely sounding, as to suggest the romancing of one whose stock of materials for invention is excessively reduced. He is however, as he actually shows himself, a definite human individual, with immense tact and patience, and great desire to please and be regarded as infallible. . . . The most remarkable thing about the Phinuit personality seems to me the extraordinary tenacity and minuteness of his memory. The medium has been visited by many hundreds of sitters, half of them, perhaps, being strangers who have come but once. To each Phinuit gives an hourful of disconnected fragments of talk about persons living, dead, or imaginary, and events past, future, or unreal. What normal waking memory could keep this chaotic mass of stuff together? Yet Phinuit does so; for the chances seem to be, that if a sitter should go back after years of interval, the medium, when once entranced, would recall the minutest incidents of the earlier interview, and begin by recapitulating much of what had then been said. So far as I can discover, Mrs. Piper's waking memory is not remarkable, and the whole constitution of her trance-memory is something which I am at a loss to understand. . . .

Her trance-talk about my own family shows the same innocence. The sceptical theory of her successes is that she keeps a sort of detective bureau open upon the world at large, so that whoever may call is pretty sure to find her prepared with facts about his life. Few things could have been easier, in Boston, than for Mrs. Piper to collect facts about my own father's family for use in my sittings with her. But although my father, my mother, and a deceased brother were repeatedly announced as present, nothing but their bare names ever came out, except a hearty message of thanks from my father that I had "published the book." I *had* published his *Literary Remains*; but when Phinuit was asked "what book?" all he could do was to spell the letters L, I, and say no more. If it be suggested that all this was but a refinement of cunning, for that such skilfully distributed reticences are what bring most credit in to a medium, I must deny the proposition *in toto*. I have seen and heard enough of sittings to be sure that a medium's trump cards are promptitude and completeness in her revelations. It is a mistake in general (however it may occasionally, as now, be cited in her favour) to keep back anything she knows. Phinuit's stumbling, spelling, and otherwise imperfect ways of bringing out his facts is a great drawback with most sitters, and yet it is habitual with him.

The aunt who purported to "take control" directly was a much better personation, having a good deal of the cheery strenuousness of speech of the original. She spoke, by the way, on this occasion, of the condition of health of two members of the family in New York, of which we knew nothing at the time, and which was afterwards corroborated by letter. We have repeatedly heard from Mrs. Piper in trance things of which we were not at the moment aware. . . .

My mother-in-law, on her return from Europe, spent a morning vainly seeking for her bank-book. Mrs. Piper, on being shortly afterwards asked where this book was, described the place so exactly that it was instantly found. I was told by her that the spirit of a boy named Robert F. was the companion of my lost infant. The F.'s were cousins of my wife living in a distant city. On my return home I mentioned the incident to my wife, saying, "Your cousin did lose a baby, didn't she? but Mrs. Piper was wrong about its sex, name, and age." I then learned that Mrs. Piper had been quite right in all those particulars, and that mine was the wrong impression. . . . On my mother-in-law's second visit to the medium she was told that one of her daughters was suffering from a severe pain in her back on that day. This altogether unusual occurrence, unknown to the sitter, proved to be true. The announcement to my wife and brother of my aunt's death in New York before we had received the telegram (Mr. Hodgson has, I believe, sent you an account of this) may, on the other hand, have been occasioned by the sitter's conscious apprehension of the event. This particular incident is a "test" of the sort which one readily quotes; but to my mind it was far less convincing than the innumerable small domestic matters of which Mrs. Piper incessantly talked in her sittings with members of my family. With the affairs of my wife's maternal kinsfolk in particular her acquaintance in trance was most intimate. Some of them were dead, some in California, some in the State of Maine. She characterised them all, living as well as deceased, spoke of their relations to each other, of their likes and dislikes, of their as yet unpublished practical plans, and hardly ever made a mistake, though, as usual, there was very little system or continuity in anything that came out. A *normal* person, unacquainted with the family, could not possibly have said as much; one acquainted with it could hardly have avoided saying more.

The most convincing things said about my own immediate household were either very intimate or very trivial. Unfortunately the former things cannot well be published. Of the trivial things, I have forgotten the greater number, but the following, *raroe nantes*, may serve as samples of their class: She said that we had lost recently a rug, and I a waistcoat. [She wrongly accused a person of stealing the rug, which was afterwards found in the house.] She told of my killing a grey-and-white cat, with ether, and described how it had "spun round and round" before dying. She told how my New York aunt had written a letter to my wife, warning her against all mediums, and then went off on a most amusing criticism, full of *traits vifs*, of the excellent woman's character. [Of course no one but my wife and I knew the existence of the letter in question.] She was strong on the events in our nursery, and gave striking advice during our first visit to her about the way to deal with certain "tantrums" of our second child, "little Billy-boy," as she called him, reproducing his nursery name. She told how the crib creaked at night, how a certain rocking-chair creaked mysteriously, how my wife had heard footsteps on the stairs, &c., &c. Insignificant as these things sound when read, the accumulation of a large number of them has an irresistible effect. And I repeat again what I said before, that, taking everything that I know of Mrs. P. into account, the result is to make me feel as absolutely certain as I am of any personal fact in the world that she knows things in her trances which she cannot possibly have heard in her waking state.[6]

After reading such a statement, Henry James could scoff at the notion of genuine trance mediumship only by scoffing also at the gullibility of members of his own family. Had he been inclined so

6. *PSPR* 6 (1890): 651–59. Bracketed materials are present as such in the original.

to scoff, it seems likely that he would have had the dignity to decline reading the letter aloud before a group of serious researchers, among them some of his own and his brother's personal friends. On November 7, a week after the event in Westminster Hall, Henry James wrote a letter to his brother:

It was a week ago today that I read you at the S. P. R., with great éclat—enhanced by my being introduced by Pearsall Smith as "a Bostonian of Bostonians." You were very easy and interesting to read, and were altogether the "feature" of the entertainment. It was a full house—and Myers was rayonnant.[7]

Henry James seems to have been pleased with the evening, and with his part in it. Could it have started him thinking seriously, and reading seriously, about subjects that had earlier not much interested him? We cannot know. All we can say with much assurance is that, if Henry James did come to feel less "outsideness" to such subjects, the change in his attitude probably dated from October 1890. It may be worth noting here that just a year later he published "Sir Edmund Orme," a story about the ghost of a spurned lover who returns with a dual purpose: to torment the woman whose rejection of him had caused him to commit suicide and to protect the interests of the young narrator, who seeks the hand of that woman's daughter. It is not a brilliant story. Though we cannot know whether or not that story derived from Henry James's experiences in October of 1890, it does seem quite possible that a later and truly brilliant story did. Henry James found himself, just seven years after his part in the "feature entertainment" at the Society for Psychical Research, hard at work on *The Turn of the Screw*.

Mrs. Piper was one of many mediums, and reports about spirit possession and the speaking of spirits through the mouths of the living were common enough. Let us consider, for example, two more American cases.

The first of these was not widely known, but it demonstrates one author's attempt to turn such cases into a good story. It is

7. James, *Letters*, ed. Edel, 3:305.

reported by Arthur Morrison in the same 1891 book, *The Shadows Around Us,* in which he had told the story of Mrs. Simpson of St. Swithin's Lane. He prefaces the story with a general comment about possession:

Instances of what has been called "possession" are not at all uncommon among stories of the unaccountable which may be fairly classed as authentic; that is to say, cases in which a departed spirit enters or seems to enter, the body of a person still living, using it in its own way, speaking with its mouth, hearing with its ears, and so forth. Many of these cases are no doubt nothing but the result of some unusual derangement of mind on the part of the person said to be "possessed," or even impositions in which that person takes the leading, or, perhaps, the sole part. But still there remain many others to which such explanations are quite inapplicable.[8]

The narrative that Morrison tells as an "authentic" story of possession is too long to give here at full length. It involves a woman named Esther who marries and moves with her husband to California, leaving behind in Massachusetts two sisters, Anne and Cecilia, this last one a married woman referred to variously as "Mrs. J." and "Cissy." Not long after Esther's arrival in California she dies of cholera. Before word of this death arrives in Massachusetts, Anne, Cecilia, and Mr. J. are spending an evening playing cards when strange things start to happen:

Mr. J. made the first deal, Mrs. J. the second. Anne F. then took the cards, and, after they had been shuffled and cut, was about to deal, when suddenly she sat back rigidly in her chair, her eyes fixed intently on those of her sister, and her whole body violently convulsed, while the hand which held the cards assumed a rapid gyratory motion, scattering them broadcast.

"Anne! What are you doing? Don't be so stupid—you'll lose the cards." No answer; the spasmodic movement continued.

"Are you ill, Anne? What is it? Come and lie on the sofa," and Mrs. J. rose to assist her.

Then, from Anne's mouth, in a strangely hollow but still a familiar voice—certainly not Anne's—came the words,

8. Morrison, *Shadows,* 49.

"I am not Anne, Cissy. I am Esther!"

"You are not well, Anne," said the husband. "You must lie down a little while. I will go for Doctor S."

"I am Esther, I am Esther! I say to you that I am Esther!" . . .

Doctor S. arrived, and Mrs. J. was removed from the room. Still Anne remained in a strange state of trance. They attempted to carry her to the sofa, but she remained perfectly rigid and straight from head to heel, no matter in what position she might be placed; and for hours there issued from her mouth at intervals that awfully familiar voice:

"Cissy, Cissy! Where is Cissy? I must tell her something."

Midnight was rapidly approaching, and Mrs. J., in her bed-room, had become fairly composed after an hour or two's rest. The doctor, who could only attribute Anne's condition to some extraordinary hysterical attack, represented that it might be advisable, since she called for her so earnestly, for Mrs. J. to go to her sister.

She did so.

There still lay Anne, motionless, save for intermittent twitchings of the limbs.

"Cissy, Cissy, I must whisper!"

Mrs. J., much agitated, approached her sister and bent down to listen.

For twenty or thirty seconds she stood so, and then, turning away with a look of dazed abstraction, seeing nothing and hearing nothing, she made her way from the room.

Whether she had heard any whisper, and, if so, what it was, nobody but herself ever knew.

Soon Anne lay perfectly motionless, and her breath came easily and regularly. It was nearly ten minutes more than four hours since her first seizure when she slowly opened her eyes, and, starting up, cried in her natural voice:

"Dear, dear! Have I been asleep? What is it? Is there anything wrong?"

And Dr. S. could find nothing in her condition indicative of anything but an awakening from a healthy sleep. ("Mrs. F. and the Visit of Esther")

Another American case—one about which Henry James is more likely to have heard—is the famous one of Mary Roff and Lurancy Vennum, reported in some detail in booklet form in 1878 by the spiritualist doctor E. Winchester Stevens, who had been personally involved in the case. Published by the Religio-Philosophical Publishing House under the title *The Watseka Wonder,* the booklet sold so well and attracted so much attention that it was revised and reissued in 1887. Let us briefly review the strange happenings it describes.

In July 1877, in the town of Watseka, Illinois, a thirteen-year-old girl named Lurancy Vennum began suffering strange attacks or "fits." She would fall to the floor, her muscles becoming rigid. Sometimes she would speak, saying that she saw her little brother and sister, who were dead, or that she was one or another strange man or woman from the spirit world. At the end of January 1878, Lurancy proclaimed that she was Mary Roff and that she wanted to go home to her parents.

Mary Roff had died in Watseka a dozen years earlier, in July of 1865. She had been eighteen at the time of her death, which had followed a long history of her own fits or attacks. Here is what Stevens had to say about Mary Roff, the dead girl, whose parents still lived in Watseka and had provided him with much of the personal history of their daughter:

In the spring of 1847, when about six months old, Mary was taken sick and had a fit, in which she remained several hours. After the fit, she became conscious and lay several days without the family having much hope of her recovery. In two or three weeks she seemed to have entirely recovered. A few weeks later she acted, on one occasion, like a child going into a fit. The pupils of her eyes dilated, the muscles slightly twitched but lasted but a few moments. From the age of about six months, she had these spells as described, once in from three to five weeks apart, all the time increasing in force and violence, until her tenth year, when they proved to be real fits, having from one to three and sometimes four or five of them within a period of three or four days, when they would cease, and she would enjoy good health until the next period approached. At these times, she for a few days would seem sad and despondent, in which mood she would sing and play the most solemn music (for with all the rest of her studies, in which she was considered well advanced, she had learned music) and almost always would sing that beautiful song, "We Are Coming Sister Mary," which was a favorite song with her.

When she was fifteen years old, and the violence of the fits had increased, the parents say they could see her mind was affected during the melancholy periods prior to the fits. Dr. Jesse Bennett, now residing at Sparta, Wis., and Dr. Franklin Blades, now Judge of the Eleventh Judicial Circuit of Illinois, and resident of Watseka, were employed to attend her. Dr. N. S. Davis, of Chicago, Illinois, and several other prominent physicians, had examined her. They kept her in the water cure at Peoria, Illinois, under the care of Dr. Nevins, for eighteen months, but all to no purpose.

In the summer of 1864 she seemed to have almost a mania for bleeding herself for the relief, as she said, "of the lump of pain in the head." Drs. Fowler, Secrest and Pitwood were called and applied leeches. She would apply them herself to her temples, and liked them, treating them like little pets, until she seemed sound and well.

On Saturday morning, July 16th, 1864, in one of her desponding moods, she secretly took a knife with her to the back yard, and cut her arm terribly, until bleeding excessively, she fainted. This occurred about nine o'clock A.M. She remained unconscious till two o'clock P.M., when she became a raving maniac of the most violent kind, in which condition she remained five days and nights, requiring almost constantly the services of five of the most able bodied men to hold her on the bed, although her weight was only about one hundred pounds, and she had lost nearly all her blood. When she ceased raving, she looked and acted quite natural and well, and could do everything she desired as readily and properly as at any time in her life. Yet she seemed to know no one, and could not recognize the presence of persons at all, although the house was nearly filled with people night and day. She had no sense whatever of sight, feeling or hearing in a natural way, as was proved by every test that could be applied. She could read blind-folded, and do everything as readily as when in health by her natural sight. She would dress, stand before the glass, open and search drawers, pick up loose pins, or do any and all things readily, and without annoyance under heavy blindfoldings.[9]

A year after this incident, Mary Roff died during one of her fits. We shall have occasion to consider the circumstances of that death in the next chapter, but for now, let us return briefly to Lurancy Vennum, whose spirit seemed to have departed and been replaced by that of this Mary Roff, who asked to be taken home to her parents. Mary Roff's parents agreed to let Lurancy Vennum come to live in their home, even though they scarcely knew either Lurancy or her parents. Lurancy stayed with them for the next three months. During that time she could remember nothing about her own home or her parents, the Vennums, but knew in precise detail virtually everything about Mary Roff and about Mary's family as it had been a dozen years earlier when Mary had still been alive. Lurancy Vennum's story is absorbing, but I shall say no more of it here except that after several months Mary Roff

9. E. W. Stevens, *The Watseka Wonder: A Startling and Instructive Psychological Study, and Well Authenticated Instance of Angelic Visitation*, 5.

left Lurancy's body, and Lurancy, having presumably been cured in the spirit world, returned to her own body and went back to live a full life as Lurancy Vennum. She eventually married and had a number of children of her own.

Strange doings, these. It is difficult for us to understand at the end of the twentieth century what some people at the end of the nineteenth century believed about such phenomena. Most people today would call the Roff-Vennum phenomenon pure insanity, and many at the time did so as well. The skeptics, however, had difficulty accounting for what seemed to be the facts of the case. No one who had observed it, for example, could quite figure out how the blindfolded Mary Roff, before she died, could in one of her fits or trances read books and letters held before her eyes. And it was difficult to explain how Lurancy Vennum, a dozen years later, could know details about incidents in the lives of Mary Roff's parents, brothers, and sisters that even they had all but forgotten.

Among those who did believe that the Roff-Vennum possession was probably genuine was William James, who devotes two pages of his 1890 *The Principles of Psychology* to the case. Although William James did not have personal contact with any of the principals involved in the case, he had read Steven's *The Watseka Wonder,* and he reports that his friend and fellow psychical researcher, Richard Hodgson, had gone to Illinois to conduct an investigation. I quote part of a footnote in William James's very influential book:

He [Hodgson] visited Watseka in April 1890, and cross-examined the principal witnesses of this case. His confidence in the original narrative was strengthened by what he learned; and various unpublished facts were ascertained, which increased the plausibility of the spiritualistic interpretation of the phenomenon.[10]

The point of all this is that spirit possession was a reasonably familiar phenomenon at the turn of the century and that accounts of spirit possession were published and considered worthy of notice by men and women of reputation. Of particular signifi-

10. William James, *The Principles of Psychology,* 1:398.

cance is that William James, the most respected psychologist of his day, did not automatically dismiss all these accounts as the ravings of insanity. None of this tells us what Henry James might have thought about such accounts, of course, but it does give us an indication that both he and his audience might have known about them, whether or not they personally believed in the "spiritualistic interpretation" of them.

So far we have been discussing mostly the good or benign spirits that took control of the bodies of the living, but there was another class of spirits. Mediums who invited the friendly spirits often found themselves beset by dangerously unfriendly ones as well, spirits whose effects could range anywhere from mildly unpleasant or disagreeable to downright malignant or diabolical. In this class of unfriendly spirits was the spirit that came to Mary Roff after she cut her arm, and the spirit of Katrina Hogan, an unpleasant sixty-three-year-old German woman who invaded Lurancy Vennum a year or so before Mary Roff did.[11] These unfriendly spirits were usually called demons. So dangerous were such demons to their subjects—variously known as hosts, victims, demoniacs, or merely the possessed—that many experienced spiritualists warned against tampering with mediumship at all. Crosland, for example, in 1873 urged that people should "believe in the verity of these manifestations, but not . . . seek them":

The undeveloped and earth-bound spirits throng about the mediums, struggle to enter into parley with them, apparently with the purpose of getting possession of their natures, or exchanging natures; and I have heard of sittings terminating from this cause in cases of paralysis or demoniacal possession. If you leave your doors open, an enemy may enter sometimes as well as a friend.[12]

Before we consider specific cases of demon possession, let us review what was generally known, or hypothesized, about this puzzling phenomenon in the last half of the nineteenth century.

11. See Stevens, *Watseka*, 3.
12. Crosland, *Apparitions*, 17.

We shall begin with Catherine Crowe, who has a few words to say about demon possession in her influential *The Night Side of Nature*. She relies, as usual, on the views of German scholars. It is worth noting in her account that cases of supposed possession were easily confused with cases of insanity. Indeed, one of the early ways of referring to insanity was to say that a person was possessed. *Magnetism*, which Crowe calls in her first sentence a remedy for possession, was an early term for what we now call *mesmerism* or *hypnotism*. I quote her cautious introductory paragraph on the subject of demon possession:

I must here observe, that many German physicians maintain, that to this day instances of genuine possession occur, and there are several works published in their language on the subject; and for this malady they consider magnetism the only remedy, all others being worse than useless. Indeed, they look upon *possession* itself as a demono-magnetic state, in which the patient is in rapport with mischievous or evil spirits; as in the Agatho (or good) magnetic state, which is the opposite pole, he is in rapport with good ones; and they particularly warn their readers against confounding this infliction with cases of epilepsy or mania. They assert, that although instances are comparatively rare, both sexes and all ages are equally subject to this misfortune. . . . Amongst the distinguishing symptoms [are] the patient's speaking in a voice that is not his own, frightful convulsions and motions of the body, which arise suddenly, without any previous indisposition . . . blasphemous and obscene talk.[13]

We shall have occasion in the next chapter to consider several of the cases Crowe cites from her German authors. First, let us consider the somewhat perplexed view of church officials. Protestants, especially, had difficulty knowing what to make of the concept of diabolic or demon possession. On the one hand, there was ample scriptural basis for belief in such phenomena. On the other hand, to believe that diabolic possession still took place was to associate oneself too closely either with the Catholic church, which still from time to time practiced rites of exorcism, or with a theologically suspicious belief in some kind of witchcraft or devil

13. Crowe, *Night Side of Nature*, 447–48.

worship. Surely, if Christ had robbed Satan of his power, we should not expect to see the devil reasserting such direct control over the bodies or wills of modern men and women. But, if the devil still did, even in isolated cases, hold some kind of direct power over the actions of the living, surely the church ought to stand ready to help, or at least to urge that prayer or belief might be an efficacious remedy. Such arguments quickly became very circuitous, if not outright contradictory, and there is no need to try to reproduce them at great length here. It may be helpful, however, to quote several paragraphs written by a divine named Henry Christmas and published in 1850 in his *Echoes of the Universe.* Christmas tends not to cite specific cases, but these paragraphs will give the general flavor of his opinions on the delicate subject of demon possession:

The notion once prevalent on the subject of demoniacal possession, and not yet entirely extinct, is, that a devil took up his abode in the body of a man, entirely suppressing the power of the man's soul, and actuating that body at its own will,—leaving, indeed, an occasional, and sometimes a perpetual consciousness of such alien domination,—and admitting, it would appear, of lucid intervals, either by the temporary departing of the evil spirit, or by allowing the spirit of the man again to govern the body.

In examining the works of those of the greatest fathers of the church who have written on this subject, it will be easy to see that their views were considerably different: they regarded the human spirit as being subjugated by the infernal, and *compelled to act* according to its will. It is a possession, not of the bodily frame only, nor yet of the human will only, but a strange and partial enslavement of *both*; as though, in fact, the demon had obtained occupation of the channels of communication between the bodily and intellectual, or spiritual, part of the man's nature. . . .

Setting aside, then, the notion of a merely corporeal possession, and coming to those views entertained by the more enlightened, we observe that the idea which *has* prevailed, which still *does* prevail, and which, because founded on truth, ever must prevail, concerning this doctrine is, that there are certain circumstances under which Satan has been suffered, or evil spirits have been permitted, to take possession of the *mind* of man, to overpower his faculties, and to use him as the instrument of their own devices—taking from him his self-control, and making him merely a servant in their hands. . . .

The question has often been asked, whether or not there are in *these* days cases of demoniacal possession. It was stated, indeed, about the middle of the last century, that there were many such cases; but an eminent physician, Dr. Antonio De Haen, who, at the request of the Austrian Government, devoted his time to the examination of those who were brought before him as demoniacs, came to the conclusion to which we now come,—namely, that he did not dare to say that such things did not exist, indeed he rather believed that they did.[14]

The books of Crowe and Christmas were dated by the time Henry James began working on *The Turn of the Screw* half a century later, but they had helped set the stage for what appeared to be, at least in certain quarters, a growing belief in demon possession. A couple of examples will indicate the extent to which spirit or demon possession was mentioned as a possible cause in what we might consider to be unlikely situations. An anonymous article in the October 16, 1886, issue of *Light* carried the title "Sin and Its Remedy." The general thesis of the article is that criminals, like errant children, should be treated with love. We should try to improve them, raise their moral standards, educate them. We should emphatically *not* put them to death, the argument goes, because their corrupt and unimproved spirits are liable to take possession of the living and thus perhaps do more harm than the criminals could have done if permitted to live:

We kill our murderers, and thereby send into the spirit world a legion of revengeful and vindictive spirits to hover around the abodes of men, filling other natures with their own inharmonious conditions.[15]

Another unlikely example of the attribution of harmful causality to demon possession appeared a few years later in the same newspaper. This example, of particular interest to us because it involves children, deals with the celebrated case of the "boy-murderers" of Liverpool. It seems that two Liverpool lads, aged eight and nine, planned and carried out a terrible murder. They brutally harassed another boy, pushed him into some water, then sat on his head to make sure that he drowned. Their only appar-

14. Henry Christmas, *Echoes of the Universe*, 296–98, 305.
15. *Light* 6 (October 16, 1886): 504.

ent motive for the murder was that they wanted their victim's clothes. In the trial the boys were found guilty but were held not responsible because of their tender ages. There was much publicity about the case, and many individuals had opinions about the cause of the depravity in the boys: bad environment, parental neglect, failure of Christian instruction, and so on. An anonymous contributor to *Light* on December 19, 1891, had his own idea that a special kind of original sin was the true cause of the murders:

But if by "original sin" we mean the subjugation of the subject of that sin to the powers of evil we have the key to the whole history of crime. Wherever there is a chance of these agents of spiritual wickedness fastening on to our humanity, that chance is seized. "Lead us not into temptation, but deliver us from evil," has a meaning of far deeper import than the small wishfulness of those who glibly utter the phrases in what they call their "devotions." . . . It is far from unusual for delicately-nurtured women, who have been kept all their lives out of the range of material impurity, to pour out streams of obscenity and blasphemy, when the usual balance of reason is lost. To say, as is said by some, that this language had been heard during the patient's sane life, and has been unconsciously garnered up in some odd corner of the memory, is but to confess utter ignorance of the matter. But if we allow that, as in the case of the boy-murderers, there was an opportunity seized by evil agents in the unseen to vent their spleen, or to exhibit themselves in order to gratify a depraved vanity, we get a solution of the difficulty.[16]

Clearly, then, notions about the malignant possibilities of demon possession were very much in the minds of certain people in the last quarter of the nineteenth century. Those notions were given additional impetus by the publication of an unlikely book by an unlikely author. John L. Nevius had spent forty years in China as a missionary. A book he had written shortly before his death was published in 1896. Entitled *Demon Possession and Allied Themes*, the book recounted, with many examples and cases, instances of demon possession among mostly unconverted Chinese. Although Nevius went to China convinced that demon

16. *Light* 11 (December 19, 1891): 606.

possession was nonsense, after talking with some Chinese he began to alter his opinion. Let us read about it in Nevius's own words:

My first home in China was in the city of Ningpo, in the province of Che-kiang, which place we reached in the spring of 1854. My first work was of course that of acquiring the language. A native scholar, Mr. Tu, was engaged to serve me as a teacher. He was a strong believer in the "supernatural," and when we could understand each other through the medium of his vernacular, spiritual manifestations and possessions formed a frequent subject of conversation. I brought with me to China a strong conviction that a belief in demons, and communications with spiritual beings, belongs exclusively to a barbarous and superstitious age, and at present can consist only with mental weakness and want of culture. I indulged Mr. Tu, however, in talking on his favorite topics, because he did so with peculiar fluency and zest, and thus elements of variety and novelty were utilized in our severe and otherwise monotonous studies. But Mr. Tu's marvelous stories soon lost the charm of novelty. I used my best endeavors, though with little success, to convince him that his views were the combined result of ignorance and imagination. I could not but notice, however, the striking resemblance between some of his statements of alleged facts and the demonology of Scripture. This resemblance I accounted for as only apparent or accidental, though it still left in my mind an unpleasant regret that it was so strong, and I should also add a feeling amounting almost to a regret that such detailed statements should have been recorded in the Bible.[17]

Nevius goes on to describe an incident involving some Chinese Christians in the Shantung province who rent a building that is available because it is haunted and no one else has been able to use it. They successfully move into the new building, but soon receive complaints that a woman in a nearby household is possessed by the angry spirit that had been driven out when the new occupants arrived. Nevius did not think much about the incident at the time, but soon began hearing about more and more cases of demon possession. Moreover, there seemed to be a certain consistency in the various reports.

Finally Nevius yielded to what appeared to be the facts and

17. John L. Nevius, *Demon Possession and Allied Themes*, 9–10.

decided to do a little informal psychical research of his own by conducting a kind of "census of possession" in China. He constructed a lengthy questionnaire and mailed it in September 1879 to his fellow missionaries, of various denominations, scattered throughout China. On the list were questions about the number of cases of possession observed or heard about, whether the victims of possession were physically strong or weak, whether the possession seemed to be voluntary or involuntary, what methods (if any) of heathen or Christian exorcism seemed to be effective, and so on. We need not dwell at any length on most of these, but I would like to mention, by way of example, Nevius's seventh question about the utterances of demon-possessed people and their ability to recollect. I select this particular question because it may have relevance to Miles's having "said things" at school for which he is apparently expelled yet of which he subsequently seems to have little recollection. Here is the question as it was put in Nevius's questionnaire:

In supposed cases of demon possession in which the subject gives forth utterances apparently proceeding from a different personality, is there any conclusive proof that this is really the case? Does the subject retain a recollection, after passing from one of these abnormal states, of what he has said or done while in it?[18]

Nevius received replies from various parts of China. I reproduce below translations from the Chinese of three of the responses to this question 7. The first is from Chen Sin Ling, reporting from the city of Fu-chow:

The words spoken certainly proceed from the mouths of the persons possessed; but what is said does not appear to come from their minds or wills, but rather from some other personality, often accompanied by a change of voice; of this there can be no doubt. When the subject returns to consciousness he invariably declares himself ignorant of what he has said.[19]

18. Ibid., 42–43.
19. Ibid., 49–50.

The second is from Wang Wu-Fang, in Shantung:

In cases of possession by demons what is said by the subject certainly does not proceed from his own will. When the demon has gone out, and the subject recovers consciousness, he has no recollection whatever of what he has said or done. This is true invariably.[20]

The third is from Wang Yng-ngen, in Peking:

It may be said in general of possessed persons, that sometimes people who cannot sing, are able when possessed to do so; others who ordinarily cannot write verses, when possessed compose in rhyme with ease. Northern men will speak languages of the south, and those of the east the language of the west; and when they awake to consciousness they are utterly oblivious of what they have done.[21]

Nevius refers to many western writers about such subjects. Indeed, he provides a useful annotated list of relevant books and articles. It may be worth mentioning that he devotes no fewer than fourteen pages to quotations from and discussion of William James's views on possession as published in *The Principles of Psychology.*

William James was sufficiently interested in demoniacal possession that in late 1896 he devoted one of the Lowell Lectures to the subject. No exact transcript of this lecture was ever made; it is possible, however, to reconstruct an accurate idea of what he said by consulting William James's handwritten lecture notes and his references in those notes to specific page numbers in published books. Eugene Taylor has recently done just that. Taylor quotes from William James's notes for the lecture on possession:

Its attacks are periodic and brief, usually not lasting more than an hour or two, and the patient is entirely well between them, and retains no memory of them when they are over. During them, he speaks in an altered voice and manner, names himself differently, and describes his natural self in the third person as he would a stranger. The new

20. Ibid., 53–54.
21. Ibid., 58.

impersonation offers every variety of completeness and energy, from the rudimentary form of unintelligible automatic scribbling, to the strongest convulsions with blasphemous outcries.[22]

I call particular attention to the fact that, according to Taylor, William James referred in his lectures specifically to cases of possession involving an eight-year-old girl and a ten-year-old boy.[23] It may not be entirely coincidental that not long afterwards Henry James wrote a story involving—if my interpretation is correct—the possession of two such children.

We cannot assume, of course, that William James's interest in possession is proof of Henry James's interest, though we should recall that the two brothers at least pretended to show an interest in each other's professional doings. I should perhaps note also that even though Henry James did not attend the Lowell Lecture on demoniacal possession, he might easily have heard about it. His brother's views on such subjects were more than a little newsworthy. When a reporter, for example, misinterpreted the speaker to have said that all spirit mediumship was demon possession, the editors of *Light* gently chided William James for confusing good spirits with evil spirits. They invited him to clarify what he meant.[24] William James did so in a brief letter he sent to *Light* shortly thereafter:

The remarks in question were in a lecture on demoniacal possession. I stood up for it on historic grounds as a definite type of affliction, very widespread in place and time, and characterised by definite symptoms, the chief of which are these: The subject is attacked at intervals for short periods, a few hours at most, and between whiles is perfectly sane and well. During the attack the character, voice, and consciousness are changed, the subject assuming a new name and speaking of his natural self in the third person. The new name may in Christian countries be that of a demon, or spirit, elsewhere it may be that of a god; and the action and speech are frequently blasphemous or absurd. When the attack passes off the subject usually remembers nothing of it. . . . I contented myself

22. Eugene Taylor, *William James on Exceptional Mental Stress: The 1896 Lowell Lectures*, 94.
23. Ibid., 101, 107.
24. *Light* 17 (March 6, 1897): 109.

with 'rehabilitating' demoniac possession as a genuine phenomenon, instead of the 'imposture' or 'delusion' which at the present day it is popularly supposed to be.[25]

William James's remarks were reprinted almost immediately by William Stead in *Borderland*.[26]

Less than a year later William James again lectured on demon possession, this time to the Neurological Society of the Academy of Medicine in New York. We no longer have a copy of this lecture, but just before he gave the lecture William James wrote a letter to Henry W. Rankin, the man who had arranged to have Nevius's book published posthumously. I quote from this February 1, 1897, letter:

I shall of course duly advertise the Nevius book. . . . The most I shall plead for before the neurologists is the recognition of demon possession as a regular "morbid-entity" whose commonest homologue today is the "spirit-control" observed in test-mediumship, and which tends to become the more benignant and less alarming, the less pessimistically it is regarded. This last remark seems certainly to be true. Of course I shall not ignore the sporadic cases of old-fashioned malignant possession that still occur today. . . . The first thing is to start the medical profession out of its idiotically *conceited ignorance* of all such matters—matters which have everywhere and at all times played a vital part in human history.[27]

Two days after William James wrote this letter, a notice of his having addressed the Neurological Society appeared in the *New York Times*.[28] If Henry James had wanted, when setting to work later that year on his famous story, to find out what the most recent authorities had to say on the subject of demon possession— even the "cases of old-fashioned malignant possession that still occur today"—he need not have looked far.

Even if Henry James was not aware of his brother's widely broadcast views on such subjects, he would probably have been

25. *Light* 17 (May 1, 1897): 211.

26. *Borderland* 4 (1897): 270.

27. As reprinted in Gardner Murphy and Robert O. Ballon, eds., *William James on Psychical Research*, 261.

28. *New York Times*, February 3, 1897, p. 7.

aware of his father's. Surely he knew, for example, that his father had in 1873 published in the *Atlantic Monthly* a review of M. J. Williamson's book, *Modern Diabolism*. As Leon Edel has pointed out, at least one critic assumed that the son, not the father, had written the review.[29] Williamson's book was about his own experiments and experiences with spirit possession. Williamson allowed himself to be controlled by assorted spirits in an attempt to discover what the next world was like. One of his controls was a depraved woman named Ellen Macauley. Others were more benign. More might be said of Williamson's book, but I am interested here in the review that Henry James, Sr., wrote of it. He was generally critical of the book, mostly because Williamson neglected to familiarize himself with the ideas of Swedenborg. Those ideas, Henry James, Sr., felt, would have provided Williamson with a philosophical framework for understanding his experiences. The most interesting part of the review, however, is the extended reference to an experience of an eminent medical doctor, a close friend of Henry James, Sr., involving demon possession:

Unlike Mr. Williamson, my friend did not invite the cadaverous crew that chased him to a premature grave. They came upon him by stealth, muffled at first in the familiar voices of nature and the cheerful sounds of industry, while he was prostrate under a long and painful affection of the optical nerve, which robbed him of his physical strength, but left his intellect and will unimpaired. Gradually they separated their voices from the sounds of art and nature, and addressed him directly, soliciting him to become the medium or instrument of a great society of illuminati in the other world, composed of the noblest and best of mankind, who really though invisibly guided the course of human history, and furnished the backbone of its various priesthoods and governments. My friend's intellectual curiosity was piqued by this extraordinary visitation, no doubt, and he gave himself up to its active scrutiny; but that for a long time was all, and I shall never forget the grim pleasantry with which he used to wrestle down any too urgent assault, and laugh the faulty logic of his tormentors to scorn. But there they were all the same, forever prating of this sublime brotherhood beyond the grave. . . . It became thus a contest for strictly personal supremacy between him and his envenomed foes, the one party backed by the total force of falsehood known to the human

29. Leon Edel, *Henry James: The Untried Years—1843–1870*, 59.

will, the other inspirited by no adequate light of truth divine, harvested by the human understanding.[30]

This account of the terrifying and destructive experience of the elder James's friend is interesting for several reasons, not the least of which is that it suggests a way in which demon possession can begin. The demons come in the guise of cheerful friendship and then, having asserted a right to at least periodic control of or conversation with the one possessed, they gradually reveal their more demonic purposes. Might this account have suggested to Henry James, the son, how Peter Quint and Miss Jessel could assert their venomous control over Miles and Flora, having appeared to them first as friends? As two orphans who had been abandoned by their guardian to the unimaginative devices of Mrs. Grose, might the children have succumbed only too readily to the proferred spirit friendship of their old cohorts? If so, they would not have been entirely unique among possessed persons, as we shall see in the next two cases.

In the first case below a mother and her daughter are both subject to possession. Of particular interest here is that though both at first invite the society of spirit friends, only the mother is strong enough to throw off the "enslavement" that seems so often to be the result of such possessions. I might mention that those who write about experiences of demon possession are particularly reluctant, for obvious reasons, to reveal names. I have resorted, then, to the unsatisfactory alternative of calling the subject of this case "Mrs. Blank." She is not, of course, to be confused with other "Blanks" we have encountered or will encounter shortly:

Just thirty years ago, the mother of several children, of whom the eldest was but eighteen, became interested in Spiritualism. She and her husband encouraged the mediumship of the little ones, and presently became enthusiastic believers. The mother was advised to seek mediumship for herself by sitting alone for development, and full of enthusiasm she sat alone at any and all hours when she could escape from

30. Henry James, Sr., "Modern Diabolism," 223.

domestic duties. But our spirit friends are not always by our side. They have occupations demanding attention, although they keep an appointment with sacred punctuality. The undeveloped, and therefore more or less unprotected medium, who has no regular hour for sitting, thus easily becomes the prey of spirit visitors, who find a ready acceptance and then outstay their welcome. There is something so sacred in spirit presence, especially to the trained orthodox mind, that any spirit is likely to be greeted as a friend. But it is only those who are very sensitive who discover their danger by painful experience.

Presently this mother became clairaudient, and then she discovered that she was rapidly becoming the slave of those who claimed to be her guides, but were apparently working to do her harm rather than good. She realised her peril in time, and for nearly two months fought a silent battle for life, liberty, and love of her husband and children. She refused to reply to the voices around her, till at last wearied and disgusted, these spirits left her. She fought her battle to victory, but sacrificed her mediumship to avoid a second contest; thus through ignorance losing that which should have proved the greatest blessing of her life. Strangely enough, she continued to encourage mediumship in her children, but giving them no warning as to any possible danger. Her eldest daughter, though sometimes giving startling tests to her parents, most naturally thought more of this world than any other, and cared little for these family circles. She grew to womanhood, was married, and had a daughter sixteen years old before she became interested in spirit return. But she was none the wiser for her mother's experiences. She was a true sensitive, and at first was much happier in her mediumship than her mother had been. It was orderly, and none but loved friends came to her inner life, until she ignorantly ran into a greater danger than her mother had experienced. She began to visit public miscellaneous circles—so dangerous to the undeveloped medium—at every opportunity, and then came sad proofs of hereditary tendencies and sensitiveness. Like her mother she heard voices. She also often saw her spirit visitors, and counting them as true friends encouraged their influence. But the old story was repeated, for she presently found herself compelled to say cruel and unkind things to her husband and daughter, whilst really devotedly attached to them. For months she was in an asylum, where her husband visited her daily, only to be insulted and attacked. Yet in his absence she was so perfectly normal, that the doctors and attendants could not realise but that she was only "making believe" to be insane. When she would beg these spirits to leave her they would reply that it was the only fun they had. ("Mrs. Blank and Her Enslaving Demon")

The second case is rather longer than most, but is worth quoting in full not only because it makes interesting reading in its own right but also because it shows a number of suggestive parallels with *The Turn of the Screw*: the victim's susceptibility to the controlling influence of the demon because he has been deprived of human love; the clearly diabolic character and purposes of the demon; the notion that the victim may be "lost" and "damned"; the narrator's notion that he is engaged in a struggle for a human soul; the mention of an "abyss" on the edge of which the struggle takes place; the victim's ambivalence about coming to the narrator in the first place (his wanting, that is, both to seek help and to spurn it); the face of the victim turning hideously ugly. I propose this case of demon possession as the one that Henry James is most likely to have both read and been influenced by. Not only did it appear in *Borderland* in 1896, just before James set to work on his famous story, but it is also told with a vividness that James would have appreciated. The narrator of the piece, none other than William Stead himself, does not describe a second- or third-hand experience but one he witnessed himself. He introduces his narrative as "an object lesson on the dangers of spiritualism," a warning that *this* is what might happen to others who carelessly dabble in the occult. Before we read the case itself, we should look at Stead's introductory comment:

Fifteen years ago, when I first began to look into the subject, I remember hearing ghastly stories both from spiritualists and anti-spiritualists of cases within the knowledge of my informants in which Englishmen living in our time had become the victims of a kind of demoniacal possession as the result of meddling with spiritualism. In some, it took the form of temporary possession by an Invisible who constrained his victim to use language or to do acts highly detrimental to his success in life and the tranquility of his home. I heard of lives that were blasted by the malignant and persistent influence of malicious intelligences, which, having gained possession of those who had ventured within range of their power, had succeeded in establishing a hold that could not be shaken off. Although I had heard of those things from others, no instance had occurred within the range of my personal observation until this month, when it was my sad fortune to be brought into contact with a case which displayed in very tragic fashion the consequences which sometimes follow from dabbling with matters beyond our ken.[31]

31. *Borderland* 3 (1896): 11.

It is perhaps worth noting that in the subsequent issue of *Borderland*, Stead published two more sentences about what he called the "modern demoniac":

I have received letters from the unfortunate gentleman whose evil case I described in our last issue begging me to say no more about him. I have no idea who he is or where he is, but it would seem that he is still a prey to his obsessing demon.[32]

Because Stead gives us no name for this unfortunate man, I shall call him in my title "Mr. Carcass," picking up a name for him given by his own cruel demon or control. Here, then, is the narrative:

One Thursday afternoon in January, when coming in after lunch, I met at the foot of the stairs a young man, who somewhat nervously asked the lift-boy whether Mr. Stead came down to the office nowadays.

"What do you want?" said I. "I am Mr. Stead."

"O!" said he, "might I speak to you?"

"Certainly," said I, and so he followed me into my office without going through the usual preliminary of sending in his name, therefore I do not know to this day who my visitor was, or where he came from. I only know that he said he was an officer in the British army, and that he is now, and has been for some time, on sick leave.

He said that he wished to speak to me because he had been interested in spiritualism and thought he could tell me something that was interesting, and at the same time he hoped I might be able to give him some advice.

Some time ago he had taken to experimenting, and had found that he had great facility in automatic writing. His hand had moved within five minutes of the time he had first taken the pen in his hand, and left it free to move as it pleased. Fascinated by the unusual phenomena he had gone on and on, neglecting his duties and abandoning himself for hours—eight, nine and ten at a stretch—to receiving the communications which were written by his hand. It became a passion with him. After a time he found that there was no necessity for him to use a pen as his hand would automatically trace the characters in the air, and he could read them wherever he might be. This after a time was succeeded by a further form of development, when he became partially entranced, and would talk under control when he was either wholly unconscious or only partially conscious. Thus by gradually sapping the mind, the invisible Intelligence which had established itself as his control, gradually gained such complete possession of his faculties that, as he said, "I no longer felt I belonged to myself. It dominates me by its will, and I do not know what the end will be."

He spoke quietly, with simple earnestness, as of a man caught in the grip of a mighty, invisible force which was bearing him irresistibly down into the abyss against which it was in vain even to struggle. I said to him at once that he had been frightfully reckless, that the one condition of safety in all such experiments was never to abandon the control of your own personality to that of any agency whatever, and that he must break with it once and for all.

He smiled sadly. "It is all very well to talk about my giving him up, but he won't give me up," said he.

"But," said I, "did the agency itself never warn you as to consequences of this frightful over-indulgence?"

"Ah!" said he, "it is not a good spirit. It is a very bad one that sticks to me, not for my good but for my harm, and I cannot shake it off."

"Nonsense!" I said. "It is all a matter of will."

"Yes," said he, "that may be, but he dominates my will. I cannot stand up against him, and he tells me that now he has got me he will never let me go until he has killed me."

"This is madness," said I; "he may tell you that a thousand times, but it is only because you give in to it."

"But," said he, "how can I help it? He seizes me when he pleases. He jerks my head from one side to the other, or forces me to go here and there at his own caprice; nay, he will suddenly drive me as it were out of himself, extinguishing my own consciousness and taking possession of my body, using it as his own."

"Do you mean to say you cannot stay him?" said I.

"No!" said he; "he has such power over me, he uses me just as if my body were his and not mine."

"But you must stop that, and at once. Otherwise you are lost."

"Yes," he said, mournfully. "I am afraid I am; at least he says so. He says that he will do me all the evil he can while I live, and that after, I am to be damned. But," said he, "will you speak to him?"

"Certainly," said I. "Will he take possession of you now?"

"At any time," he replied.

I paused for a moment; but I thought that as the Evil Spirit was in the habit of seizing him without his will at all times and to his own detriment, it would be permissible to allow him to enter in by an act of his own volition when he was with one who might possibly be the means of helping in his deliverance; so I said, "Yes, if he will talk he may come."

My visitor walked across the room and sat down without saying a word in a large easy chair. In a moment he became convulsed, his eyes closed, he fell backwards with his head on the couch, his chest heaved, rising and falling, while his body writhed as if convulsed. Not a word was said. I stood watching him silently, nor did he speak or make a sound beyond a low moan when the convulsions became more violent. After waiting for two or three minutes standing over him, I at last said, "Well!"

Then there was another writhing movement of the prostrate form before me, and a very curious voice, quite different from that of my visitor, said to me,

"Well! A b—— queer fellow it is, is it not?"

"Who are you?" I said.

"I will tell you," said he, as the body was more violently contorted. "I will tell you. I am the grandfather of a girl, that d—— carcass . . ." Then he writhed again and the voice ceased.

"Come," I said sharply; "why can't you talk decently and tell me who you are and what you want? Will you talk to me?" I said.

"Yes," said he, and then with another shuddering convulsion he raised himself upon the chair, and said,

"Yes, I will tell you. I am the grandfather of a girl who was a d—— pretty girl, whom this b—— carcass, ugh . . ."

Once more the convulsions recommenced, and he flung himself back with his head on the couch writhing and moaning.

"Come, come," I said; "why do you play the fool like that? Sit up straight and talk to me like a gentleman."

He continued, however, lying as he was.

"Talk to you respectably?" said he. "Talk to you like a gentleman, and this d—— carcass . . ."

His head jerked backwards violently over the side of the chair. Then he was silent for a moment, apparently collecting himself.

He said, "I like to do that, it hurts him; it hurts this old carcass, doesn't it, ugh." Then he struck himself a violent blow on the chest. The face twinged with pain. "Does it not hurt him? I like to do it. I am going to kill him, kill him; yes, kill him. D—— him, d—— him!"

"Nonsense," I said. "You will not kill him, or do anything of the kind."

"Won't I, though! You will see. He knows. He dare not shave himself for fear he will cut his throat. Ho! I have got him. I have got him."

I replied, "What is the meaning of all this? Who are you? Why have you got him? And what is it all to you? Can't you speak straight and tell me without all this?"

"Are you a father?" he said. "You can understand then what I feel towards this brute. Ugh! How I loathe having to touch him. I only do it to torment him. Well, you know my granddaughter."

"What about your granddaughter?"

"Pretty girl, very pretty girl. Well this brute . . ."

He writhed again.

"What about her? What happened?"

"He made love to her for four months. For four months he did, d——
him, and for four months I have had him. I have tortured him night and
day, and for four months more I will make his life horrible. Oh, yes, I will
cut his throat, I will, and he will be damned for ever, and serve him
right."

"Now," I said, "how dare you talk like this? You are only making your
own torment worse."

"What do I care? I would willingly be tormented for eternity to have
the joy of punishing him."

"But," I said, "what right have you?"

"Right!" said he. "Listen. My granddaughter, a lady, girl of good
family, one of the best families. Oh, yes! and this d—— carcass came
along, made love to her he did. Such a nice young man! D—— fool, don't
you know—always says 'Don't you know'—came along and made love to
her."

"Did he marry her?"

"Wanted to," said he. "Would now if he could get the chance, but he
never will. He will never see her again. Don't know what would happen.
D—— swine, he is as ugly as sin; ugly, yes. Yet, she is such a fool that if
she saw him again I don't know what would happen. They will never
meet again. Never! Never! I take care of that."

"But," I said, "what is the matter? He wanted to marry her, made love
to her. There is no wrong in that. I can't understand. Did he ruin . . ."

"Ruined her. Seduced her. Lived with her for four months. Nobody
knew. Nobody. Then she turned round and sent him away. She said, 'You
have made me a beast. I will have nothing more to do with you.' And he
goes, the wretch, the carcass."

Again there was a convulsion. The breast heaved, and again he struck
himself a heavy blow on the chest, writhing with passion, and continued,

"I can do anything with him now. Anything. He is mine, altogether. I
make him go where I like, talk to him when I like; night and day torment
him. Keep it up. O! yes, keep it up. And in four months cut his throat."
And as he said so, he drew his hand across his neck, making a hideous
gurgling sound in his throat.

"Nothing can save him," he said. "Nothing."

"You are quite wrong," I said. "You have no business to torment him in
this way whatever wrong he has done, and he will turn you out."

"Turn me out! Ho! Ho!" he cried out. "The other day he called on God to have mercy on him. Did I not laugh? He did not talk much to God before I took him in hand. No! he is mine and I keep him."

"But," I said, "where is the girl now? Would he marry her now?"

"Of course he would. But she won't have him, and he will never get the chance. Never! never!"

"How long have you been on the other side?"

"Fifty years!" he said. "Fifty years."

"In fifty years," said I, "you ought to have made better progress than to be giving way to all this hideous passion. What have you been doing all the time?"

"I have been in Hell," said he. "In Hell, tormented, going about everywhere, doing this kind of thing."

"But," I said, "are you all alone?"

"Yes, all alone."

"Well," I said, "how did you come to get hold of him?"

"Listen," said he. "I was an officer in the army in my time, and I think I ruined more women than any man I know. Then I came over here, and for fifty years what have I had to do but to go about seeing girls, pretty girls, falling in love with them, not being able to speak to them. What could they do to me? What could I do to them? I could not touch them, but the desire was there all the time, and I go about seeing it all. Tormented with desire that could never be satisfied, and then to go and see my relations doing as I did. My granddaughter, to see her ruined! D—— him! d——! and he will be d——. Oh curse it!" he said, striking his head against the edge of the couch, "to think of it, this carcass, oh this carcass. But I will pay him out. Four months more, night and day, night and day, and then to be d—— with him for ever. That is good." And he laughed a hideous, hollow laugh.

"But," I said, "is there no one to care for you at all?"

"None!" he said, "no."

"But," I said, "you must have loved many women."

"Seduced them, you mean," he said. "They are in Hell, all in Hell. Do you think they love me? No, they curse me."

"No," I said, "I don't believe they are in Hell, and if they were—women are very good, and some of them must have loved you."

"No; none!"

"But," I persisted, "you are quite wrong. No one knows how deep, how great is a woman's love. But did you never do an unselfish thing in your life?"

"Never! never! I pleased myself."

"Poor wretch," I said. "I am awfully sorry for you."

A violent convulsion shook the frame of my unfortunate visitor.

"Don't," he said, in a ghastly grating voice. "Don't pity me! Don't pity me. I can't bear it."

"But I do pity you," I said. "I am awfully sorry for you. It must be ghastly to go on like this."

"I don't want pity, I want vengeance, and I am taking it now. Don't I take it out of him, and won't I take it out of him?"

"No," I said, "you have taken enough out of him. You will have to go."

"Who will make me go?"

"He will."

"He has no will."

"May I ask you a question?"

"Yes," said he, "ask what you like."

"Did you approve of him coming here?"

"No," said he, "that I did not."

"Then," I said, "why did he come?"

"Because," he said, speaking as if with reluctance, "because in what that d—— fellow calls his mind—*his* mind . . . it is mine, not his—there is one little bit that sometimes makes him do what he pleases."

"Then," I said, "that means he came here in spite of you."

"That is it," he said. "He did," writhing and making horrible faces. His lips would be protruded until they almost became like a pig's snout, not round, but with a circular protrusion very hideous to see.

"Well," I said, "the same will that brought him here against you will drive you out."

"Ha! ha!" said he. "Never! never! He is mine. I can do with him what I like. I say to Carcass, turn your head to the right, he turns it. Lay it on the right shoulder, he lays it. I turn his head right round. I say, Carcass, turn to the right! he does; to the left, he does. I can use his body as I please, this d—— carcass, it is mine."

"How did you gain possession of it?"

"I will tell you," he said. "Listen. There is some b—— nonsense called spiritualism. He tried with the Ouija Board, got answers from somebody, then thinks he will try handwriting. Takes a pen. I see him, I see him. I am passing, I see what he is doing. Remember about my granddaughter. Pretty girl, pretty girl, and this d—— ugly carcass."

"Never mind that. Go on."

"I wait, I think I can get at him. So one day he thinks he will try automatic handwriting. Takes a pen in his b—— old fist, ugh!" and he writhed. "I took his hand and wrote. Called myself 'Lucy,' I did. Lucy, nice girl, always said her prayers, beautiful spirit; come to lead him into the paths of virtue. Ho! did I not fool him! I wrote, 'Your perseverance is rewarded.' Then I tell him. What do I tell him? Oh! I write with his hand and tell him everything that he thinks is only known to himself about his girl and himself. He writes and writes for hours together. I torture him by everything that I can think of to give him pain, even when I am 'Lucy,' then he goes on and on. B—— fool that he is; always say b—— fool, 'don't you know.' Nice young man; nice young officer. But at last I get hold of him, and he can't shake me off."

"Oh! yes he could," I said. "He could banish you by his will."

"He hasn't got one. I have it. It is mine. You see how I use his old carcass. I use it, I hate it, curse it!—I hate it! I have tortured him for four months; I will torture him for another four, then I will cut his throat!—yes, I will!"

"No," I said, "you won't! You will do nothing of the kind. What is more, now, you will have to clear out; you have been here quite long enough."

He did not speak again. A few convulsive movements followed, a long sigh, and then my visitor slowly rose to his feet, rubbing his eyes.

"Well," he said. "You see he can use me as he likes."

I said, "He has told me a great deal about you."

"What has he told you?" said he.

"He told me first about himself. He says he is the grandfather of a lady whom you ruined. Of course, I know nothing at all about it; I only tell you what he said."

He was silent.

"Well?" I said, "is there any truth in what he said?"

"Well, yes," he said, "I am afraid there is."

"Then," I said, "my friend, I think, you are in a position of great difficulty, for which it will be absolutely necessary for you to escape at once."

"But how can I?" said he.

"By simply declining to obey him," said I. "You can banish him if you will it."

"I can't. He comes and talks to me whether I like it or not; he uses my hand to write what he wishes to say in the air."

"But," I said, "the moment he begins to use your hand put it in your pocket."

"But he will talk to me."

"Then," I said, "don't answer him back; don't listen to him. You can't pull on with this any longer; you have to fight it tooth and nail, as if you were fighting for your immortal soul."

"Yes," he said. "I am fighting for my life. I know that perfectly well. I dare not shave now."

"Yes," said I. "He told me that. I told him it was all bosh. But the question is this. He has overrun your territory, but the citadel is still intact. You came here in spite of his will. Regard this as the turning point of your destiny. Never do anything he wants you to do; and every time you baffle him and assert your own will you weaken his forces and strengthen yourself."

"But," I said, "what about the lady?"

He said, "I don't wish to speak about her. She is not in this country. It is all off between us."

"But," I said, "would you marry her if you had the chance?"

"Would I not?" said he. "But she will not hear of it."

"How was it broken off?"

"O!" he said. "She had a great spasm of repentance, bitterly upbraided me, and would not see me any more."

"Does no one know about it?"

"No one but she and me."

"Well," I said; "if she really repented, as I have no doubt she has, she must help you to escape from this domination. You must tell her."

He seemed for a moment as if he were going to be controlled; then he said, with a shudder: "Do you know what he says to me now?—'I will kill you to-night if you do. Kill you to-night.' "

I will break off the narrative at this point. I saw my unknown visitor once again. His control was more blasphemous and more defiant than before. The convulsions were worse and the contortions more violent. It was a ghastly sight to see him writhing on the floor, tossed about until he was stiff and sore.

It may have been incipient insanity. It certainly was not fooling. When the control passed the victim was calm and sane. If it be madness it was madness resulting from excessive experimentalizing with spiritualism. But I wish any materialistic doctor would take the man in hand. He would, I am sure, be less scornful in his comments upon that "exploded superstition Demoniacal Possession." ("Mr. Carcass and His Obsessing Demon")

We do not know what ever became of Carcass. We do know that a year after the story of his possession was published, Henry James was at work on *The Turn of the Screw*. It is time we took a closer look at James's story and try to apply to a reading of it— particularly of its final scenes—what we have learned about the strange phenomenon of spirit possession. In doing so we shall have reason to refer again to some of these same people and to take an occasional glance at a number of other possessed people about whom Henry James might have read.

6
VOICES FROM OUTSIDE
AND FAR AWAY

Having seen what was generally known or believed about spirit mediums and demon possession, and having considered several examples of reportedly factual cases, we are ready to apply what we have learned about demons to a reading of *The Turn of the Screw*. In doing so, I have to make what many readers will consider to be a fatal assumption: that we can trust most of what the governess tells us about what happens at Bly. I am aware that readers who are convinced that the governess is insane or deluded will reject outright such an assumption. All I can ask from such readers is a temporary suspension of their disbelief. I am aware, also, that the validity of my reading will depend heavily on the slippery evidence of parallels between cases like those I have been citing and the events described by the narrator of *The Turn of the Screw*. Even though the evidence is slippery, that evidence is still worth presenting if we hope to approach something like an accurate or complete reading of the story.

I shall proceed by attempting to answer those eight questions I raised at the beginning of the fifth chapter, questions that the advocates of both the crazy-governess and the evil-ghost readings of the story have difficulty answering convincingly. In offering my own answers to those questions, I shall from time to time make reference to cases already presented and shall cite appropriate passages from relevant additional cases of demon possession. We shall consider Flora first.

FLORA ACROSS THE LAKE

Why does Flora go across the lake? Is it to find a few moments of respite from the stifling attentions of a lunatic governess? Is it to gather withered ferns? No. Flora goes because Miss Jessel compels her to go by taking possession of her body. The enslavement of the body of the living by the spirits of the dead is, of course, what possession is all about. Cases abound in examples of that enslavement. We have already seen—for example, in "Mrs. Blank and Her Enslaving Demon"—cases in which the possessing spirits literally enslave their victims, forcing them to do or say things they would never do or say in their normal state. Here is an example from another case:

That I, a man in the full vigor of health, should be a slave to this demon, is the trial of my life. ("Mr. Kwo and His Irresistible Demon")

Sometimes a dominant spirit enslaves not only the victim, but also other or conflicting spirits vying for control of the victim. The following case involves a ten-year-old girl:

This spirit spoke generally in the plural number, for he said she had another beside himself, a dumb devil, who plagued her most. "He it is that twirls her round and round, distorts her features, turns her eyes, locks her teeth, &c. What he bids me, I must do!" ("Miss Wildin and Her Raging Demon")

Cases of involuntary possession or spirit enslavement of children are reasonably frequent. The following case, for example, was reported in India (I cite only the opening of the case):

A young girl, who had attended a certain festival, on her return home, exhibited undoubted symptoms of involuntary possession. Up to that time her behaviour had been in all respects exemplary. The habits of a confirmed drunkard developed rapidly in her, and she, who had formerly been sober and industrious, degenerated into an idle and dissolute character. She was continually in a state of intoxication and all efforts to reform her proved ineffectual. . . . Her hair, which was very long, frequently touched the ground when she bent forward in her contortions, and before long it became a disheveled mass in which sticks, straws, and refuse of every description were entangled. The poor victim presented in truth a disgusting yet pitiable object. ("Miss Blank and Her Drunken Demon")

In a sense, saying that Flora crosses the lake because Miss Jessel

enslaves her and forces her to go merely begs the question of
motivation, for we are left wondering why Miss Jessel wants her
to cross the lake. Two cases we looked at in the last chapter
suggest possible motives on the part of the possessing demons. In
"Mrs. Blank and Her Enslaving Demon" the demons possess the
living because, as they put it, it is "the only fun" they have. In
"Mr. Carcass and His Obsessing Demon" the malicious invader
suggests that he does it for several reasons: to prevent Carcass
from rejoining his granddaughter; eventually to get revenge by
killing him; and "to torment . . . to have the joy of punishing
him." In an additional case the deceased former fiancée of an
unfortunate bridegroom possesses his bride on their wedding day
to let him know that she is a bit jealous:

On the night of the wedding and after the wedding ceremony, when most
of the guests had left the house, the bridal pair were conducted to their
apartments, and left to drink wine together, as is the custom with us in
our neighborhood. At this time the bride, changing to an unnatural
appearance, and with the voice and manner of the deceased daughter-in-
law Li, and a strength almost superhuman flew upon the unfortunate
bride-groom in a fury of passion, and seized him by the throat, exclaiming, "You never treated me in this fashion; you never gave me wine to
drink." ("Mrs. Chu and Her Jealous Demon")

Other cases suggest other motives. With Miss Jessel, however, we
are apparently meant to trust the governess's own intuition. She
speculates to Mrs. Grose, we recall, that Peter Quint and Miss
Jessel want to attract the children to them "for the love of all the
evil that, in those dreadful days, the pair put into them. And to
ply them with that evil still, to keep up the work of demons, is
what brings the others back" (p. 49). Later the governess says that
Miss Jessel wants Flora to join her and to suffer with her "the
torments of the damned" (p. 60). That motive fits well enough,
incidentally, with Frederic Myers's idea that the two ghosts have a
"natural desire" to carry the children off to hell (see the letter
printed at the end of chapter 3). There are hints that Miss Jessel's
motive is more specifically sinister and that she may intend for
Flora to drown, out of the sight of the governess and others, at the

far side of the pond. Mrs. Grose asks the governess if she thinks Flora is *in* the pond. The governess answers, "She may be, though the depth is, I believe, nowhere very great" (p. 68). I am aware of one reported case of possession in which a young man is driven by his demon to try to drown himself in a pond:

A Chefoo boy of fifteen was going on an errand. His path led through fields where men were working at their crops. When he came up to the men, and had exchanged a word or two with them, he suddenly began to rave violently; his eyes rolled, then he made for a pond which was near by. Seeing this, the people ran up to him, stopped him from drowning himself, and took him home to his parents. When he got home he sprang up from the ground to such a height as manifested almost superhuman strength. After a few days he calmed down and became unusually quiet and gentle; but his own consciousness was lost. The demon spoke of its friends in Nan King. After six months the demon departed and the boy recovered. ("Mr. Blank and His Drowning Demon")

The governess cannot *know,* of course, why Miss Jessel brings Flora alone to the lake, and it appears that Henry James wanted to leave Miss Jessel's motivation somewhat unspecified. There is no reason, however, to deny the possible motives the governess suggests or to deny that those motives are sufficient to cause the "pale and ravenous demon" (p. 71) to lead Flora across the lake. There is also no reason not to suppose that the arrival of the governess and Mrs. Grose frustrates whatever diabolic plans Miss Jessel might have had for Flora.

FLORA'S STRENGTH

How does Flora maneuver a boat that is too heavy for her? We should recall that when Henry James first wrote the story he was thinking of Flora as a highchair-and-bib child of six, an age that would make her action even more remarkable. The governess's explanation of Flora's "prodigious" feat is that "at such times she 's not a child: she 's an old, old woman" (p. 69) and we might recall that Mrs. Grose says that Flora is "every inch of her, quite old" (p. 74). What can this mean but that Flora is possessed by, and so has the strength of, an adult? It was a common phenomenon for possessed people to be unusually strong. We have just seen, in the passages cited from "Mrs. Chu and Her Jealous Demon" and "Mr. Blank and His Drowning Demon," references to the super-human strength of possessed people. And we have seen in the last chapter how Mary Roff, in one of her fits, could nearly overpower five strong men, even though she weighed a mere one hundred pounds herself and should have been even weaker than normal from loss of blood. There are many, many more instances of the superhuman strength of victims of possession. Here are three:

The first struggle took place in the person of her sister Catherine, who at times was possessed of such superhuman strength that it took several men to hold her. ("Miss Dittus and Her Strong Demon")

In the case of Rosina Wildin, aged ten years . . . the demon used to announce himself by crying out, "Here I am again!" Whereupon the weak exhausted child, who had been lying like one dead, would rage and storm in a voice like a man's, perform the most extraordinary movements and feats of violence and strength, till he would cry out, "Now I must be off again!" ("Miss Wildin and Her Raging Demon")

Her strength during such attacks was that of a maniac. The strength of a strong man was tried to the utmost to prevent her from injuring herself or others. ("Miss Linda and Her Demon Struggle")

FLORA'S UGLINESS

Why does Flora suddenly turn hideously ugly? The governess sees Flora come out of the woods. She asks Flora where Miss Jessel is—the first time the name of the previous governess has passed between them. At that moment the face of the lovely Flora undergoes a marked change. It takes on a "smitten glare . . . an expression of hard still gravity, an expression absolutely new and unprecedented"; it becomes a "mask," and her "childish beauty" vanishes; the "dreadful little face" turns "hideously hard . . . common . . . ugly" (pp. 71–73). How are we to account for this dramatic physical change? The answer would have been obvious enough to readers familiar with spirit possession, for facial changes were common in the reports. Oliver Lodge, for example, described Mrs. Piper's face as having taken on, during her trances "distinctly altered and hardened features."[1] We have seen, in "Mr. Carcass and His Obsessing Demon," a possessed man "making horrible faces . . . very hideous to see." Other demoniacs also underwent facial changes when they went into trance:

Whenever this demon wished to speak the countenance of the girl immediately and very strikingly changed, and each time presented a truly demoniacal expression. ("Miss B. and Her Blasphemous Demon")

The faces changed back when out of trance:

The transformation was astounding, from the disfigured demoniac countenance to a purely human, cheerful one. ("Miss Grombach and Her Demon Monk")

FLORA'S SPURNING OF THE GOVERNESS

Why does Flora so suddenly and so vehemently turn against the governess? The governess has, after all, done Flora no demonstrable ill and is eager only to do her good. Why then should Flora, who has up to then been a model and loving pupil, suddenly turn upon the governess with the cutting words, "I think you're cruel. I don't like you!" and then, with a "furious wail," demand that Mrs. Grose "take me away—oh take me away from *her*!" (p. 73)? Is it because Flora knows that the governess is dangerously crazy? Or is it because Flora is possessed by the spirit of Miss Jessel, who knows that her own corrupting influence is diminished by the proximity of the governess? My questions are of course rhetorical, but if we are not to think that those words come from Miss Jessel through the mouth of Flora, why does the governess tell us that "the wretched child had spoken exactly as if she had got *from some outside source* each of her stabbing little words" (p. 73, italics mine)? Perhaps Miss Jessel is

1. *PSPR* 6 (1889): 444.

like the demon in the sad case of "Mr. Carcass and His Obsessing Demon" who does not want his victim to visit William Stead. Perhaps Flora suddenly turns on the governess, her surrogate mother, for the same reason that, in "Mrs. Blank and Her Enslaving Demon," the mother "found herself compelled to say cruel and unkind things to her husband and daughter, whilst really devotedly attached to them." Possessed people were known suddenly and unaccountably to do verbal and sometimes physical injury to those who loved them most and whom they had reason to love most. Here is one more example:

My father hearing the state of things came from his home to see me. As he entered I seized a fowling-piece, which I had secreted under my bed, and fired it at him. ("Mr. Kwo and His Irresistible Demon")

FLORA'S SHOCKING LANGUAGE

Why does Flora use such shockingly vile language? Since the governess herself is not present to hear it and Mrs. Grose is too proper to repeat it, we never learn just what Flora says. But Mrs. Grose does report that Flora speaks "horrors" in "appalling language" that is "really shocking." It is so shocking that, just thinking of it, Mrs. Grose drops "with a sudden cry" and collapses on the sofa at "all the anguish of it" (p. 77). Why should such shocking language come from the mouth of a very young girl who has until then been so angelic and proper? My answer will be no surprise: the language is Miss Jessel's. Mrs. Grose has, after all, "heard some of it before!" (p. 77)—apparently from the former governess. Terrible, blasphemous language, uncharacteristic of the speaker in his or her normal state, is, as we have seen, one of the most characteristic features of the various reported cases of possession. Here are a few more corroborative citations:

A strange voice proceeded from her, which assumed to be that of an unblessed spirit, who had formerly inhabited a human form. Whilst these fits were on her, she entirely lost her own individuality, and became this person; on returning to herself, her understanding and character were as entire as before. The blasphemy and cursing, and barking and screeching, were dreadful. ("Mrs. Blank and Her Barking Demon")

On Monday, the twenty-first of January [Miss B., aged eleven] assumed a deep bass voice. . . . On the evening of the twenty-second of January another commenced to speak in a tone distinctly different from the aforementioned bass voice. . . . There was no confusion or incoherence in the words of the voice, but great consistency was shown in answering all the questions logically, or in skilfully evading them. But that which principally distinguished these sayings was their moral, or rather their immoral character. They expressed pride, arrogance, mockery, or hatred of truth, of God and of Christ. The voice would say, "I am the Son of God, the Saviour of the world—you must adore me," and immediately afterwards rail against everything holy—blaspheme against God, against Christ, and against the Bible; express a violent dislike towards all who follow what is good; give vent to the most violent maledictions a thousand times repeated. ("Miss B. and Her Blasphemous Demon")

From August 25th her struggles with the Black Spirit gradually became more violent, and he entered her body and spoke out of her mouth. . . . She lost consciousness and individuality. Her voice was no longer her own, but that of the monk's. The speeches which she uttered when in this state were worthy of a demon. ("Miss Grombach and Her Demon Monk")

He certainly exhibited . . . a duality of vocalisation, Mr. B. from time to time talking in his natural voice, and then suddenly—and often with blasphemous expressions utterly foreign to his natural disposition—in a totally different voice, and with a totally changed expression of countenance. ("Mr. B. and His Blasphemous Demon")

The unfortunate girl is . . . coarse and repulsive in her language and manner during the attack using oaths and other expressions foreign to the sensitive pure nature of her normal life. ("Mrs. Blank and Her Coarse Demon")

I am aware that Flora's shocking language cannot be considered proof that she is possessed. It could mean, for example, merely that she repeats language she remembers hearing Miss Jessel use. In all of these questions, we are speaking of possibilities, of suggestions, not of certainties.

These five questions about Flora as a possible victim of possession suggest still another: is she saved by being rescued from Bly at the end of the story? If I am right in my reading of the scene across the lake, then the decision to take Flora away from the governess is not, as many critics have suggested, a fortunate one. Far from saving Flora from the corrupting influence of a dangerous governess, the move plays precisely into the plans of the corrupting demon, Miss Jessel. Indeed, if I am right, it is Miss Jessel who, through Flora's mouth, demands that Flora be taken away from the governess, both at the lake and later, when alone with Mrs. Grose, who reports to the governess that Flora wants "never again to so much as look at you" (p. 75). In permitting Flora to leave the next day, the governess and Mrs. Grose seem unwittingly to participate in a demon-inspired plan that cannot augur well for Flora. Although certain ghosts were sometimes thought to be able or willing to haunt only certain specific locations, possessing spirits were able to follow their subjects at will. Phinuit, for example, was able to speak through Mrs. Piper not only in Boston but also in London and Liverpool. Sending Flora away from Bly will presumably be no more effective than sending Miles away to school. Peter Quint, after all, seems to have followed Miles to boarding school and then back again to Bly. We can then assume as well that Peter Quint would have followed Miles to the new school to which Miles asked to be sent so that he could get away from the governess and be with his "own sort" (p. 56).

It is now time to turn to Miles, to see whether a knowledge of demon possession helps us to make sense of certain puzzling questions about his behavior. It appears that the basic facts of possession are as applicable to Miles as they are to Flora, although the degree of possession may be quite different. Miles does not yield completely, as does the younger and more easily controlled Flora. Miles does not, for example, grow ugly in his final scene, and he does not speak, at least to the governess, openly blasphemous words. He seems, rather, to maintain at least partial self-control throughout that final scene, never yielding fully to the spirit of Peter Quint, who seeks to dominate his will. We shall come to that final scene in a moment. Let us first discuss an earlier incident that took place when Miles was somewhat younger and so perhaps less able to resist Peter Quint's domination.

MILES'S EXPULSION FROM SCHOOL

Why was Miles expelled from school? Just as we shall never know precisely what shocking things Flora said to Mrs. Grose, so we shall never know what shocking things Miles said to his friends at school. It is easy enough, however, to speculate that he said them while possessed by Peter Quint or, rather, that Peter Quint said them while possessing Miles. At any rate, Miles's inability to recall what he said or to whom he said it is characteristic of the victims of possession. I could cite numerous additional cases in which such victims have no recollection of what they said or did while under the spirit control of another, but the point has been sufficiently made already.

We must keep in mind that Miles might have done almost any terrible thing while possessed by the spirit of a man who, in life, had been prone to "strange passages and perils, secret disorders, vices more than suspected" (p. 28). Frederic Myers's supposition that Miles was "expelled from school for obscenity" (see full passage quoted at end of chapter 3) may be true. It may, however, greatly underestimate the nature of the offense. Even if we take into account the "victorian" prudishness of Victorian schoolmasters, it is difficult to imagine that a tuition-paying student would have been expelled for a few four-letter obscenities said to his friends, even if those friends were disloyal enough to report the incident to the school authorities. The governess herself, sheltered as she had been, seems to think that merely saying things to one's friends is not sufficient cause for expulsion. "Stuff and nonsense!" is all she can say when Miles "confesses" why he was expelled (p. 87). And if Miles merely had blurted out a few obscenities, it is difficult to understand why the schoolmaster would not have indicated as much in the letter of expulsion to Miles's Harley Street uncle. At any rate, if we are to understand that Miles's offense was really Peter Quint's offense, then of course our imaginations run as wild as Henry James apparently wanted them to, and we are free to conjure up any sort of offense that we think would have been bad enough to account both for Miles's expulsion and for the headmaster's silence about the reasons for that expulsion.

We must also realize that Miles's statement that he "said things" to "those I liked" (pp. 86–87) may not be Miles's statement at all, but Peter Quint's. Let us recall the scene. The governess has just asked Miles whether he took her letter. Her question to Miles, like her earlier lakeside question to Flora about the whereabouts of Miss Jessel, is a direct question about possible wrongdoing. And just as the governess's direct question to Flora had earlier seemed to bring on Miss Jessel's appearance to the governess and her possession of Flora, so this question to Miles seems to bring on Peter Quint's appearance to the governess and his possession of Miles. As soon as she asks her question the "white face of damnation" appears at the window and the governess senses that she is "fighting with a demon for a human soul" (p. 85). Miles apparently senses the same struggle, for he becomes pale and feverish, reminding us of the physical symptoms that sometimes accompany trance situations. Then Miles speaks. The governess, however, does not say that he "speaks." Rather, she refers to "a sound" that came from Miles, "not low nor weak, but as if *from much further away*." The sound says that Miles took the letter. A moment later, when the governess asks Miles if he stole at school, Miles appears to have trouble concentrating and "to be thinking of something *far off*." When she asks him what he did do, if not steal, Miles answers as if he is "standing *at the bottom of the sea*" (pp. 85–86, italics mine). Why does James tell us that Miles speaks from so far away, if not to suggest that Miles's words in that scene are not his own, but Peter Quint's? And if they are Peter Quint's, then of course Miles's confession that he "said things" is not his confession at all, but one that Peter Quint puts into his mouth, possibly as a means of diverting the governess's attention from more serious offenses or of preventing Miles from making a true confession of the sort that might allow him to throw off the controlling influence of Peter Quint.

Returning then to the original question, Miles does not know and therefore cannot tell us what big or little crimes he committed, while possessed by Peter Quint, at school. Peter Quint probably knows but is unwilling to reveal, through Miles, the full story. We are left to imagine any terrible thing we want to, any terrible thing that Peter Quint, for the love of all evil, was capable of doing.

MILES'S DEATH

What kills Miles? This is one of the crucial questions of the story, a question even more perplexing than the question of why Miles was expelled from school. The answers that have been proposed vary in detail, but they cluster around two poles: choking and fright. If it is choking, then the killer is the governess, who chokes Miles either accidentally in some sort of seizure or deliberately to prevent Miles from tattling to his uncle. If it is not choking, then Miles dies of some sort of sudden fright or heart attack. I should like to propose a third alternative: Miles dies from the violence of dispossession.

I would point out, first of all, that Miles's death is not so sudden as most critics make it out to be. A close look at the last two chapters of *The Turn of the Screw* shows that Miles becomes *progressively* more and more agitated, nervous, and sick, that his condition *gradually* worsens. When we look at the signals by which Henry James reveals the approaching death of Miles, we cannot help noticing that those signals are keyed to the governess's requests for information—that is, for a confession—in that final interview in the dining room. The left-hand column below shows statements the governess makes and questions she asks just before Miles shows the growing signs of illness, which we see quoted in her description of him in the right-hand column. All quotations are taken, in order, from the last two chapters of the story (pp. 82–88). The scene begins, we recall, with the end of dinner and with Miles looking "not comfortable . . . anxious" through the window:

"What else should I stay on for [but your company]?"	The expression of his face, graver now . . .
"Don't you remember how I told you . . . that there was nothing in the world I would n't do for you?"	more and more visibly nervous . . .
"Out, straight out."	quiver of resentful passion . . .
"There could n't be a better place or time."	uneasily . . . the approach of . . . fear . . .
"You want to go out again?"	flushing with pain . . .
"Tell me if . . . you took . . . my letter."	a perfect dew of sweat . . . as white as the face against the glass . . . the sudden fever . . . the tremendous pulse . . .
"You opened the letter?"	the ravage of uneasiness . . .
"And you found nothing!"	his forehead . . . was drenched . . .
"What, then, did you do?"	vague pain . . . drew his breath, two or three times over, as if with difficulty . . .
"And did they repeat what you said?"	still breathing hard . . . unspeakable anxiety . . .
"The masters? They did n't— they 've never told. That 's why I ask you."	fevered face . . .
"It's *there*—the coward horror."	a frantic little shake for air and light . . . a white rage . . .
"Whom do you mean by 'he'?"	convulsed supplication . . .
"There, *there*!"	jerked straight round . . . uttered the cry of a creature hurled over the abyss . . . his little heart, dispossessed, had stopped.

And *then* Miles is dead. It is anything but a sudden death. It takes seven pages of anxiety, fear, pain, fever, paleness, racing pulse, shaking, sweating, convulsion, and suffocation. One does not need to be a doctor to see that Miles's death is a gradual thing, not a sudden choking, suffocation, or paroxysm of fear. And if it is a gradual thing, the usual explanation of a sudden paroxysm of fear or of a violent choking will not hold, and we are left to consider whether what we see in that final scene is Miles's gradual dispossession of the controlling spirit of Peter Quint.

One of the more curious phenomena in the history of criticism of *The Turn of the Screw* is that readers have for the most part ignored the implications of the word *dispossessed* in the final sentence. It is the governess's word, of course, but we must assume that James chose it carefully for her. Given the common use of the word in contexts relating to possible interactions between the living and the dead, and given Henry James's own personal knowledge of the mediumship of Mrs. Piper, it is puzzling that so many readers simply pass over the word. Those who do not pass over it tend to give it quite surprising meanings. Matheson, for example, trying to prove that the insane governess smothers Miles, transforms its meaning into "dispossessed of air."[2] In light of all that we have been saying in this and the previous chapter, is it not more likely that *dispossessed* means that the possessing demon has departed and that the violence of dispossession has robbed Miles of his life?

What kills spirit-possessed people in the various reported cases? First, we must recognize that in reported cases of demon possession the victims almost never die in the course of the narrative. One reason may be that one of the few proofs of possession is that the possessed person becomes dispossessed and thus becomes *living* evidence that he or she is not simply insane. The victims of possession in the reported cases usually somehow outgrow or outlive their possession, or resist their possessor and free themselves. In many cases reported by people of

2. Terence J. Matheson, "Did the Governess Smother Miles? A Note on James's *The Turn of the Screw*," 174. More recently, JoAnn P. Kreig, "A Question of Values: Culture and Cognition in *The Turn of the Screw*," p. 152, says that the line means that Miles's mind has been "dispossessed of its intellectual freedom."

the church, the possessing demon is exorcised by one of a half-dozen methods, Christian or other. Occasionally we find reports of the death of possessed persons, but these tend to be general reports, not specific cases. Nevius, for example, reports that a Baptist missionary in Chefoo had reported the following about Chinese and Mongolian people possessed by demons:

This infliction comes on very suddenly, sometimes in the day, sometimes in the night. The demoniac talks madly, smashes everything near him, acquires unusual strength, tears his clothes into rags, and rushes into the street, or to the mountains, or kills himself unless prevented. After this violent possession the demoniac calms down and submits to his fate; but under the most heart-rending protests. These mad spells which are experienced on the demon's entrance, return at intervals, and increase in frequency, and generally also in intensity, so that death at last ensues from their violence.[3]

And here is an almost humorous report from India showing that death can result from a primitive kind of exorcism:

Occasionally flogging is resorted to, to induce the spirit to depart—the theory being that the blows *repercuss* on the ethereal body of the possessing entity. This method is, however, not always attended with the happiest results, the involuntary mediums having in some cases been thrashed so severely that they have died![4]

Some modern readers of *The Turn of the Screw* come close to accusing the governess of either physically or emotionally flogging Miles to death. West suggests, for example, that she kills him with "psychopathic compulsive violence" or at least engages in "an exuberant debauch of violence that contributes to the sudden death of little Miles" (note the adjective *sudden*).[5] And more recently, Renner says that Miles is destroyed because he is "trapped in the psychosexual undertow of the mother-son relationship."[6]

Most critics, however, prefer the theory that Miles somehow

3. Nevius, *Demon Possession*, 64.
4. *Borderland* 4 (1897): 411.
5. Muriel West, "The Death of Miles in *The Turn of the Screw*," 187–88.
6. Stanley Renner, "Sexual Hysteria," 194.

dies "of fright." Such a view is not without some support in cases involving ghosts, as distinguished from possessing demons. Mysterious deaths were sometimes vaguely attributed to the shock of seeing or hearing ghosts of one kind or another. This case, for example, involved a child of five:

"Well," I said, "she has been dreadfully frightened," and I thought, but did not say, if she dies, it will be as much from fright as any other cause. A few days after, I was called away to a very important case. My little patient lived only two or three days after my departure. More than once since then I have asked myself this question, "Was she frightened to death"? ("Mrs. H.'s Nurse and the Lady at the Partition")

In the following case a boy of thirteen was thought perhaps to have died of fright from having heard a ghost:

One night in September, 1879, when H. T., a boy of thirteen, had been ill for many months, and was sleeping in the back dining-room, with Mrs. T. in the same room to attend upon him, they both heard a noise as of a door opening into a third room on the dining-room floor being opened, and the window of that room being thrown open. The door then banged, and a match was heard to be struck outside. All the household were upstairs in bed, and the boy became ill with fright. . . . From this time, until the date of the boy's death, a fortnight or three weeks afterwards, the noises were louder than at any other time, and disturbed the boy's rest at night. ("Mr. T. and the Ghosts in West Brompton")

A girl of seventeen was also thought to have died of fright in this case:

On one occasion when she was left alone in the house she saw the shadow of a man on the blind. . . . Since then she had several times at night said she had seen the ghost of her cousin, who has been dead about two years. . . . Dr. Alford gave it as his opinion, having heard the history of the excitement from which the girl suffered, that she died in a fainting fit brought on by excessive fright—in short, that she died from syncope. The jury returned a verdict accordingly. ("Miss Bishop and the Ghost of Her Cousin")

Cases such as these, in which the death of children may possibly be caused by the presence of ghosts, may somewhat parallel Miles's death. For a number of reasons, however, the parallels do not convince me that Miles, by analogy, might also have died of fright. First, in each of these cases the children were ill before the ghosts came, not after; Miles is not ill before the scene in which he dies. Second, these other children die after—some days after—seeing or hearing a ghost; Miles not only dies that very evening, but he also apparently never sees or hears a ghost.

Two special features of Miles's death—his convulsions and his scream—find many parallels in reports of the behavior of those undergoing either possession or dispossession. Let us consider first Miles's convulsions. James has the governess three times in the last twenty-five lines of the story use words suggesting that Miles shakes convulsively: his head gives "a frantic little shake for air and light"; his face gives a "convulsed supplication"; and his body is "jerked straight round" (p. 88). In describing Miles thus, James would have reminded readers familiar with demon possession of one of the most common symptoms of possession. We need not seek far for examples. One observer described Mrs. Piper going into a trance in this way: "Her fingers began to twitch and then her whole body, and she groaned and ground her teeth."[7] Stead uses some form of the word *convulsion* several times in describing the behavior of Carcass. For example, when Carcass goes into possession, "in a moment he became convulsed . . . his body writhed as if convulsed . . . the convulsions became more violent . . . another shuddering convulsion." When Carcass comes out of his trance he also gives "a few convulsive movements." Here are other descriptions of the convulsions that accompany a victim's going into, or coming out of, possession:

Margaret B., at eleven, of lively disposition, but a godly, pious child was on the nineteenth of January, 1829, without having been previously ill, seized with convulsive attacks. ("Miss B. and Her Blasphemous Demon")

A child suffering from spasms of choking. . . . Presently there were added convulsive agonies frightful to witness. ("Miss Linda and Her Demon Struggle")

7. *PSPR* 6 (1889): 101.

She fell into convulsions, which sometimes lasted as long as four hours. ("Miss Dittus and Her Strong Demon")

She was seized with the most extraordinary convulsions. ("Mrs. Blank and Her Barking Demon")

In some cases the convulsions accompanying possession or dis-possession are referred to in somewhat different terms, but they are nonetheless a relatively common feature. The following instance is taken from M. J. Williamson's *Modern Diabolism,* a book Henry James might well have been familiar with:

This time there occurred violent palpitation of the heart, at least I know not what else to call it, but my whole breast heaved with *terrible* violence and rapidity. Some one said, "You are going, sir," and, for a few moments, I thought I was dying. ("Mr. Williamson and His Unwanted Spirits")

Involuntary cries, like convulsions, sometimes accompanied the transition between possession and dispossession. There are numerous parallels with Miles's final cry. In cases of demon possession these are associated with both going into and coming out of a trance of possession. We recall, for example, that Mrs. Piper "groans" when going into her trance, and that Carcass utters a "low moan" when going into his trance and a "long sigh" when coming out. In other reported cases the sound is more pronounced:

Suddenly his young son was possessed by a demon, writhed in agony, . . . and with a loud cry fell down insensible. ("Mr. Hieh and His Agonizing Demon")

One night after hours of prayer Blumhardt commanded the demon to come forth, when a fearful outcry was heard by hundreds of people penetrating to a great distance. ("Miss Dittus and Her Strong Demon")

Some victims of possession utter these involuntary cries both upon being possessed and upon being dispossessed. The following case demonstrates not only the two cries, but also a parallel with Miles's fear of an unseen presence. Concerning this last similarity, we should recall Miles's "looking through the haunted pane for something he could n't see," his looking round the room "uneasily," and his look of "fear" (pp. 82–84) as he comes closer to his decision to talk openly with the governess:

In the year 1871, or 1872, the following experiences were met with in the village of Chu-mao in the district of Ping-tu. There was a native school there in which was a boy named Liu, about twelve years of age, who was supposed to be at times possessed by an evil spirit. When the attacks occurred he would start and cry out with fear, as if conscious of some unseen presence, and then fall down insensible. On these occasions a woman in the village who was believed to be a spirit-medium, or exorcist, was immediately sent for. On the recurrence of one of these attacks another of the pupils ran to call the exorcist. On his way he met a man named Liu Chong-ho, who had recently been to Teng-chow fu, as an "enquirer," and had, after studying the Scriptures there for a month or more, been baptized. On learning the boy's errand he told him not to summon the exorcist; and at once returned with him to the school. Requiring all the pupils to kneel with him, he earnestly called on Jesus for help. Then turning to the prostrate boy he said in almost Scriptural words: "I command you in the name of Jesus Christ to come out of him!" The boy uttering a piercing cry, was at once restored to conscious-ness. . . . When the boy above referred to was interrogated as to the reason for his crying out, he said it was because the spirit in leaving him hurt him. ("Mr. Liu and His Evil Demon")

The shakes, convulsions, jerks, and cries that so often accom-pany the passage into or out of trance do not usually signal death, as they do for Miles. But sometimes they do. There was at least one case on record in which, apparently, it did. I am referring to the most famous case of them all, Mary Roff's. It is pertinent to note that during her fits Mary Roff would "twitch" and exhibit various degrees of convulsive behavior. Her death took place during such a fit, and like Miles, she cried out just before death. Here is how Stevens words it in his widely disseminated booklet:

On July 5th, 1865, while her parents were at Peoria, Ill., on a three days' visit, she ate a hearty breakfast, and soon thereafter lay down on her bed, and in her usual health went to sleep. In a few minutes she was heard to scream, as was usual on taking a fit. On approaching her bedside, they found her in a fit, and in a few moments she expired.[8]

What does all this prove? It proves nothing, conclusively, but these various parallels do seem to hold clues, for readers aware of the behavior of people going into or coming out of trances, that Miles dies not because he is frightened and not because the governess chokes him but because of the wrenching physical and spiritual violence of dispossession.

I should like to cite one more case of what might be called a cry of dispossession followed immediately by death. This one is different from the others I have cited because it appeared in a piece of fiction, not in a factual report. I feel justified in citing it, however, because the fiction is a short story by Henry James. "Sir Edmund Orme," published in 1891, ends with the death of Mrs. Marden, a distraught mother who has been tormented by the ghost of a rejected lover. At the moment of Mrs. Marden's death, the narrator of the story, a young man who has been courting Mrs. Marden's daughter, hears a sound like "the wail of one of the lost." The narrator wonders whether the dying woman makes the sound or whether, as he thinks more likely, the spirit of Sir Edmund Orme makes it. The narrator puts it this way: "Was the sound I heard . . . the despairing cry of the poor lady's death-shock or the articulate sob (it was like a waft from a great storm) of the exorcised and pacified spirit? Possibly the latter, for that was mercifully the last of Sir Edmund Orme."[9] And there the story ends, with typical Jamesian ambiguity. "Sir Edmund Orme"— written shortly after James read his brother's Piper letter—is a suggestive preview of several motifs later to appear in *The Turn of the Screw.* I call attention here only to the mournful wail of an "exorcised" spirit at the death of the living person troubled by that spirit. Although Mrs. Marden does not appear to be spirit-possessed in the way that I have suggested Flora and Miles at times are, the term *exorcised* is a companion-term to *dispossessed.* A living person is dispossessed; a spirit is exorcised. Is it too much to

8. Stevens, *Watseka,* 6.
9. Henry James, *Stories of the Supernatural,* ed. Leon Edel, 172–73.

suggest that in having the spirit of Sir Edmund Orme exorcised as a cry is uttered, Henry James was writing a kind of preview of an ambiguous scene for a later and more powerful story in which Miles is dispossessed as a similar cry is emitted?

MILES'S SALVATION

Is Miles "saved" by the governess at the end? That can be several questions. To the question "does the governess save Miles?" the answer is that she does not. She tries to, and she perhaps thinks she does, but I see little evidence that she does more than set the stage for salvation by encouraging him to try to answer certain questions. If we cannot hold the governess responsible for Miles's death, neither can we credit her with having saved him. She is more of an observer, a witness, than an effective force for change. To the question "does Miles enter the kingdom of God forever?" I have no answer to propose. There is little evidence for an answer, and no evidence that Henry James meant for us to ask the question, at least in that way. But if the question is "does Miles free himself from demonic influences?" then James has given us the raw materials for an affirmative answer. Miles's death is not an entirely unfortunate thing, and we have reason to complete our reading of the story feeling horrified that Miles has died but also pleased that he has shown the strength to repudiate the blighting influence of Peter Quint.

The very fact that Miles exhibits those convulsive shakes and jerks just before his death may tell us that he is trying to resist or fend off the force that attempts to possess or control him. Nevius, the missionary who was at first skeptical about the possibility of demon possession and who later wrote a book describing it in action, has something to say about the "paroxysms," as he called them, that accompanied the act of going into or coming out of possession. Having studied a large number of cases, Nevius summarizes the "facts" about demon possession. The third of those facts has to do with what Nevius called the "transition" between the states of possession and dispossession:

During transition from the normal to the abnormal state, the subject is often thrown into paroxysms, more or less violent, during which he sometimes falls on the ground senseless.[10]

For our purposes, however, the more interesting fact is Nevius's fifth one:

During the transition period the subject often retains more or less of his normal consciousness. The violence of the paroxysms is increased if the subject struggles against, and endeavors to repress the abnormal symptoms. When he yields himself to them the violence of the paroxysms abates, or ceases altogether.[11]

The more a victim resists the transitional symptoms, the more violent are the paroxysms. The more yielding the victim is, the less violent they become.

Most critics would agree that Miles struggles. I contend, however, that he struggles not against the governess who attempts to smother or choke him, but against Peter Quint who attempts to dominate his will and control his actions. Such struggles are commonplace in the reported cases of demonic possession. Perhaps the most enlightening case is that of Carcass, the weak young man who wants desperately to be free of his possessing demon and who even comes to William Stead in what appears to be a desperate plea for help. Here is Stead's advice to him: "You can banish him if you will it. . . . You have to fight it tooth and nail, as if you were fighting for your immortal soul. . . . Every time you baffle him and assert your own will you weaken his forces and strengthen yourself." It appears that Carcass lacks the strength of will or character to fight the battle successfully, but the battle, the struggle of wills, is unmistakable. More successful is the mother in "Mrs. Blank and Her Enslaving Demon." In her "silent battle for life, liberty, and love," this stalwart woman learns to resist her demon, thereby fighting "her battle to victory."

10. Nevius, *Demon Possession*, 143–44.
11. Ibid., 144.

The concept of a battle or a struggle of the will was common in cases of demon possession. Here are two more examples:

The battle had raged for a year when I first met Linda, and was introduced to her parents. I soon became intensely interested, for I found that I was watching a battle between invisible giants for possession of a young maiden just budding into womanhood. . . . Presently at all hours she not only sensed the struggle, but it produced spasmodic contractions of the muscles of her arms and limbs that were very painful. ("Miss Linda and Her Demon Struggle")

He certainly exhibited all the phenomena of diabolical possession . . . above all the strange duality of consciousness with a struggle between the two wills. ("Mr. B. and His Blasphemous Demon")

Does Miles win his struggle? Does he, by asserting his will, cast off the influence of Peter Quint and thus save himself before he dies? The answer lies in an interpretation of Miles's closing epithet: "Peter Quint—you devil!" (p. 88) What is the antecedent of the pronoun *you*? Many critics argue, not without some persuasiveness, that because Miles is directly answering the governess's question ("Whom do you mean by 'he'?"), the *you* refers to her. Thus, vexed by her prodding, the anguished Miles, just before he dies, turns on the governess by calling her a devil. On the other hand, some critics argue that Miles's *you* refers to the closer antecedent, "Peter Quint." Thus, vexed by Peter Quint's poisonous presence, Miles hurls his dying condemnation at his former friend by spurning him and calling him a devil. Still other critics argue that the ambiguity is intentional, and that both referents are equally and simultaneously valid.

There is some merit to arguments that tales of the supernatural require a measure of ambiguity if they are to maintain the sense of mystery that gives them their power. It is entirely possible, then, that Henry James may have intended a measure of ambiguity about the referent of "devil." Miles, however, is not ambiguous about his own intentions. He does not, after all, say "you devils!" Miles knows what devil he refers to, and our initial job as readers is to try to determine whom *Miles* meant by the singular "you devil!" It is he, after all, whose triumph or defeat we are trying to determine.

I cannot accept the view that Miles means to call the governess a devil. He has, for one thing, no motive for doing so. If Miles at that moment is strongly possessed by the spirit of Peter Quint and therefore is not responsible for words that come out of his mouth, then he might, like Flora the day before, want to condemn her. But why would Peter Quint, speaking through Miles's mouth, name "Peter Quint" as the coward horror in answer to the governess's question? No, Miles never fully yielded to Peter Quint's control that evening in the dining room. If he had, he would presumably not be with the governess at all now, let alone trying to answer her questions about certain compromising behaviors in his own past. He would rather, like Flora under the control of Miss Jessel, have removed himself from her presence.

Unlike Flora, however, Miles seeks out the governess when he does not need to and stays with her longer than he is required to. Miles seems to know that the governess has been kind to him, and wants only what is best for him. Surely the governess *has* been kind to Miles. She welcomed him to Bly, offered him security, friendship, approval, help, and even love. She refrained from pressing him earlier about delicate subjects. She respected his right to have his own room. And she just recently gave him total freedom from her. Critics who refer to the governess as Miles's "jailer," neurotic or otherwise, seem to forget that Miles "had his freedom now" (p. 74, and again on p. 80). Even Miles admits, on the evening of his death, that "I've never been so free" (p. 82). What does Miles do with his freedom? He joins the governess by the fire the night after her traumatic scene across the lake with Flora: "He wanted, I felt, to be with me" (p. 74). And the next night he stays with the governess in the dining room long after he is free to excuse himself. Miles engages in a battle with his demon, then, not because the governess forces him to or refuses to let him go, but because he *wants* to. He wants to stay and stay, and talk and talk. When questions get too close to forbidden subjects, such as stealing and expulsion from school, Peter Quint shows up to provide his answers, but Miles never yields full control to his demon. With the help and support of the governess, he seems to succeed in regaining that self-control that is the very antithesis of demon-control. Having stayed voluntarily in her presence and having permitted the governess to participate in, or at least to witness, his struggle, Miles would have no reason to call *her* a devil.

If Miles has no reason to call his governess a devil, he has, on the other hand, ample reason to call Peter Quint one. Peter Quint has used Miles to commit unnamed crimes and offenses for the love of all evil, and Peter Quint tries, as Frederic Myers put it, to lead Miles off to hell.

Miles's "you devil!" fits Peter Quint exactly. It is, of course, impossible to *prove* the intended referent for an uncertain or careless pronoun reference. I might point out, however, that immediately after Miles utters his "you devil!" he looks around the room for Peter Quint, and then asks *"Where?"* Since the individual on Miles's mind both just before and just after he says the word *devil* is Peter Quint, the referent most likely meant at that moment is Peter Quint.

The source of much of this difficulty in determining the antecedent lies in Henry James's use of the dash as a mark of punctuation between "Peter Quint" and "you devil!" Just what relationship between the two halves of Miles's speech does the dash indicate? I have found no precisely parallel construction in *The Turn of the Screw* that might throw light on the function of the dash in this instance. I have found, that is, no lines in which a speaker identifies someone by name and then after a dash immediately uses the second-person pronoun to refer either to the person identified or to the person addressed. James often, however, uses the dash in direct speech. It might be helpful to see some examples. They are culled, I wearily point out, from the more than six hundred instances of the dash in *The Turn of the Screw*. When Henry James uses a single dash within a direct speech or piece of dialogue he uses it to indicate a pause or hesitation. The pause is sometimes caused by a shift in sentence plan, indicating that the speaker changes his or her mind in mid-sentence, either from an ability to think of the right word or from an unwillingness to speak directly of a delicate subject. Here are a few examples of the dash used to indicate such a shift in sentence plan:

Douglas: "For dreadful—dreadfulness!" (p. 2)

Governess: "He's—God help me if I know *what* he is!" (p. 22)

Mrs. Grose: "And afterwards I imagined—and I still imagine" (p. 33)

Miles: "If I did n't—and you too" (p. 56)

More often James uses the single dash within a direct speech to indicate simply a pause or hesitation on the part of the speaker, the mere passage of time between the utterances of the two parts joined by the dash:

Mrs. Grose, "slowly": "Miss Jessel—*was* infamous" (p. 32)

Governess: "You must tell me now—and all the truth" (p. 47)

Miles: "Well—I want to see more life" (p. 56)

Governess: "Well—tonight" (p. 62)

In other words, Henry James uses the dash to indicate the kind of pause more recent writers would indicate with ellipses: "For dreadful . . . dreadfulness!"; "Miss Jessel . . . *was* infamous." If we read Miles's "Peter Quint—you devil!" as "Peter Quint . . . you devil!" we are closer to the meaning James suggests. That pause between the two pairs of words is sufficient then to support—though of course it does not prove—the theory that Miles speaks the first two words to the governess, and the last two to Peter Quint.

In uttering that epithet to his former friend, Miles distances himself from his fiendly enemy, asserts his independence of him, and is free. Utterance—as anyone familiar with the reported cases of demon possession would have known—was often a prerequisite to ridding oneself of demons:

On the forenoon of the twenty-sixth, January, at eleven o'clock, these attacks ceased. The last thing which was heard was a voice from the mouth of the patient, which said, "Depart, thou unclean spirit, from this child—knowest thou not that this child is my well-beloved?" Then she came to consciousness. ("Miss B. and Her Blasphemous Demon")

"Lord Jesus help me." . . . She spoke the words, and immediately all convulsions ceased. ("Miss Dittus and Her Strong Demon")

Miles's impassioned utterance is different from those of Miss B. and Miss Dittus. Miss B.'s mouth speaks the words of a friendly spirit who has apparently gained dominance within her over an unfriendly one. Miss Dittus repeats a phrase given to her by a Christian exorcist. Miles, in an utterance both more tragic and more heroic, uses his own words to cast out his demon. And then he dies.

I have found no reported cases of demon possession that offer a close parallel to Miles's self-reliant verbal casting out of his demon—a fact that suggests that James wanted Miles not to be like the passive victims of demon possession described so often by writers on the subject. Or, if Miles is such a victim at the start of the story, he grows sufficiently by the end so that, in responding willingly to the governess's request for information, he can, in his own way and without the help of religion, save himself. He does so at the cost of his life, but at least he has, like the heroes and heroines of many a fictional story before *The Turn of the Screw,* made the right choice, and made it *himself.*

There are many literary antecedents to Miles's sacrifice of life to gain freedom from destructive influences. Although the purpose of this book is to trace not literary antecedents to *The Turn of the Screw* but rather historical and intellectual ones, I would like to refer to a novel of the occult written by a writer contemporary with Henry James. Edward Bulwer Lytton's novel *A Strange Story,* first published in 1861, is a romance of love, travel, reincarnation, trance, witchcraft, medicine, mystery, mesmerism, murder, manuscripts, and immortality. As those various terms suggest, *A Strange Story* is too complicated to summarize here. I shall content myself with saying that its narrator and hero is a medical doctor named Fenwick who discovers that his bride is possessed and controlled by the diabolical Margrave. This Dr. Fenwick gradually rejects his youthful "scientific" skepticism about occult powers. I shall quote here only three sentences in the novel. They convey Dr. Fenwick's ruminations about two mysterious events: the murder accomplished by a man who had no motive for committing it and who claimed afterward to have been possessed by a demon when he did it; and the burning of an ancient manuscript by an old housekeeper who had no motive for burning it and who also claimed to have done the act while possessed by a demonic force she could not resist. While pondering these two mysterious acts, the doctor suddenly recalls some old reports of witchcraft he had heard in his youth. I quote from the first chapter of the second volume:

Then, there came over me confused recollections of tales of mediaeval witchcraft, which I had read in boyhood. Were there not on judicial record attestation and evidence, solemn and circumstantial, of powers analogous to those now exercised by Margrave,—of sorcerers instigating to sin through influences ascribed to Demons; making their apparitions glide through guarded walls, their voices heard from afar in the solitude of dungeons or monastic cells; subjugating victims to their will, by means which no vigilance could have detected, if the victims themselves had not confessed the witchcraft that had ensnared, courting a sure and infamous death in that confession, preferring such death to a life so haunted? Were stories so gravely set forth in the pomp of judicial evidence, and in the history of times comparatively recent, indeed to be massed, pell-mell together, as a *moles indigesta* of senseless superstition,—all the witnesses to be deemed liars; all the victims and tools of the sorcerers, lunatics; all the examiners or judges, with their solemn gradations—lay and clerical, from Commissions of Inquiry to Courts of Appeal,—to be despised for credulity, loathed for cruelty; or, amidst records so numerous, so imposingly attested, were there the fragments of a terrible truth?[12]

I cite this passage in part because it refers, although in fictional context, to an earlier "factual" tradition of possession by evil personages who override the wills of others, and to the "fragments of a terrible truth" that might be found in the discredited old stories of witchcraft and supernatural control of unwilling

12. Edward Bulwer Lytton, *A Strange Story,* 2:5–6.

victims. I cite the passage particularly, however, because of its relevance to our discussion of Miles's "confession." Dr. Fenwick recalls that in old tales and judicial reports the victims of witches and sorcerers could cast away the terrible influence by confessing the evil that had ensnared them. In making their confession, the doctor recalls, they willingly selected a sure death as preferable to a haunted life. That death was normally death by execution, the usual fate for confessed witches in the old witchcraft trials.

Although Miles is not judicially executed, he nevertheless dies for his confession. Does Miles sense that by naming and denouncing Peter Quint as a devil he will bring about his own death? Does he, like the victims in the old judicial trials, prefer "such death to a life so haunted"? We must not press the parallels too far, but I would point out that James does have the governess call Peter Quint an "executioner" (p. 87).

In his final scene Miles asserts his own will, makes his confession, and having decided against living a haunted life, heroically dispossesses himself of his diabolical executioner. Henry James, then, has written a wonderfully affirmative story, a story that exhibits faith in the power of human will to assert itself against almost overpowering forces of evil. By personal strength and assertiveness, the brave little soldiers of the world can gain at least a partial victory over those forces.

So much for my answers to the eight questions about the children in *The Turn of the Screw*. If I am right in reading the two key scenes at the end of *The Turn of the Screw*—Flora across the lake and Miles in the dining room—as scenes in which demons possess those children, then we are led inevitably to additional questions. Of major importance among these is whether the governess who witnesses and describes those scenes recognizes the demon possession herself. Does she know that Flora is possessed by the spirit of Miss Jessel and that Miles is possessed by the spirit of Peter Quint?

My own answer is that she does not fully understand, though she at times nibbles at the edges of understanding. She sees and carefully records how the children look, what they do, and what they say—or seem to say. She tells us that Flora's cutting words seem to come from an outside source and that Miles's seem to come from far away. She seems to sense Miles's struggle with a demon. She seems to have a kind of intuitional understanding that it would be good for Miles to confess the truth about stealing the letter, about what happened at school, and about his past or present relationship with Peter Quint. She even seems to know, either at the time or upon reflection some years later when writing her narrative, that the word *dispossessed* is an appropriate one to use in reference to Miles's death, though she mistakenly applies it to his heart rather than to his body or spirit. She sees the symptoms of possession but never quite puts all her data together correctly. If her eyes are unsealed to the ghostly presences of Peter Quint and Miss Jessel, those eyes remain sealed to the full implications of their relationship with the children. Indeed, the governess's perception is limited by the very fact that she *can* see the ghosts of Peter Quint and Miss Jessel. Because she can see them, she thinks that the only danger they present to the two children is the possibility of the children's also seeing them.

The governess's inability to recognize the existence of other than visual spirits is obvious enough from her own statements. Shortly after she sees Peter Quint, the governess develops the theory that it would be terrible if Miles should also see him. When Mrs. Grose asks the governess, "What if *he* should see him?" the governess replies that Peter Quint "wants to appear" to the children (p. 26). By a curious chain of logic, the governess decides that so long as *she* sees Peter Quint, the children will not see him: "Something within me said that by offering myself bravely as the sole subject of such experience, by accepting, by inviting, by surmounting it all, I should serve as the expiatory victim and guard the tranquility of the rest of the household" (p. 26). The governess thinks of herself as a screen shielding the children from seeing the ghosts: "The more I saw the less they would" (p. 28). Although the logic of her conviction is neither clear nor convincing, she never seems to shake her belief that it would be terrible indeed if the children saw the ghosts. In the first scene by the lake with Flora, the governess's heart stands still "with the wonder and terror of the question whether she too would see" (p. 30).

Later she finds it impossible to get rid of "the cruel idea that, whatever I had seen, Miles and Flora saw *more*—things terrible and unguessable" (p. 53). Even in the final scene with Miles, the governess is still intent on keeping Miles from seeing what she sees. When Peter Quint appears to her at the window, the governess tries to keep Miles "with his back to the window." She thinks that her finest act is "to keep the boy himself unaware" (p. 85).

In her way, then, the governess is as literal in her interpretation of what happens at Bly as Mrs. Grose is. It seems never to occur to her that the danger lies not in seeing a visible ghost of the dead but in being possessed by a spirit of the dead. The governess's eyes are unsealed to more than Mrs. Grose's, and her imagination is more vivid, but in the end she seems as unable as Mrs. Grose to understand the real danger the spirits of Peter Quint and Miss Jessel pose for the children. If she had understood, she would not have let Flora leave Bly, and she would perhaps have been less persistent in her questions to Miles, questions the answers to which would lead to his death.

Some readers will want to condemn the governess for not seeing beyond the appearance of the ghosts. It may be, indeed, that her inability to see the truth is really her *refusal* to see it. It may be that she does not ask the headmaster of Miles's school why Miles was expelled because she does not really want to know the worst about her little angel. It may be that she is so caught up with her own need to secure the love of the Harley Street uncle that she does not fully sense the prior need of his niece and nephew for that same love. It may be that in agreeing to shield their uncle from the emotional demands of the two children she has already given up all chance of shielding the children from the blighting demands of the spirits of Peter Quint and Miss Jessel. It may be that she refuses to see past the visible ghostly masks of Peter Quint and Miss Jessel because she cannot face the truth about her inability to shield the children from evil.

All these may be. I refuse, however, to join the chorus of readers who seek to blame the governess for all the evil at Bly. Perhaps the governess hesitates to write to the headmaster because she does not want to be influenced by an outsider's negative view of Miles, preferring to allow him a fresh start now with her. Can we really blame her for her loyalty to, even her infatuation with, the Harley Street uncle? And if she fails to recognize the real danger posed by Peter Quint and Miss Jessel, well, why would we expect her to recognize it? How could the governess, raised in a country parsonage with only a small and very select library, have learned about demon possession except from the Bible? But Protestant country parsons before mid-century were not likely to preach that the demon possession of biblical times was still a fact of life in nineteenth-century Christian England. And even if her library had been more complete or her curiosity greater, we must remember that the works I cite in this and the last chapter were all written after the governess's experiences at Bly. It would have been impossible for her to know what subsequent research or observation might reveal to readers in the 1890s.

We may want to blame the governess, harshly or mildly, for being so self-centered at the end of *The Turn of the Screw,* for being as concerned about her own welfare as about the welfare of the children at Bly. We may be troubled that she confesses to an "appalling alarm" at the momentary thought that Miles had been innocent of any serious offense at school, "for if he *were* innocent what then on earth was I?" (p. 87). We may be troubled that she tends to think that Miles's victory at the end is her own victory and that Miles's heroic saying of the name of Peter Quint is merely Miles's tribute to her own devotion. We must refrain, however, from condemning the governess for her inability to identify the actions of Flora and Miles as the symptoms of demon possession. Her ignorance is forgivable.

By calling attention to the importance of understanding demon possession for a proper interpretation of *The Turn of the Screw,* I have opened the story to new avenues of interpretation. Some of these avenues are promising. For example, it seems quite likely that James wanted us to think that Miles is possessed by Peter Quint the night he leaves his room at midnight and goes out onto the lawn. And it is quite likely that we are later to see Miles as possessed the night the governess visits him in his room and asks questions about what happened at school. That night, we recall, Miles takes on the attitude of "an older person" (p. 63) who, when she kneels at his bedside and says she wants to "save" him, gives out a "loud high shriek" (p. 65) and then cleverly says it was he who blew the candle out. Some avenues of interpretation opened up by the concept of demon possession, however, promise to lead creative readers in false directions. I should like to mention three of these avenues in an effort to direct the attention of readers away from them and toward more substantial matters.

First, some readers may think that the governess should have tried to save Miles and Flora by invoking the name of Jesus. As a parson's daughter, she might be expected to know about the most highly touted method for exorcising demons; yet it never occurs to her to try it. Because she does not think to try the obvious solution, she participates in the downfall of her two charges. I shall say only two things about this view. First, if the governess does not understand that the children are possessed by demons, why would she have thought of exorcising those demons by applying techniques that even experienced Protestant parsons would have been reluctant to apply? Second, *The Turn of the Screw* could scarcely have ended, without being ludicrous as literature, with the governess trying to pray away the demons. Miles does quite well enough without a deus ex machina, and Henry James does quite well enough without giving his story the heavily Christian orientation such an ending would have lent it.

Second, some readers may think that Miles does not die at all, but merely, like many possessed persons, goes into a death-like catatonic trance often mistaken for death. Indeed, the subjects of such trances were sometimes given a premature burial. If Miles's "death" is merely catatonic trance, then there may be some point to the speculations of certain critics that Douglas is really Miles grown up, and that the governess's narrative is a very personal statement to Douglas about certain events in his youth. I find this reading quite unconvincing. Not only does it answer few questions that are not answered more simply by other readings, but it also forces us to continue James's story past the point where he ended it. *The Turn of the Screw* ends at its climax with a stopped heart. We have no right to write its denouement by setting that heart beating again.

And third, some readers may think that the governess herself is possessed. This position has already been presented by Donal O'Gorman. *The Turn of the Screw,* he claims, is not really about the children Miles and Flora, but about "a first-person narrator who is possessed by the Devil."[13] I cannot here undertake a full-scale refutation of O'Gorman's long and closely argued reading of the tale, a reading that places O'Gorman squarely within the tradition of critics who insist on seeing the governess not as a reporter of strange events but as the deluded central actor in those events. I may say, however, that O'Gorman's reading of the governess as a diabolically possessed witch is inconsistent with the known facts of demon possession as they were understood in the last half of the nineteenth century.

O'Gorman, for example, is wrong in at least one of the principles on which he bases his argument about the governess's being possessed: that Miles and Flora cannot be the ones possessed because they "are too young to be victims of possession."[14] As several of the cases I have cited show, Miles and Flora are by no means too young to have been possessed.

Another problem with O'Gorman's argument is that it ignores the fact that if the governess had been herself possessed by a demon, she would have remembered nothing of the events that transpired. One of the most persistent facts about possession is that the victims of possession do not recall what happens while they are in trance, and so cannot tell anyone what happened. It is a basic inconsistency, then, for the governess to be both a victim of possession and the first-person narrator of what happened during that possession. O'Gorman is aware of this inconsistency but lamely suggests that James "chose to ignore" it: "It should be noted that [James] chose to ignore one frequently mentioned fact about possession, namely, that the sufferer comes out of the seizures with little or no remembrance of what he has said or done during them. This departure from the norm was of course unavoidable: once James had opted for his first-person narration there could be no question of blotting out the narrator's memory."[15]

13. Donal O'Gorman, "Henry James's Reading of *The Turn of the Screw,*" 245.
14. Ibid., 250.
15. Ibid., 251.

My own view, of course, is quite different. I believe that it is the children, not the governess, who are at times possessed, and Henry James used, rather than ignored, the fact that the possessed do not remember what they did while under possession. The inability of Miles and Flora to recall what happened during possession is part of the plot of the story, not a violation of a medically and psychologically accepted fact about possession.

Still another crucial weakness in O'Gorman's reading is that it forces him to gloss over one of Henry James's own statements about the story. In writing to Dr. Louis Waldstein on October 21, 1898, shortly after publication of the story, James said of his "bogey-tale" that "the exposure indeed, the helpless plasticity of childhood that isn't dear or sacred to *some*body! That *was* my little tragedy." O'Gorman passes this statement off by saying that "James was speaking loosely" and so blithely ignores James's own quite explicit comment about the focus of his story.[16] I contend, of course, that James was speaking anything but loosely when he announced that the "exposure" of Miles and Flora was the real subject of his story.

In having written *The Turn of the Screw,* Henry James said all he needed to say about the governess, the ghosts, and the children. Yet Henry James said more. After the story was in print he wrote letters about it to people who asked questions, and then wrote an extended preface for the New York Edition published a decade after the first publication of the story. It is now time to turn to these post-story Jamesian documents to see, first, whether Henry James is likely to have agreed with what I have said of his story and, second, whether what I have said of his story sheds light on the meaning of some of his post-story comments.

16. James, *Letter,* ed. Edel, 4:84; O'Gorman, "James's Reading," 256.

"MY BAD THINGS"
James on James

Critics of both the evil-ghost and the deluded-governess persuasions are prone to seek corroboration for their theories by quoting Henry James's extratextual statements about the story. They point to his letters to his friends, and they cite his lengthy preface about the story, prepared a decade after the first publication of the story and published as part of the New York Edition in 1908. Some critics of both persuasions find what they think of as ample support for their readings in these after-the-fact authorial statements. Where James's comments do not support their readings, they call him "evasive" or else proclaim all extratextual comments to be "irrelevant" to an explication of the text. Of course, James's comments after he wrote *The Turn of the Screw* are often both evasive and irrelevant: evasive because he probably found it demeaning to be utterly explicit about explaining his own work; irrelevant because the story does, after all, speak for itself. Still, certain of James's after-the-fact comments are worth looking at in connection with the present study, partly because they sometimes illuminate now ambiguous intentions and partly because some of what I have been saying in previous chapters may shed light on what James meant by certain of his comments about the story.

Let us consider, for example, a couple of comments Henry James made about the governess. On December 9, 1898—just a year after he finished writing *The Turn of the Screw*—James replied to a letter (now lost) in which H. G. Wells had apparently gently criticized *The Turn of the Screw*. Wells particularly wished that James had more fully characterized the governess. In his reply Henry James described his story as "essentially a pot-boiler and a *jeu d'esprit*," but did give a more specific reply to Wells's comment about the weakly characterized governess. I quote here that portion of James's reply to Wells:

Bless your heart, I think I could easily say worse of the T. of the S., the young woman, the spooks, the style, the everything, than the worst any one else could manage. One knows the *most* damning things about one's self. Of course I had, about my young woman, to take a very sharp line. The grotesque business I had to make her picture and the childish psychology I had to make her trace and present, were, for me at least, a very difficult job, in which absolute lucidity and logic, a singleness of effect, were imperative. Therefore I had to rule out subjective complications of her own—play of tone etc.; and keep her impersonal save for the most obvious and indispensable little note of neatness, firmness and courage—without which she would n't have had her data.[1]

James's comment to Wells about having ruled out subjective complications of his narrator might be noted by those who insist upon reading the story as nothing more than the subjective complications of his narrator. James's comment that he needed "my young woman" to be firm and courageous in order for her to get data seems, in the light of what we have been saying about the science of psychical research, to mean simply that James needed a narrator who would not run trembling from the first evidence of the supernatural or of danger, for she would then not have stayed at Bly long enough to gather the data that were to form the heart of her narrative about children and "spooks." All this suggests that James thought of the governess primarily as a means to get a story told, rather than as the central character in that story.

One other comment should be made about the governess's courage. Much has been said about her love for or infatuation with the uncle in Harley Street, especially by critics who desire to emphasize her faults—her general unreliability, her "sexual repression," her desire to draw attention to her "slighted charms," and so on. We might do well to recall that the narrator of the frame story tells us that her desire not to disappoint the "splendid" man who put so much trust in her "gave her the courage she afterwards showed" (p. 4). It is unfortunate that whereas the narrator emphasized the infatuation as explanation for the courage she showed at Bly, many critics have emphasized the infatuation as

1. James, *Letters*, ed Edel, 4:86.

explanation for her lunacy. Henry James's letter to Wells suggests that he might have sided with his frame narrator in emphasizing her courage.

It may well be that a decade later Henry James was recalling this exchange of letters with H. G. Wells when he referred to a reader who had complained about the incomplete characterization of the governess. I quote the remark from the 1908 preface:

I recall for instance a reproach made me by a reader capable evidently, for the time, of some attention, but not quite capable of enough, who complained that I had n't sufficiently "characterised" my young woman engaged in her labyrinth; had n't endowed her with signs and marks, features and humours, had n't in a word invited her to deal with her own mystery as well as with that of Peter Quint, Miss Jessel and the hapless children. I remember well, whatever the absurdity of its now coming back to me, my reply to that criticism—under which one's artistic, one's ironic heart shook for the instant almost to breaking. "You indulge in that stricture at your ease, and I don't mind confiding to you that—strange as it may appear!—one has to choose ever so delicately among one's difficulties, attaching one's self to the greatest, bearing hard on those and intelligently neglecting the others. If one attempts to tackle them all one is certain to deal completely with none; whereas the effectual dealing with a few casts a blest golden haze under cover of which, like wanton mocking goddesses in clouds, the others find prudent to retire. It was 'déjà très-joli,' in 'The Turn of the Screw,' please believe, the general proposition of our young woman's keeping crystalline her record of so many intense anomalies and obscurities—by which I don't of course mean her explanation of them, a different matter."[2]

This passage is of particular interest for two reasons. First, James again explains that it simply was not his purpose in *The Turn of the Screw* to offer a full characterization of the governess. He was concerned, rather, with the affairs of "Peter Quint, Miss Jessel and the hapless children." He could not do everything in one story and therefore chose to "intelligently neglect" the governess, to let her "retire." All he wanted was to have her keep "crystalline" her "record" of the events at Bly. He felt he could not do that

2. James, *The Turn of the Screw* (New York: 1908), 120–21.

if he also tried to endow her with complex signs, marks, features, humors, and mysteries of her own.

Second, James makes an important distinction between the governess's record of the events at Bly and "her explanation of them, a different matter." If the reading I have been proposing is right, this remark suggests that James wanted to have his narrator record what she observed with as much accuracy and clarity as he could manage, but he did not want her fully to understand or be able to explain the meaning of all that she observed. To be more specific, this remark suggests that he wanted her to see the ghosts of Peter Quint and Miss Jessel and he wanted her accurately to sense that they are somehow out to "get" the children. But he wanted her to be wrong in thinking that the mere visibility of the ghosts is a threat and that to protect Miles and Flora all she has to do is continue to see the ghosts. She does not, in any case, recognize the real danger to the children: that the malignant spirits of Peter Quint and Miss Jessel can possess her young charges and in that manner lure them into evil, into death, and into damnation. The governess does, to be sure, give some early hints that the children might possibly at times be possessed. For example, she notes her puzzlement that Miles is able to do so very well in his lessons, his feats of entertainment, his memorizing, his acting. She speaks of having "the impression, if I had dared to work it out, that he was under some influence" (p. 39). Henry James does not want her to dare to work it out, at least not yet, but she nevertheless leaves this hint, for readers who do want to work it out, of the possibility that the "influence" may involve possession. Rather than have her "explain" everything that is going on, he wants her to get on with her record of the events in the story. She does so. Her record of what happens is generally reliable; her explanation of what happens is not always reliable.

And why should her explanation be reliable? It would scarcely have served James's literary purposes to have the governess fully understand and accurately explain all the mysteries at Bly. That would have made the reader's job too easy and would have shed light into too many corners James preferred to leave shadowy. The governess has much in common with other Jamesian "unreliable narrators." The purpose of the unreliability here, however, is not to direct the reader's attention to her own flaws but rather to create ambiguity regarding the exact nature of the mysterious phenomena she witnesses. James speaks in several places about his desire to leave unspecified the precise evil of Peter Quint and Miss Jessel. Nowhere, however, does he speak more directly than in the 1908 preface:

Only make the reader's general vision of evil intense enough, I said to myself—and that already is a charming job—and his own experience, his own imagination, his own sympathy (with the children) and horror (of their false friends) will supply him quite sufficiently with all the particulars. Make him *think* the evil, make him think it for himself, and you are released from weak specifications.[3]

For the governess to be more reliable, to understand more accurately or completely the mysteries at Bly, would have reduced Henry James to giving those "weak specifications." He wanted the governess to understand Peter Quint and Miss Jessel only partially, because he wanted the reader's imagination, the reader's own horror of them, to provide details of the utmost evil possible. James thought one of his primary tasks in *The Turn of the Screw* was to *avoid* letting his narrator tell too much about his "bad things." He had seen fiction fail too often from that very fault. To quote again from the preface:

One had seen, in fiction, some grand form of wrong-doing, or better still of wrong-being, imputed, seen it promised and announced as by the hot breath of the Pit—and then, all lamentably, shrink to the compass of some particular brutality, some particular immorality, some particular infamy portrayed: with the result, alas, of the demonstration's falling sadly short. If *my* bad things, for "The Turn of the Screw," I felt, should succumb to this danger, if they should n't seem sufficiently bad, there would be nothing for me but to hang my artistic head lower than I had ever known occasion to do.[4]

3. Ibid., 123.
4. Ibid., 122.

Henry James can scarcely have known that in leaving the doings of his "bad things" so unspecified and imparticular, he was to invite his readers to imagine that it was rather his narrator who was the only truly bad thing in the story.

More specifically, what did Henry James have to say, after he wrote *The Turn of the Screw,* about Peter Quint and Miss Jessel, his "bad things" at Bly? He says, for example, that his ghosts are not the kind of ghosts reported in the annals of psychical research:

I had for instance simply to renounce all attempt to keep the kind and degree of impression I wished to produce on terms with the to-day so copious psychical record of cases of apparitions. Different signs and circumstances, in the reports, mark these cases; different things are done—though on the whole very little appears to be—by the persons appearing; the point is, however, that some things are never done at all: this negative quantity is large—certain reserves and proprieties and immobilities consistently impose themselves. Recorded and attested "ghosts" are in other words as little expressive, as little dramatic, above all as little continuous and conscious and responsive, as is consistent with their taking the trouble—and an immense trouble they find it, we gather—to appear at all. Wonderful and interesting therefore at a given moment, they are inconceivable figures in an *action*—and "The Turn of the Screw" was an action, desperately, or it was nothing. I had to decide in fine between having my apparitions correct and having my story "good"—that is producing my impression of the dreadful, my designed horror. Good ghosts, speaking by book, make poor subjects, and it was clear that from the first my hovering prowling blighting presences, my pair of abnormal agents, would have to depart altogether from the rules. They would be agents in fact; there would be laid on them the dire duty of causing the situation to reek with an air of Evil. Their desire and their ability to do so, visibly measuring meanwhile their effect, together with their observed and described success—this was exactly my central idea; so that, briefly, I cast my lot with pure romance, the appearances conforming to the true type being so little romantic.[5]

That is a rich passage, worth reading for a number of reasons. It reveals, for example, that Henry James was undeniably familiar with the reports of the Society for Psychical Research. More important, it reveals that he thought the immobile ghosts of the

5. Ibid., 121.

psychical research reports, though perhaps "wonderful and interesting" at a given moment, simply would not be sufficient for an effective or extended story requiring action. In saying all that, James reveals just what kinds of ghosts he thought *would* be effective in his story, his "action": "expressive," "mobile," "dramatic," "responsive," "active," "purposeful," "continuous," "conscious," and "romantic" ghosts. "Good" ghosts, the "true type" of ghost found in the psychical research reports, simply could not provide him with the "hovering prowling blighting presences" he had in mind. Although the official reports could provide him with certain static details about ghostly appearance and demeanor, James's "abnormal agents" must be not the merely telepathic agents that men like Frederic Myers and Edmund Gurney described, but "agents in fact." Critics have generally ignored the implications of that phrase, but what can "agents in fact" mean except nontelepathic, nonsubjective ghosts? Peter Quint and Miss Jessel are not merely illusionary images or thought-transferred memories of dead persons. They are real agents come back from the dead for what James called in his preface "a second round of badness."[6]

When he says, "I cast my lot with pure romance," Henry James means not that he abandoned the visual appearance or behavior of the "recorded and attested" modern ghosts, but that he gave Peter Quint and Miss Jessel the motives and the power for action of the older-style fictional ghosts. He offers some illuminating alternative terms or synonyms for the kinds of ghosts he is talking about:

Peter Quint and Miss Jessel are not "ghosts" at all, as we now know the ghost, but goblins, elves, imps, demons as loosely constructed as those of the old trials for witchcraft; if not, more pleasingly, fairies of the legendary order, wooing their victims forth to see them dance under the moon.[7]

Surely there is nothing less evasive in James's preface than that

6. Ibid., 122.
7. Ibid.

statement. Peter Quint and Miss Jessel are not the kinds of ghosts discussed in the modern psychical cases presented by Myers and Gurney, but are beings of an older, more romantic, order: demons, elves, fairies, goblins, imps. Have we forgotten what those terms mean?

I quote below from the *Oxford English Dictionary*, omitting those meanings that are utterly irrelevant in the present context and omitting all illustrative examples:

Demon. A supernatural being of a nature intermediate between that of gods and men; an inferior divinity, spirit, genius (including the souls or ghosts of deceased persons). Applied to the idols or gods of the heathen, and to the "evil" or "unclean spirits" by which demoniacs were possessed.

Elf. The name of a class of supernatural beings, in early Teutonic belief supposed to possess formidable magical powers, exercised variously for the benefit or the injury of mankind. They were believed to be of dwarfish form, to produce diseases of various kinds, to act as *incubi* and *succubi*, to cause nightmares, and to steal children. . . . Sometimes distinguished from a "fairy": (a) as an inferior or subject species; (b) as a more malignant being, an "imp," "demon."

Fairy. One of a class of supernatural beings of diminutive size, in popular belief supposed to possess magical powers and to have great influence for good or evil over the affairs of man.

Goblin. A mischievous and ugly demon.

Imp. A "child" of the devil, or of hell. . . . Applied to . . . petty fiends or evil spirits . . . . A little devil or demon, an evil spirit.

These definitions, of words Henry James himself used to describe Peter Quint and Miss Jessel, help us to determine more clearly that he had in mind creating malignant spirits who interfered, with evil intent, in the affairs of the living. When we put such definitions together with the reference, in the last passage quoted above from the preface, to the children as "victims" of these spirits, there seems little reason to doubt that one of James's primary purposes in *The Turn of the Screw* was to portray two innocent children beset by the most malicious evil he and his readers, between them, could conjure up.

I should like now to consider one other phrase in that last sentence quoted above from the preface: that Peter Quint and Miss Jessel are "demons as loosely constructed as those of the old trials for witchcraft." I have for the most part refrained in earlier chapters from referring to witchcraft. I have been concerned rather to show that Henry James knew, drew on, and carefully selected among much more recent phenomena reported by contemporary psychical researchers and spiritualists. But now that James himself has given the cue, I feel that I must remind modern readers about what some of the seventeenth-century witchcraft cases were like. I can best do so by quoting selections from three of those old cases. My quotations are all taken from George Burr's *Narratives of the Witchcraft Cases, 1648–1706.* Although Burr's book was published in 1914, just two years before Henry James's death and thus too late for James to have read it before writing *The Turn of the Screw,* it merely gathers together and republishes cases that were in print much earlier and so available in a number of sources. Because Burr's introductory essays and notes will inform interested readers about the publication history of the narratives, I shall say little more about that history here. My own concern is with the cases themselves, because they shed light on Henry James's comment about one of the traditions that he acknowledges as providing background for his conception of Peter Quint and Miss Jessel.

The first witch case I cite was reported by Increase Mather in his 1684 *Essay for the Recording of Illustrious Providences.* It involves the demon possession of a sixteen-year-old girl in Groton, Massachusetts:

Another thing which caused a noise in the Countrey, and wherein Satan had undoubtedly a great influence, was that which hapned at Groton. There was a Maid in that Town (one Elizabeth Knap) who in the Moneth of October, Anno 1671, was taken after a very strange manner, sometimes weeping, sometimes laughing, sometimes roaring hideously, with violent motions and agitations of her body, crying out Money, Money, etc. . . . Six Men were scarce able to hold her in some of her fits, but she would skip about the House yelling and looking with a most frightful Aspect. . . . And now a Daemon began manifestly to speak in her. Many words were uttered wherein are the Labial Letters, without any motion of her Lips, which was a clear demonstration that the voice was not her own. Sometimes Words were spoken seeming to proceed out of her throat, when her Mouth was shut. Sometimes with her Mouth wide open, without the use of any of the Organs of speech. ("Miss Knap and Her Accusing Demon")

The case of Elizabeth Knap shows that victims of witchcraft often behaved very much like the victims of spirit or demon possession, showing great strength, uttering strange speech, and generally behaving very unlike their normal selves.

A somewhat different case is that of Bridget Bishop, reported by Increase Mather's son Cotton in his *Wonders of the Invisible World*. A longtime resident of Salem Village, Bridget Bishop was the first of the Salem witches to be tried (on June 2, 1692) and the first to be executed (on June 10). Cotton Mather's account of her trial is interesting to us for several reasons. Most important, it demonstrates the bad effects that witches were supposed to have on children. Note particularly that Bridget Bishop was accused of having caused the deaths of the Stacy child and the Gray child, as well as the illness of the Shattock child. For readers of James's story familiar with such accusations leveled at witches, the illness of Flora and the death of Miles might have had particular resonances. And I wonder if the last name of the members of the Bly family who testified against Bridget Bishop could have suggested to Henry James the name he gave to the country manor in which his mysterious story is set. I reproduce only selections from Cotton Mather's long account of the Bishop trial:

I. She was Indicted for Bewitching of several persons in the Neighbourhood, the Indictment being drawn up, according to the Form in such Cases usual. And pleading, Not Guilty, there were brought in several persons, who had long undergone many kinds of Miseries, which were preternaturally Inflicted, and generally ascribed unto an horrible Witchcraft. . . .

VI. Samuel Gray testify'd, That about fourteen years ago, he wak'd on a Night, and saw the Room where he lay full of Light; and that he then saw plainly a Woman between the Cradle and the Bed-side, which look'd upon him. He Rose, and it vanished; tho' he found the Doors all fast. Looking out at the Entry-Door, he saw the same Woman, in the same Garb again; and said, In Gods Name, what do you come for? He went to Bed, and had the same Woman again assaulting him. The Child in the Cradle gave a great schreech, and the Woman Disappeared. It was long before the Child could be quieted; and tho' it were a very likely thriving Child, yet from this time it pined away, and after divers months dy'd in a sad Condition.

VII. John Bly and his Wife testify'd. . . .

IX. Samuel Shattock testify'd, That in the Year 1680, this Bridget Bishop often came to his house upon such frivolous and foolish errands, that they suspected she came indeed with a purpose of mischief. Presently whereupon his eldest child, which was of as promising Health and Sense as any child of its Age, began to droop exceedingly; and the oftener that Bishop came to the House, the worse grew the Child. As the Child would be standing at the Door, he would be thrown and bruised against the Stones, by an Invisible Hand, and in like sort knock his Face against the sides of the House, and bruise it after a miserable manner. Afterwards this Bishop would bring him things to Dy, whereof he could not Imagine any use; and when she paid him a piece of Money, the Purse and Money were unaccountably conveyed out of a Lock'd box, and never seen more. The Child was immediately hereupon taken with terrible fits, whereof his Friends thought he would have dyed: indeed he did almost nothing but cry and Sleep for several Months together; and at length his understanding was utterly taken away. . . .

XI. William Stacy . . . testify'd, that he verily Believed, the said Bishop was the Instrument of his Daughter Priscilla's Death; of which suspicion, pregnant Reasons were assigned.

XII. To Crown all, John Bly and William Bly Testify'd, That being Employ'd by Bridget Bishop, to help take down the Cellar-wall of the old House, wherein she formerly Lived, they did in Holes of the said old Wall find several Poppets, made up of Rags and Hogs Brussels, with Headless Pins in them, the Points being outward. Whereof she could give no Account unto the Court, that was Reasonable or Tolerable. ("Mrs. Bishop and Her Salem Witchery")

There were, of course, many more witch trials at Salem, but I need cite no more of them here. The Bishop case is more or less typical and, as the first and most prominent, set the tone both for the later trials and for the reports about them.

I would like to refer to one more case, an earlier one than these last two, that has particular relevance to a discussion of *The Turn of the Screw*. Not only is it about the diabolical temptation of a boy who reminds us of Miles, but it also reveals a number of parallels with Miles's experiences: the boy's being cut off from his parents; the distant concern, through letters, of an uncle; the speaking through the boy's mouth of words not his own; the devil's attempt to prevent the boy from making confessions that would free him; the boy's blurted rebuke of "the devil!"; the astonishing noise made by the devil as he leaves the boy's body after the tormented boy confesses. Even the special circumstances of publication of the narrative remind us of James's story. The narrative, published by Cotton Mather in his 1689 *Memorable Provinces, Relating to Witchcrafts and Possessions,* concerns events that had happened some thirty years before publication. Cotton Mather claimed not to know what finally happened to the boy of the narrative, for he was limited in his knowledge to an account of the incidents written in his own grandfather's hand. "I have the Manuscript," he reports in an introductory note, "from whence I have caused it to be Transcribed." *The Turn of the Screw,* we recall, was also said to have been published from a transcribed copy of a faded manuscript written many years earlier in its author's own hand. Here is Cotton Mather's grandfather's narrative:

The Boy was for his'natural Parts more than ordinary at seven years old. He with many others went to see a Conjurer play Tricks in Holland. There it was strongly suggested to him, He should be as good an Artist as he. From thence to eleven year old he used the Trade of inventing Lyes, and Stealing mony, Running away from his Father, spending of it at Dice, and with the vilest Company; and his Trade he used in that space (he confessed) above Forty times at least, and many strange Instances he gives of it. His Father following him with constant Instruction, and Correction, he was desperately hardned under all, and his heart sett in a way of Malice against the Word of God, and all his Father did to restrain him. When he was about ten or eleven years old, he ran away from Rotterdam, to Delph; and the Devil appeared to him there in the shape of a Boy, counselling him not to hearken to the Word of God, nor unto any of his Father's Instructions, and propounding to him, to Enter into a Covenant with him. Being somewhat fearful at first, desired that he would not appear to him in a shape, but by a voice, and though his heart did inwardly consent, to what the Devil said, yet he was withheld that he could not then Enter into a Covenant with him. His Father not knowing this, but of his other Wickedness, being a godly Minister, procured many Christians to join with him in a day of Humiliation; confessed and bewailed his Sins, prayed for him, and sent him to New-England and so committed him to God. From that time to this, being now about Sixteen years old, the Devil hath constantly come to him by a voice; and he held a constant Discourse with him. . . . Still the Devil would not away, nor could he get from him. Then out of Fear he cryed out, "Lord, Jesus, rebuke the devil!" . . . He would fain then have confessed his sins, but when he was about to do it the Devil still held his mouth, that he could not. He entreated God, to release him, promising to confess and forsake his Sins, and the Lord did so; but he being well, grew as bad, or worse than ever. About six weeks since, his Convulsion Fits came again three times most dreadfully, with some Intermissions, and his former Horrours and Fears. He would have confessed his Sins but could not. It pleased God to put it into the heart of one to ask him, Whether he had any Familiarity with the Devil? he got out so much then as, Yes. He fetching Mr. Pierson, the Convulsion Fits left him, and he confessed all, how it had been with him. That very night the Devil came to him, and told him, Had he blabbed out such things? He would teach him to blabb! and if he would not then write and seal the Agreement, he would tear him in pieces, and he refusing, the Devil took a corporal Possession of him, and hath not ceased to torment him extremely ever since. If any thing be spoken to him, the Devil answereth (and many times he barks like a Fox, and hisseth like a Serpent) sometimes with horrible Blasphemies against the Name of Christ; and at some other times the Boy is sensible. When he hath the Libertie of his Voice, he tells what the Devil saith to him, urging him to seal the Covenant still, and that he will bring Paper, Pen and Ink in the night, when none shall see, pleading, that God hath cast him off, that Christ cannot save him: That When He was upon earth He could cast out devils, but now He is in Heaven He cannot. Sometimes he is ready to yeild to all in a desperate way. Sometimes he breaks out into Confession of his former sins, as they come into his mind; exceedingly judging himself and justifying God in His for ever leaving of him in the hands of Satan. Once he was heard to Pray in such a manner so sutable to his Condition, so Aggravating his Sin, and pleading with God for mercy, and in such a strange, high enlarged manner, as judicious godly persons then present, affirm they never heard the like in their lives, that it drew abundance of tears from the eyes of all present, being about twenty persons. But his torment increased upon him worse after such a time; or if any thing were spoken to him from the Word of God by others, or they pray with him. The last week after he had confessed one strange

Passage, namely that once in Discourse he told the Devil, that if he would make his Spittle to scald a dog, he would then go on in a way of Lying and Dissembling, and believe that he should do it, which he said, he did with all his heart, and so spit on the dog, and with that a deal of Scalding Water did poure on the Dog. In pursuance of his Promise, he went on in a way of Lying and Dissembling: That when he was urged about it, that he had done some mischief to the dog, then he fell down into a Swound, as if he had been dead. As soon as he had confessed this, the Devil went out of him with an astonishing Noise, to the terrour of those then present. . . . And the Devil entered unto him again a Second time, railing upon him, and calling him, Blab-tongue, and Rogue! he had promis'd to keep things secret, he would teach him to blabb, he would tear him in pieces. Since, he hath kept his Body in continual Motion, speaking in him, and by him, with a formidable Voice: sometimes singing of Verses wicked and witty, that formerly he had made against his Father's Ministry, and the Word of God, etc. ("Mr. Blank and the Devil Who Tempts Him")

Perhaps these narratives of witchcraft cases can help us to understand what Henry James meant when he spoke of "demons as loosely constructed as those of the old trials for witchcraft." It is not, of course, that James *believed* in witchcraft. Indeed, in his 1908 preface he calls his story everything but true or factual: "irresponsible little fiction . . . flower of high fancy . . . sinister romance . . . exercise of the imagination . . . fairy-tale pure and simple . . . piece of ingenuity pure and simple . . . pure romance . . . fable." James says nothing of his belief or disbelief in witchcraft, and we have no need to speculate about that belief or disbelief. What he does do, and what he later said he did, is *use* for his own artistic ends some of the narrative characteristics associated with witchcraft. Wanting his story to "reek with an air of Evil," he turned to old stories of witchcraft for models of the greatest imaginable evil: the Satan-tormented demoniac, the destroyer of innocent children, the devil acting directly as tempter and motivator.

Evil motive, the ultimate in sinister malignancy, was of course what witchcraft was all about. James in his preface expressed his need to make his "demon-spirits," Peter Quint and Miss Jessel, seem convincingly motivated by evil:

The essence of the matter was the villainy of motive in the evoked
predatory creatures; so that the result would be ignoble—by which I
mean would be trivial—were this element of evil but feebly or inanely
suggested. Thus arose . . . the question of how best to convey that sense
of the depths of the sinister without which my fable would so woefully
limp. Portentous evil—how was I to save that, as an intention on the part
of my demon-spirits, from the drop?[8]

Henry James's concern in this and in most of his other remarks
in his preface seems to have been with the artistry of his story,
with the literary effect rather than with the literal factuality of his
materials. Near the beginning of his 1908 preface, he laments the
end of the good, old, horror-producing ghost story:

The good, the really effective and heart-shaking ghost-stories (roughly
so to term them) appeared all to have been told, and neither new crop
nor new type in any quarter awaited us. The new type indeed, the mere
modern "psychical" case, washed clean of all queerness as by exposure
to a flowing laboratory tap, and equipped with credentials vouching for
this—the new type clearly promised little, for the more it was respectably
certified the less it seemed of a nature to rouse the dear old sacred terror.[9]

In view of this and James's other statements about his intentions,
and in view of the story he wrote, can there be any doubt that in
The Turn of the Screw Henry James attempted to tell a ghost story
about the old type of ghost? He knew the new type, the modern
psychical ghost, but he wanted to write something more heart-
shaking, something to stir up "the dear old sacred terror." Some
readers may think that James has failed to stir their hearts or to
inspire them with terror. Others may think ghost stories in general are too trivial to be taken seriously as literature. Others may
think that James should have tried for more subtle characterization, or a more complicated plot, or a more fully characterized
governess. Others may simply not enjoy a fable about how inex-
perienced goodness pales in the presence of absolute evil, or a
story about how an innocent youth is corrupted, then grows to
manhood but dies in the process. These are all quite legitimate

8. Ibid.
9. Ibid., 117–18.

responses to *The Turn of the Screw*. It should, however, be enough for such readers to say simply, "I don't like it." Instead, many of them have felt obliged to proclaim, "James did better than that." Instead of taking Chaucer's age-old advice to turn over the leaf and choose another tale, they try to recast this one into something less "lazy," more "rich," and more "modern."

I have tried to argue in these pages that Henry James's *The Turn of the Screw* is a ghost story. Whether it can also be, simultaneously, the story of an insane governess who merely imagines that she sees ghosts, I must leave to others to decide. It would be attractive, perhaps, to attribute to Henry James, the master craftsman of modern fiction, the ability to write the story in such a way that both the evil-ghost and the deluded-governess stories are simultaneously plausible. Certainly some modern critics have made just that claim.[10] Other readers will find this claim unconvincing. Their instincts tell them that this story is to be read one way or the other, but not both ways. A healthy ambiguity they can appreciate in questions about why Ahab chases the whale or why Dimmesdale refuses to join Hester on the scaffold or why the governess stays at Bly. The various ways of answering those questions will seem, to such readers, not to tear the characters asunder but to enrich them. These readers, however, will feel differently about the question of whether the governess is sane or insane. If she is sane and sees ghosts, that is one story; if she is insane and only imagines that she sees ghosts, that is another. These readers will feel uncomfortable trying to have it both ways, for they will feel that the governess cannot be both sane and insane, cannot both see and imagine the ghosts.

It is obvious that I am not comfortable with the deluded-governess reading, at least as I described that reading in my introduction. I find the evil-ghost reading to be more satisfactory, especially if we think of it as the governess's own "reading" of what happens at Bly. It tells us what she sees, what she understands. Most of what she sees and what she understands is what we

---

10. See, for example, Paul N. Siegel, "Miss Jessel: Mirror Image of the Governess," 30, and Christine Brooke-Rose, *A Rhetoric of the Unreal*, 229.

readers are to see and understand. In at least one important way, however, the evil-ghost reading is insufficient and needs to be supplemented—but not supplanted—by a reading that did not occur to the governess. We might call this the "possessed-children" reading. Peter Quint and Miss Jessel are, to the governess, what she thinks they are: ghosts, and evil. To Miles and Flora, however, they are something different, and a great deal more dangerous. Whereas they appear merely *to* the governess, they appear *through* the children. They are diabolical presences who have taken advantage of two love-starved orphans and have tempted them into an early experience of evil. They are demonic forces that can supplant the children's own spirits and coerce them into doing and saying things they would not normally think of doing or saying. Although the governess does not understand all this, she observes the phenomena and reports them carefully enough so that readers aware of the concept of demon possession and of certain ancient and modern instances of it can read past her ignorance to a finer understanding than she has of what goes on in the story she tells. One of the purposes of my book has been to acquaint modern readers with that concept and with some of those instances so that they can more fully understand *The Turn of the Screw* as Henry James seems to have meant for them to understand it.

In 1889 Henry James wrote an introduction to a translation of *The Odd Number,* a collection of thirteen tales by Guy de Maupassant. Although one of the tales is of more than passing interest to us because it is about a ghost (see "A Ghost"), my primary concern here is with certain remarks that James made in his introduction. James talked about the difficulty readers of one nation have in understanding the writers of another nation:

It is so embarrassing to speak of the writers of one country to the readers of another that I sometimes wonder at the complacency with which the delicate task is entered upon. These are cases in which the difficult art of criticism becomes doubly difficult, inasmuch as they compel the critic to forfeit what I may call his natural advantages. The first of these natural advantages is that those who read him shall help him by taking a great many things for granted; shall allow him his general point of view and his terms—terms which he is not obliged to define. The relation of the American reader to the French writer, for instance, is, on the contrary, so indirect that it gives him who proposes to mediate between them a great deal more to do. Here he has in a manner to define his terms and establish his point of view.[11]

The same might be said for writers of one generation reading a work written for another generation. A special understanding, a special definition of terms, a special point of view is needed. As Henry James attempted to "mediate" between English-speaking audiences and Guy de Maupassant, so have I attempted in this book to "mediate" between readers of my own generation and Henry James. By ferreting out and reproducing for modern eyes some documents that help us understand Henry James's terms and his point of view, I have tried to aid readers in discovering the story Henry James wrote at the end of the nineteenth century as distinct from the one readers may think they read at the end of the twentieth.

The task I set for myself was to show how *The Turn of the Screw,* fiction though it is, derives from factual traditions about ghosts and demons. We cannot fully understand James's story without knowing some of the reported cases upon which he based it. If I have succeeded, then I have shown that almost every characteristic associated with Peter Quint and Miss Jessel—every detail of appearance, every action, every motive—was derived directly or indirectly from some "factual" tradition.

It may seem quixotic to suggest, after so much has been said by so many distinguished critics, that there is a correct way to read a work as rich and as ambiguous as *The Turn of the Screw.* Certainly I have no delusions that this will be the final word on the story, or that many readers who have grown to like the story another way will be swayed by what I have said and will now read it my way.

I am fully aware that many readers simply will not accept from Henry James a Gothic story about evil ghosts and demons tormenting innocent women and threatening innocent children. For such readers I have nothing more to say. I am fully aware that for

11. Henry James, Introduction to Guy de Maupassant, *The Odd Number,* vii–viii.

some readers my insistence on taking the focus of the story off the governess and placing it on two corrupt servants and two corruptible children will seem like an attempt to steal away much of the pleasure they have taken in the story. For such readers I have nothing more to say. I am fully aware that for some readers my interpretation will seem to reduce the rich story they have been enjoying into an unimaginative account based on contemporary psychical theory. For such readers I *do* have a little more to say.

I do not view *The Turn of the Screw* as in any sense unimaginative. It is obvious that although Henry James drew from contemporary "factual" accounts, we no longer read those accounts—whereas we still read, and with renewed interest, *The Turn of the Screw*. The factual accounts focus on event, James's story on character. They focus on fact, this on theme. They are boring, this gripping. They are earthbound, this soars. If, by attempting to direct readers' attention to the factual sources from which Henry James drew some of his material, I have given the impression that Henry James's story is unoriginal, then I have done him a great disservice. I consider *The Turn of the Screw* to be amazingly original.

Surely it is wrong to call unoriginal a work that combines elements from so many traditions into something so unique, a piece of fiction so distinctive and so rich in texture that readers are still having difficulty naming its genre. Peter Quint and Miss Jessel are so strikingly original that readers have seen no precedent, in either fact or fiction, for such ghost-demons. Surely it is wrong to call unoriginal an author who channeled three streams into a single new river, an author who took some old-style ghosts of romance, gave them the visual appearance and demeanor of the new-style ghosts of psychical research, then gave them power by allowing them to take possession of the bodies of the living. The result is an ambiguity bordering on confusion. It may seem improbable that the spirits of dead persons can be visible to one person and at the same time be taking demonic possession of another, but it is surely not unoriginal. I am aware of no other narrative—factual or fictional—in which visible ghosts were also possessing demons. Indeed, Peter Quint and Miss Jessel are so strikingly original, so strikingly ambiguous, that many readers, unaware of the three separate traditions—the romantic, the scientific, and the demonic—that made them, have decided that the real ambiguity lies less in these strange ghost-demons than in the character of the young woman who, not quite understanding them herself, describes them.

And surely it is wrong to call unimaginative a work that incorporates such a wealth of gentle ambiguity, a work in which ghosts are also demons, in which their victims are both innocent and corrupt, in which the narrator is both accurate in her descriptions and inaccurate in her explanations. And surely there is nothing fact-bound or slavishly unoriginal in the way Henry James satisfied both the demands of an audience familiar with the facts of ghostly and demonic phenomena, and the demands of an audience that sensed that the best fiction—even the best realistic fiction—needed an element of the mysterious, the unspecified, the unexplained.

BIBLIOGRAPHY OF CASES

Listed below are the ghost and demon cases cited in this book. I have assigned all titles. The person whose name is mentioned first in the title is usually the person who perceives a ghost or who is possessed by a spirit visitant. This ghost or spirit visitant is referred to after the "and" in the title. The titles are alphabetized according to the name or initial of the percipient, or subject, of the visitation. Alphabetization ignores personal titles of address such as "Miss," "Rev.," or "Squire." Thus, "Mr. Addison" is listed before "Capt. Ayre." Names given only by initial are grouped at the start of each letter category. Where no names or initials are given in the case, I use the name "Blank," alphabetized under "B." Basic publication information is given for each case. For cases taken from books the last name of the first author is given (for example, Gurney), along with page references. Readers will find the full entry for such books, including date of publication, in the bibliography of Works Cited immediately following this list. For cases cited from periodicals—*Borderland, Light,* and the two publications of the Society for Psychical Research, its *Journal (JSPR)* and its *Proceedings (PSPR)*—I give volume and year in this listing. All the cases cited were in print before James completed *The Turn of the Screw* in the fall of 1897. The vast majority—fully 85 percent of the 135 cases—were published (or republished) in the dozen years before 1897. For cases in print in more than one location by 1897, I list first the one from which my own quotations come. When either Roellinger or Sheppard (two modern scholars) make significant reference to a work I cite, I note that fact.

"Mr. A. and the Ghost in His Bed." *Light* 2 (1882): 378.
"Rev. A. and the Parsonage Imp." Stead, 296–300.
"Miss Adams and the Man by the Fireside." Gurney, 2:237–38.
"Mr. Addison and the Dark Specter." Stead, 214–18.
"Miss Anderson and the Invisible Attackers." *Light* 8 (1888): 188.
"Capt. Ayre and the Ghost of Hunt's Father." Gurney, 2:256.
"Miss B. and Her Blasphemous Demon." Nevius, 122–25. The case was
    originally given in Griesinger, 243–44.
"Mr. B. and His Blasphemous Demon." *Light* 11 (1891): 316.
"Mr. B. and the Face Looking In." Gurney, 1:524–25.
"Mr. B. and the Ghost of His Wife." *Light* 12 (1892): 120.
"Miss B. and the Lady in the Tower." Lee, *More Glimpses,* 118–23.

"Gen. Barter and the Ghost of Lieutenant B." Stead, 195–97.

"The Beaminster Boys and the Ghost of Daniel." Ingram, 10–13.

"Rev. Bellamy and the Apparition of Miss W." Gurney, 2:216–17.

"Mrs. Bettany and the Night Visitor." Gurney, 2:204–5.

"Mrs. Bishop and Her Salem Witchery." Burr, 223–29.

"Miss Bishop and the Ghost of Her Cousin." *Light* 14 (1894): 106.

"Mrs. Blank and Her Barking Demon." Crowe, 448.

"Mrs. Blank and Her Coarse Demon." *Light* 11 (1891): 508.

"Miss Blank and Her Drunken Demon." *Borderland* 4 (1897): 411.

"Mrs. Blank and Her Enslaving Demon." *Light* 11 (1891): 508.

"Mr. Blank and His Drowning Demon." Nevius, 64–65.

"Rev. Blank and His Friend." Gurney, 2:122–23.

"Mr. Blank and the Devil Who Tempts Him." Burr, 136–40.

"Miss Blank and the Dining Room Ghost." Stead, 304–8.

"Miss Blank and the Ghost of Mr. B." Gurney, 2:580–81. See also *Light* 3 (1882): 58.

"Mrs. Blank and the Mailed Figure." Ingram, 98–100.

"Mrs. Blank and the Man at Her Bedside." *PSPR* 3 (1885): 101–2. See also Podmore, pp. 290–91.

"Mr. Blank and the Phantom Cavalier." Ottway, 169–73.

"Mrs. Blank and the Sallow Woman." *PSPR* 3 (1885): 114–15.

"Miss Blank and the Visit of Her Mother." Gurney, 2:581.

"Mr. Blank and the White Lady." Ingram, 360–67.

"Mrs. Bolland and the Ghost of Ramsay." Gurney, 1:542–44. Sheppard discusses this case on 165–66.

"Mr. Bruggeling and the Ghosts at Silverton Abbey." *Borderland* 3 (1896): 284–96.

"Mr. Butler and the Face of His Friend." Lee, *Sights*, 125–29.

"Miss C. and the Black Lady." *PSPR* 3 (1885): 119–22. Roellinger refers briefly to this case.

"Mr. C. and the Ghostly Man." *Light* 1 (1881): 375.

"Mrs. C. and the Staring Woman." Parish, 346.

"Mr. Canning and the Face at the Window." *Light* 11 (1891): 197.

"Mr. Carcass and His Obsessing Demon." *Borderland* 3 (1896): 11–14.

"Mrs. Chapman and the Woman at the Window." Ingram, 37–43. Referred to earlier in Crowe, 332–36.

"Mrs. Chu and Her Jealous Demon." Nevius, 407–13.

"Mrs. Clarke and Her Father's Face." Gurney, 2:455–56.

"Mrs. Claughton and the Lady in White." *PSPR* 11 (1895): 547–59. See also Lang, *Book of Dreams*, 175–84.

"Mrs. Clerke and Her Brother's Appearance." Gurney, 1:60–61.

"Mrs. Clerke and the Old Padrona." *PSPR* 5 (1889): 466–67.

"Mr. Colchester and the Ghost of His Grandmother." *PSPR* 1 (1883): 130–31.

"Capt. Colt and the Ghost of His Brother." Gurney, 1:556–59.

"Mr. Cox and the Little Girl's Father." Gurney, 2:555.

"Col. D. and the Cadaverous Lady." Ottway, 193–98.

"Mrs. Davies and the Ghost of Lillias Muir." *Borderland* 4 (1897): 99–100.

"Mrs. Davies and the Ghost of Mary Jeffs." *Borderland* 4 (1897): 256–58.

"Mrs. Davies and the Seduction of Doris D." *Borderland* 3 (1896): 207–9.

"Mrs. de Gilibert and Her Great Aunt." *PSPR* 6 (1889): 22–23. See also *Light* 10 (1890): 66.

"Miss Dittus and Her Strong Demon." Nevius, 111–16.

"Mr. Drury and the Groom." Ingram, 323–26.

"Miss Du Cane and the Pale Visitor." *JSPR* 5 (1892): 223–26. See also Podmore, 275.

"Mr. Durham and the Coal-Yard Man." Stead, 210–14.

"Mr. Eustace and the White Face." Lee, *More Glimpses,* 108–12.

"Miss F. and the Visit of Esther." Morrison, 49–57.

"Mrs. F.'s Maid and the Ghost of Louise." Owen, 378–81.

"Dr. Farquhar and the Castle Ghost." Ingram, 336–41.

"Miss Farrand and the Face of Mrs. Robinson." Gurney, 2:244–47.

"Mr. Frith and the Woman in His Room." *Light* 13 (1893): 607.

"Mrs. G. and the Two Ghosts." *PSPR* 6 (1889): 259–64. See also Podmore, 324–27, and Lang, *Cock Lane,* 146–49.

"Mr. Garling and His Friend's Visit." Gurney, 2:149–51.

"Mr. Grey and the Swimming Ghost." Stead, 219–20.

"Miss Grombach and Her Demon Monk." Stead, 163–67.

"Mr. Gunn and the Match-Blower." Stead, 323–27.

"Dr. Gwynne and the Draped Figure." Gurney, 2:202–3. See also Lang, *Book of Dreams,* 185–86.

"Rev. H. and the Apparition of Mrs. B." Gurney, 2:516–19.

"Mrs. H.'s Nurse and the Lady at the Partition." *PSPR* 3 (1885): 122–26. Roellinger refers to this case briefly.

"Mr. Hall and the Man at the Desk." *PSPR* 6 (1889): 53.

"Mrs. Harrison and the Lady on the Veranda." *PSPR* 3 (1885): 140.

"Mr. Hernaman and the Little Old Woman." Gurney, 1:562.

"Mr. Hieh and His Agonizing Demon." Nevius, 424.

"Mr. Hill and the Ghost in Jamaica." *PSPR* 3 (1885): 137–41.

"Mr. Horlock and the Lady in His Room." *JSPR* 2 (1886): 249–58. See also Podmore, 321–23.

"Mr. Husbands and the Ghost in His Room." *PSPR* 5 (1889): 416–17. See also Podmore, 289–90.

"Mr. J. and the Face in the Library." *PSPR* 6 (1889): 57–59.

"Rev. Jessopp and the Man at His Desk." Lee, *Glimpses,* 71–77. See also Ingram, 161–65.

"Joseph and the Willington Mill Ghosts." *JSPR* 5 (1892): 331–48.

"Miss Knap and Her Accusing Demon." Burr, 21–23.

"Mr. Kwo and His Irresistible Demon." Nevius, 17–27.

"Mr. L. and His Tormentor." Owen, 447–53. See also Crowe, 455–56.

"Mrs. L. and the Dead Child." Crowe, 330–32. See also Ingram, 180–83.

"Miss L. and the Ghost of Her Great Uncle." Gurney, 1:559.

"Miss L. and the Lady on the Bed." *PSPR* 5 (1889): 418–20. See also Podmore, 291–92.

"Miss L. and the Wet Candle." *PSPR* 11 (1895): 557.

"Dr. Leslie and the Friend at Tavistock." Gurney, 2:252–53. See also *Light* 1 (1881): 343.

"Miss Linda and Her Demon Struggle." *Light* 11 (1891): 499–500.

"Miss Lister and the Apparitions." *PSPR* 5 (1889): 444–47. Roellinger refers briefly to this case.

"Mr. Liu and His Evil Demon." Nevius, 12–14.

"Mr. Lofthouse and the Woman by the Pond." Ingram, 33–36. See also Andrew Lang, "Ghosts before the Law." *Blackwood's Edinburgh Magazine* 155 (1894): 215–16.

"Rev. Louis and the Ghost in the Sunlight." Stead, 150–51.

"Miss M. and the Lady on the Stairs." Gurney, 2:582–83.

"Mrs. M. and the Sobbing Girl." *PSPR* 8 (1892): 178–79.

"Miss Marchand and the Ghostly Man." *PSPR* 6 (1889): 43–45. Translated from the French by author. This case is discussed in Sheppard, 151–52.

"Mr. Matthews and the Reappearance of Susan." Gurney, 2:179–81.

"Miss Montgomery and the Figure in White." Gurney, 2:196–97.

"Miss Morris and the Lady in Black." *PSPR* 6 (1889): 255–59. Sheppard discusses this case on p. 164.

"Miss Morton and the Widow in Black." *PSPR* 8 (1892): 311–32. See also Lang, *Book of Dreams*, 198–200; Podmore, 311–12; and *Light* 12 (1892): 457–58. Sheppard discusses this celebrated case on 206–7.

"Mrs. Oliver and the Lady in Blue." *JSPR* 2 (1886): 258–62. See also Podmore, 323.

"Miss P. and the Wailing Child." *Light* 4 (1884): 146.

"Mrs. Pickering and the Man at the Door." *Light* 2 (1882): 222.

"Mrs. Pittar and the Man at the Desk." *PSPR* 6 (1889): 53–54.

"Mr. Potocnik and the Staring Man." *Light* 11 (1891): 15–16.

"Mr. Proctor and the Willington Mill Ghost." Stead, 261–75.

"Miss R. and the Face in Her Room." Gurney, 1:527–28.

"Mrs. R. and the Sobbing Lady." *PSPR* 3 (1885): 115–17. See also Lang, *Book of Dreams*, 196–98.

"Mrs. Richards' Friend and Her Mother." Gurney, 2:513–14.

"Mr. S. and the Ghost of Mr. L." Gurney, 1:210–11.

"Mr. Searle and the Face of His Wife." Gurney, 2:35–36.

"Mr. Smith and the Music-Room Visitor." Gurney, 2:200–202.

"Mr. Smith and the Sad Woman." *Borderland* 3 (1896): 443. See also *Light* 16 (1896): 473.

"Mrs. Stone and the Horseman." *PSPR* 6 (1889): 247–48.

"Mr. T. and the Ghosts in West Brompton." *PSPR* 3 (1885): 132–36.

"Miss T. and the Sad Man." *Light* 14 (1894): 23.

"Mr. Tandy and the Face of Canon Robinson." *PSPR* 5 (1889): 408–9.

"Mrs. Taunton and the Ghost of Her Uncle." Gurney, 1:37.

"Squire Theed and the Ghost of His Victim." Lee, *Glimpses,* 40–44.

"Rev. Thomas and the Old Beggar." Stead, 200–203.

"Mrs. Vatas-Simpson and the Two Ghosts." *PSPR* 3 (1885): 126–32. Morrison retells the narrative in his own words on 94–103. In his 1949 article, Roellinger refers to this case, though only to a small supporting account given by Mrs. Vatas-Simpson's daughter.

"Miss W. and the Ghost of Mercy Cox." Gurney, 2:253–55.

"Mrs. W. and the Man with the Pale Face." *PSPR* 3 (1885): 102–4.

"Mrs. W. and the Pointing Lady." *Light* 8 (1888): 456.

"Rev. Ware and the Boarding-School Spirits, *Light* 17 (1897): 455–56, 469, 479–80, 487–88, 500–501, 511.

"Miss Wildin and Her Raging Demon." Crowe, 449.

"Mr. Wilkins and the Ghost of Mr. P." Jarvis, 69–78. See also Ingram, 256–62.

"Mr. Williamson and His Unwanted Spirits." Williamson, 72–74.

"Mrs. Wilson and the Ghost of Mr. Tisdale." *PSPR* 8 (1892): 229–31. Sheppard discusses this case on 164–65.

"Mrs. Wilson and the Old Man in Her Bedroom." *Light* 17 (1897): 435.

"Miss X. and the East Riding Ghosts." *Borderland* 4 (1897): 254–56.

"Mr. X. and the Woman in Night Attire." *PSPR* 5 (1889): 442–44.

"Mr. Z. and the Ghost in His House." *PSPR* 6 (1889): 276–81. See also Podmore, 314–18.

WORKS CITED

Allen, Gay Wilson. *William James: A Biography*. London: Rupert Hart-Davis, 1967.

Banta, Martha. *Henry James and the Occult: The Great Extension*. Bloomington: Indiana University Press, 1972. A useful review by Joseph M. Backus appeared in *Journal of the American Society for Psychical Research* 67 (1973): 407–15.

Beecher, Charles. *A Review of the "Spiritual Manifestations."* New York: Putnam, 1853.

Beidler, Peter G. "The Governess and the Ghosts." *PMLA* 100 (1985): 96–97.

Benson, Arthur Christopher. *The Life of Edward White Benson*. 2 vols. London: Macmillan, 1899.

Brooke-Rose, Christine. *A Rhetoric of the Unreal*. Cambridge: Cambridge University Press, 1981.

Burr, George Lincoln. *Narratives of the Witchcraft Cases, 1648–1706*. New York: Charles Scribner's Sons, 1914.

Christmas, Henry. *Echoes of the Universe*. London: Bentley, 1850.

Cranfill, Thomas Mabry, and Robert Lanier Clark, Jr. *An Anatomy of "The Turn of the Screw."* Austin: University of Texas Press, 1965. A useful bibliography appears at the back.

Crosland, Newton. *Apparitions: An Essay Explanatory of Old Facts and a New Theory*. London: Trubner, 1873.

Crowe, Catherine Stevens. *The Night Side of Nature: or, Ghosts and Ghost Seers*. London: T. C. Newby, 1848; Routledge, 1852.

Curtis, Anthony. Introduction to *The Aspern Papers* and *The Turn of the Screw*. Middlesex: Penguin, 1984.

Dyer, T. F. Thistleton. *The Ghost World*. London: Ward and Downey, 1893.

Edel, Leon. *Henry James: The Untried Years—1843–1870*. London: Rupert Hart-Davis, 1953. For works edited by Leon Edel, see under "James, Henry," below.

Ferriar, John. *An Essay Towards a Theory of Apparitions*. London: Cadell and Davis, 1813.

Fussell, Edwin. "The Ontology of *The Turn of the Screw*." *Journal of Modern Literature* 8 (1980): 118–28.

Gauld, Alan. *The Founders of Psychical Research*. London: Routledge and Kegan Paul, 1968.

Goddard, Harold C. "A Pre-Freudian Reading of *The Turn of the Screw*." *Nineteenth-Century Fiction* 12 (1957): 1–36. Reprinted in Robert Kimbrough, ed., *The Turn of the Screw*, Norton Critical Edition (New York: Norton, 1966), 181–209, and Gerald Willen, ed., *A Casebook on Henry James's "The Turn of the Screw,"* 2d ed. (New York: Crowell, 1969), 244–72.

Griesinger, W. *Mental Pathology and Therapeutics.* Translated by C. Lockhart Robertson and James Rutherford. London: New Sydenham Society, 1867.

Gurney, Edmund, Frederic W. H. Myers, and Frank Podmore. *Phantasms of the Living.* 2 vols. London: Trubner, 1886.

Harris, George. "Supernatural Visitations." *Human Nature* 6 (1882): 169–75.

Harrison, William H. *Spirits Before Our Eyes.* London: W. H. Harrison, 1879.

Hassall, Christopher. *A Biography of Edward Marsh.* New York: Harcourt Brace, 1959.

Hibbert, Samuel. *Sketches of the Philosophy of Apparitions; or, An Attempt to Trace Such Illusions to Their Physical Causes.* Edinburgh: Oliver and Boyd, 1824.

Ingram, John H. *The Haunted Homes and Family Traditions of Great Britain.* Illustrated. London: W. H. Allen, 1890. An earlier, nonillustrated edition appeared in 1884.

James, Henry. *The Complete Notebooks of Henry James.* Edited by Leon Edel and Ryall H. Powers. New York: Oxford University Press, 1987.

———. "Introduction." In Guy de Maupassant, *The Odd Number: Thirteen Tales.* Translated by Jonathan Sturges. New York: Harper and Brothers, 1889.

———. *Letters.* Edited by Leon Edel. 4 vols. Boston: Harvard University Press, 1974–1984.

———. *The Notebooks of Henry James.* Edited by F. O. Matthiessen and Kenneth B. Murdock. New York: Oxford University Press, 1947.

———. *Stories of the Supernatural.* Edited by Leon Edel. London: Barrie and Jenkins, 1971.

———. *The Turn of the Screw.* Originally serialized in *Collier's Weekly,* January–April, 1898. All page references to the novel in the present study are to the text (based on James's 1908 revision for the New York Edition) in Robert Kimbrough, ed., Norton Critical Edition (New York: Norton, 1966), 1–88.

James, Henry, Sr. "Modern Diabolism" (review of M. J. Williamson's *Modern Diabolism* [London: Trubner, 1873]), *Atlantic Monthly* 32 (1873): 219–24.

James, William. *The Principles of Psychology.* 2 vols. Boston: Henry Holt, 1890.

Jarvis, T. M. *Accredited Ghost Stories.* London: J. Andrews, 1823.

Kenton, Edna. "Henry James to the Ruminant Reader: *The Turn of the Screw.*" *The Arts* 4 (1924): 245–55. Reprinted in Gerald Willen, ed., *A*

Casebook on Henry James's "The Turn of the Screw," 2d ed. (New York: Crowell, 1969), 102–14.

Kerr, Howard. *Mediums, and Spirit-Rappers, and Roaring Radicals: Spiritualism in American Literature, 1850–1900.* Urbana: University of Illinois Press, 1972.

Kimbrough, Robert, ed. *The Turn of the Screw.* Norton Critical Edition. New York: Norton, 1966.

Krieg, JoAnn P. "A Question of Values: Culture and Cognition in *The Turn of the Screw." Language and Communication* 8(1988): 147–53.

Lang, Andrew. *The Book of Dreams and Ghosts.* London: Longmans, Green, 1897.

———. *Cock Lane and Common-Sense.* London: Longmans, Green, 1894.

Lee, Frederick George. *Glimpses in the Twilight.* Edinburgh: William Blackwood, 1885.

———. *More Glimpses of the World Unseen.* London: Chatto and Windus, 1878.

———. *Sights and Shadows.* London: W. H. Allen, 1894.

Lytton, Edward Bulwer. *A Strange Story.* 2 vols. New York: Athenaeum, 1893.

Matheson, Terence J. "Did the Governess Smother Miles: A Note on James's *The Turn of the Screw." Studies in Short Fiction* 19 (1982): 172–75.

Maudsley, Henry. *Natural Causes and Supernatural Seemings.* London: Kegan Paul and Trench, 1886.

Miall, David S. "Designed Horror: James's Version of Evil in *The Turn of the Screw." Nineteenth-Century Fiction* 38 (1984): 305–27.

Molesworth, Mrs. *Four Ghost Stories.* London: Macmillan, 1888.

———. *Uncanny Tales.* London: Hutchinson, 1896.

Morrison, Arthur. *The Shadows Around Us: Authentic Tales of the Supernatural.* London: Simpkin, Marshall, Hamilton, Kent and Co., 1891.

Murphy, Gardner, and Robert O. Ballon, eds. *William James on Psychical Research.* New York: Viking, 1960.

Nevius, John L. *Demon Possession and Allied Themes.* Chicago: Revell, 1896.

O'Gorman, Donal. "Henry James's Reading of *The Turn of the Screw." Henry James Review* 1 (1980): 125–38, 228–56.

Ottway, T. *The Spectre; or News from the Invisible World.* London: Joseph Smith, 1836.

Owen, Robert Dale. *Footfalls on the Boundary of Another World.* Philadelphia: Lippincott, 1869.

Parish, Edmund. *Hallucinations and Illusions.* London: Walter Scott, 1897.

Podmore, Frank. *Studies in Psychical Research.* New York: G. P. Putnam's Sons, 1897.

Renner, Stanley. "Sexual Hysteria, Physiognomical Bogeymen, and the

'Ghosts' in *The Turn of the Screw*." *Nineteenth-Century Fiction* 43 (1988): 175–94.

Roellinger, Francis X. "Psychical Research and *The Turn of the Screw*." *American Literature* 20 (1949): 401–12. Reprinted in Robert Kimbrough, ed., *The Turn of the Screw*, Norton Critical Edition (New York: Norton, 1966), 132–42.

Sheppard, E. A. *Henry James and "The Turn of the Screw."* Oxford: Oxford University Press, 1974. A useful review by Joseph M. Backus appeared in the *Journal of the American Society for Psychical Research* 72 (1978): 49–60.

Siegel, Paul N. "Miss Jessel: Mirror Image of the Governess," *Literature and Psychology* 18 (1968): 30–38.

Sikes, Wirt. *British Goblins*. London: Sampson Low, Marston, Searle, and Rivington, 1880.

Stead, William T. *Real Ghost Stories*. London: Grant Richards, 1897.

Stevens, E. Winchester. *The Watseka Wonder: A Startling and Instructive Psychological Study, and Well Authenticated Instance of Angelic Visitation*. Chicago: Religio-Philosophical Publishing House, 1878. Reprinted, with several alterations and revisions, 1887.

Taylor, Eugene. *William James on Exceptional Mental States: The 1896 Lowell Lectures*. Amherst: University of Massachusetts Press, 1984.

Tuveson, Ernest. "*The Turn of the Screw*: A Palimpsest." *Studies in English Literature* 12 (1972): 783–800.

Weatherly, Lionel A. *The Supernatural?* Bristol: J. W. Arrowsmith, 1891.

West, Muriel. "The Death of Miles in *The Turn of the Screw*." *PMLA* 79 (1964): 283–88. See also West's more extended study, *A Stormy Night with "The Turn of the Screw."* Phoenix: Frye and Smith, 1964.

Willen, Gerald, ed. *A Casebook on Henry James's "The Turn of the Screw."* 2d ed. New York: Crowell, 1969.

Williamson, M. J. *Modern Diabolism*. London: Trubner, 1873.

Wilson, Edmund. "The Ambiguity of Henry James." Published in various states of revision, in various volumes, in 1934, 1938, and 1948. The final version, as it appeared in the revised and enlarged edition of *The Triple Thinkers* (New York: Oxford University Press, 1948), 88–132, is reprinted in Gerald, Willen, ed., *A Casebook on Henry James's "The Turn of the Screw,"* 2d ed. (New York: Crowell, 1969), 115–52, along with a 1959 postscript.

INDEX

I exclude from this index references to the characters and events in *The Turn of the Screw*, and to all but a few famous or important persons identified in narratives of ghosts and demons.